My bag contents at the conclusion of my cycling trip
(for the cycle purists)

Camera, pump seal, BA nuts and bolts, helmet and visor, waterproof coat, trousers and spats, thermal pants, spanner ends, chain tool, cycling trousers, granddad dress shirt, universal plug, cycle shoes, door wedge, first aid kit, two cycle bags, wind jacket, front brake cable, rear brake cable, cycle gloves, cycle shorts x 2, puncture repair kit, sun hat, thermal vest, allen keys, adjustable spanner, swimming costume, sun lotion (two tubes), flip flops, tin opener, rear light, handlebar bag, sunglasses, derailleur cable, log book, front light bracket, sponge and rag, nail clippers, thermal gloves, screwdriver ends, tyre levers, screwdriver, thermal cycle vest, wet wipes, cycle computer, sewing kit, biocide tablets, water bottles x 3, maps, comb, pencil, Vaseline, tyre, tape, razor, soap, torch, knife, spoon, fork, shoelaces, pump, towel.

The above included all my clothes.

I never fitted a bell. I would recommend a bell; in some countries they are compulsory. The pannier bags should be waterproof. The Raleigh Randonneur is, in my opinion, a good safe solid bike. I wrote to Raleigh customer services department at the end of my trip and mentioned a few related problems. One was the nylon nut and bolt holding the rear mudguard; this is a safety-related item in my opinion. The bolt holding my mudguard snapped; I replaced it with a steel BA nut and bolt. Also, the brakes could have worked more easily than they did; I found the brake levers hard to apply. One had to apply a lot of hand pressure. I wrote to Raleigh enclosing my serial number and a photograph. They never acknowledged my letter or returned my card or photo. A company is only as good as its employees.

2

long and hard on this question. In my opinion, the folk seemed to be non-residents; only living there on a temporary basis and constantly looking for their historical roots. They were also very able, friendly and helpful. The question was asked, 'what did it take to cycle that far?' My reply was to follow two very important pointers in life: persistence and determination.

The big question was, 'what did you get out of it personally?' It's not easy to answer; there are so many nondescript answers. I still don't know if I've really managed to answer the question. Contentment; achievement; rewarding self-discovery; adventure; a global insight leading to greater understanding of humanity. This last I feel goes a long way to describe what I got out of the experience.

The Blue Goose arrived three days after I did, unannounced; I found the box in the garage. I was a happy man; the team had been reunited. Do you know the most asked question? 'What's your next trip?' Who said those most appropriate words, 'stop the world, I want to get off'? I found what I was looking for in the Orkney Islands. It was there all the time. Many thanks, Mac Petrie.

Mr Mac
and the
Blue Goose

Mr Mac and the Blue Goose,
first published in 2006 by Mac Petrie
Quoylet, Holm, Orkney. KW19 2RS

Edited by Pam Beasant

Cover design and layout by Iain Ashman

Printed by The Orcadian Ltd
Hell's Half Acre
Hatston
Kirkwall
Orkney KW15 1DY

Mr Mac
and the
Blue Goose

Mac Petrie

Dedicated to Alf and May

'On the road again; just can't wait to get on the road again.'

Acknowledgements
My thanks to so many who helped me achieve my dream:

My wife, Gill, and all my family
My daughter Alison, who nagged me to write this book
Dr Steven Beaven
Dr George Drever
Doctors, nurses and staff at the Forrester Hill Hospital, Aberdeen
Staff at the Royal Bank of Scotland, Kirkwall
Staff at Going Places, travel agent, Kirkwall
Paterson's bike shop, Kirkwall
The Orkney Library staff
Swimming pool staff, Kirkwall
CTC staff
Arnie, Les, Mike, Martha, Martin, Marica, Jeff Sim, Roy McGhee
The Inner Man
Someone Up There

That's all folks. Many thanks for your help.

Contents
and route summary

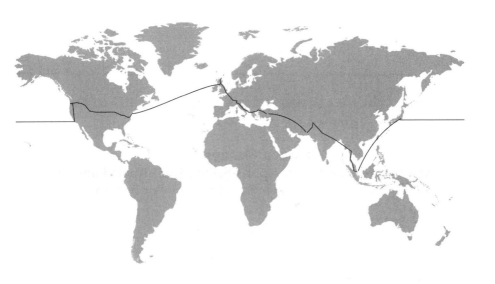

Introduction

I remember the apprehension when I first mouthed the words, 'cycle the world'. Everything else became secondary. 'Cycle the world, Mac.' I fully realise now that I'll need the same determination and persistence to write my adventures as to cycle the countries that I did.

'Come on, Mac – start now.' That's the Inner Man telling me to get on with it. You do what your mind tells you to, right or wrong; you act on it at the time. The Inner Man gives a second opinion – sometimes the same action to take – but more positive, with clarity. So, whenever I refer to the Inner Man, it's a positive reaction and second opinion I'm after.

October, 1993. The Orkney winter was early, cold, wet, windy and dark. Geese were still flying south: one could hear the ganders calling, as if to say 'this way, Mac'. I was 58 years old, cycle fit, contemplating early retirement, as I'd put all my eggs in one basket for the big 60. Cycling the world became the foremost thought in my mind.

Could I really do it? I weighed up all the pros and cons for a month and concluded with positive thinking that yes, I could and would cycle the world.

I'd read books on travel; individuals completing what seemed like impossible tasks. I concluded that the glossy brochures from the travel agents do not convey the reality of a country.

My conviction was and still is: if they can do it, so can I. My biggest hurdle was now to convince my wife, Gill, and family that I was sane and would be safe cycling the world.

I was no stranger to cycling. When I was young, a bicycle was the only form of transport available as I lived in the country. Gill reintroduced me to cycling, as she and her friend, Hannah Stove, regularly cycled the Orkney roads for both fitness and pleasure. A few bike runs and I was hooked. Miles piled on miles, dreams became reality and distance was no object. Weather was mixed; cold, wind and rain being my biggest dislike. Orkney to me is a landscape of ever-changing scenery and beauty; when the sun shines it all transforms into a rare jewel in Technicolor.

Orkney can boast the best training facilities, second to none. During my early, 'born again' cycling days, one man stood out as my guru. His name is John Legget. What can I say about John? Cycling to him seems to be a religion. When travelling by boat to work, even in the worst possible weather, when sitting with John, time would be spent talking about cycling. Bike problems? John was Mr Fixit; nothing was too much trouble. He would repair a bike any time. He was also a mine of advice. Thanks, John.

I am a lone traveller and I understood, as I thought, the many dos and don'ts of cycle touring. As the trip plan progressed, many more became apparent.

The first thing I needed was a 'master plan'; a staged directive. To jump on the bike half-cocked was a sure fire non-starter heading for positive failure.

The master plan

It's funny – when you are planning something, there seems to be nothing on the market to give you the full insight and directive you need. It's up to you to work it out for yourself. My best source of information came from reading all sorts of literature and information on cycle travel, looking at maps and the tales of travellers in many lands. Videos are also now available on travel.

At the start, I realised the need for a common format sheet. This I devised and found invaluable.

The local library became my main source of information in the early planning stages. I had to include all the countries I would cycle through. The appropriate detail was filled on to my format sheets, the details applicable to the individual countries: religion, passport, visa, monies, opening times of banks, post offices, shops, international phone numbers, accommodation, health requirements, basic language relating to hotels/motels, bed-and-breakfasts, and, most importantly, the route. With an attached map, these sheets became a great help, as I could edit them with ease when compiling the final travel requisites.

As the weeks and months went by, I slowly convinced my wife and family that my trip was safe. This was not an easy task.

My decision to cycle the world was a well-kept secret. Only the family and a few close friends knew of my plans. When told I would cycle alone, some were horrified and spoke of it being not safe; some thought it was downright crazy. But I was determined to go alone.

Questions about self-preservation were asked. I had already thought long and hard about the issue and concluded I would carry no deterrent whatsoever. If the worst came to the worst, I thought, I would give up my bike and bags rather than endanger my life. I also concluded that I would not 'take on' anyone, or show any sign of affluence; no gold, rings, watches, bracelets or neck chains. Ultimately, however, I have great faith in humanity.

My tour route

I compiled my tour route early, to allow planning – with the understanding it could change if needed.

> John O'Groats – Dover/Folkestone
> France – Switzerland – Italy
> Greece – Turkey – Pakistan – India
> Thailand – Malaysia – Singapore
> USA: Oregon, Idaho, Montana, Wyoming -
> Colorado – Kansas – Missouri – Illinois -
> Kentucky – Virginia

At this point I was still reading in detail all I could on the countries I planned to visit. I became a magpie, collecting this and that – suggestions from authors whose books I had read. I decided early in the planning stage not to 'tent'. I would 'B&B', motels, hotels – sleep where I laid my hat. The reason for not tenting was the weight factor. If I cycled with a tent, sleeping-bag, groundsheet, pots and pans, I would become a cycling donkey.

The bike

What to go for? That was the question. The answer: hand-built, direct from the manufacturer. I gave much thought to this problem. I was keen to have a hand-built model. The decisive factor was that I lived in the Orkney Islands and travel costs to and from the islands are high. Raleigh had just brought out a new model Randonneur, and I like Raleigh products.

Bike details for the purists:

Name	Raleigh Randonneur
Frame	Reynolds 708 Touristique, custom tubeset, precision cast head and seal lugs
Forks	Reynolds taper gauge, wide oval blades. Hollow, precision cast, crown offset, cantilever bosses
Gears	Shimano deore LX, with bar end shifters
Brakes	Shimano LX cantilever
Rims	Mavic T 261 AL
Hubs	Simano deore LX, parallax heavy duty double-sealed mechanism
Freewheel	11.28T, 8-speed hyperglide cassette
Tyres	Continental top touring 700X35c
Chainset	Sugino fuse 500
Headset	Champagnolo Veloce
Seat pin	Kalloy alloy micro adjust
Handlebar	ITM Randonneur with Cinelli cork ribbon tape, SR custom stem
Saddle	Brooks B17 premium grade leather with bag loops
Pedals	MKS AR2 with satae AC51L clips and Crisophe black leather straps
Features	Blackburn carriers 4 point fixing rear and lo-rider front ESGE chromoplastic mudguards
Colour	Blue Avio
Weight	13.5 kg (approx)

CTC and insurance

Like most cyclists I am a member of the CTC (Cyclist Touring Club). The help given me proved invaluable, from the latest information on the countries that I planned to visit to the insurance cover necessary for a world trip. I would fully recommend CTC membership to cyclists, especially those who intend to travel. My thanks to the CTC staff.

The insurance I took out covered me for six months, with the option of extending the cover if required. Yes, it was costly, but at least I was covered if problems occured.

Money

Help! What money should I take was the big, big question. Who would give me the information? Conclusion: see the bank. The Royal Bank of Scotland. A good question, said the bank – one we are not asked often. Leave it with us, we'll give you a call. I concluded that this bank does care. In a few days they rang asking me to call in. There were many questions: yes, we can; no, we can't; don't know, we'll find out. Conclusion:
American Express travellers' cheques
American Express credit card
Visa with pin number
Mastercard

The above I found adequate to cover all circumstances. Many thanks Jonnie Johnston and Andrew Green, the Royal Bank of Scotland, Kirkwall.

Personal fitness

I'm a very stocky person. I look at food and put on weight. Although I was still working in the day, evenings found me keeping fit, cycling indoors; weekends, weather-permitting, cycling outdoors. Alternately I would swim or lift weights. My aim was to build on my stamina.

All was going to plan. I could see things taking shape: answers to questions were forthcoming, material requisites started to appear as if by magic. Physically, I looked and felt good.

At work I had the call to attend my yearly medical. I was checked out by the works doctor and nurse. Knowing the doctor, George, he and I sat down over a cup of tea and chatted. During the conversation I mentioned some slight problems I had with my water works. I could see some concern. George examined me there and then and extracted blood samples for analysis. Two weeks later the phone rang. 'Mac – George here.' The results of those blood samples: positive. I could have cancer of the prostate. My reaction: 'Damn, that's my world cycle trip over.' Funny reaction, you might say. I agree.

My world took a dive. I found myself in freefall. Unplanned territory. After many tests it was confirmed that I had prostate cancer. After many months I had my prostate removed. Whilst in hospital, foremost in my mind was my world cycle plan; it kept my mind active. 'Positive thinking.' It gave me a goal to strive for. During hospital convalescence I strove to keep fit. I marked out a 'corridor walk', as I called it: 1,760 yards. I walked this every day, with my water bottle which I called my 'dog'. I was 59 years old and had lost my physical structure, yet I wanted to get back to training. My own doctor played a big part in my recovery. Many thanks to both Dr S. Beaven and Dr G. Drever.

The first time on my bike, I was like a child with a new toy. Very slowly, and sorely, I mounted the bike. My God, will I ever cycle again? Perseverance and determination provided the big 'YES'. My thanks to all at Forresterhill Hospital, Aberdeen.

My recovery was slow. Nature must take its own pace. I gained confidence on my training bike, then came the big test – to actually cycle on the road. My butt was sore in the seat and as I increased the miles I felt laboriously slow and out of condition. Would I ever be able to cycle my 20-40 training miles with the same gusto again? I did have doubts in my mind but persistence won the day. It's strange to describe, but one day whilst on a 20-mile training ride, I had the sensation of physical power. I was, as they say, back in the driving seat. Again, I set myself training tasks: weights, swim, walk, cycle; all with the aim of conditioning my body and improving my stamina.

Christmas 1994 was upon us. I accepted early retirement, reaching the big 60. What a great feeling. For the first time in my life I was my own boss. As free as a bird. Christmas presents included pannier bags (Kirtland make). These proved to be an important acquisition for their positive fixing to the bike, size and waterproofing. I settled for two rear panniers and a handlebar bag.

I planned to travel light, so what I could carry depended on the size of the bag. Family Christmas presents also included many of my other wants. Materially, I was now progressing. Cycle training continued. The only bike I rode was the Randonneur; it was becoming part of me. As I rode, I adjusted the bike's settings to my body's requirements. Cycling along one day, I thought of the wild geese I'd seen in the autumn. The bike, I thought, should have a name. Horses have names – why not my bike? Inspiration. 'Blue Goose.' What a good name. In future, when I refer to Blue Goose, it's my bike.

Whilst putting pen to paper the weather has been atrocious, but looking out of the window, the sun shines. I can't sit here. I'm off on a quick 20-mile ride on Blue Goose. That's better. I call it a fix because my wife says it's like a drug to me. Where were we? Oh, yes.

New Year 1995 had come and gone. It was now time to set a positive departure date. After much thought, I chose May 1, 1995. I concluded that to leave earlier than May might result in cold, wet weather in the UK. To leave later would result in cold weather on the final stages of the trip in the States.

The date was fixed. I questioned myself: it was time for a complete check on all my requirements. Now I knew my departure date, I could book my injections and speak to the doctor about my necessary medical kit. What had I forgotten? Visas, with departure dates. I needed to work out approximate times of entry to and departure from these countries. Had I left it too late? I asked the local travel agent. Yes, maybe you have left it too late, but we'll do our best. Many thanks to staff at Going Places, Yvonne and Sarah – the visas arrived in time.

OK, said I – let's check what the magpie has accumulated. This I did, following the age-old cycling tradition of laying everything out on a double bed, at the same time warning my wife not to touch or disturb anything. I stood back in amazement. My God – did I collect all that? I'd need a 5cwt-van to transport that lot, and if I did manage to bag it, I'd have to be a cycling donkey to move it. Conclusion: travel light, Mac. Reduce the collected items. Night after night I'd sit and study the lay-out, trying all combinations. I removed things, then put some of them back. What are the heavy items, I asked myself. The personal radio, the dog dazer. Oh, not that? Yes, it had to go. I purchased the dog dazer from America; the high frequency sound transmitted from it was meant to disorientate the offending dog. I don't know if it worked, I never tried it.

Tools needed to be reduced, so out went both spanners and screwdrivers. Clothes I reduced, socks, pants – also a cycle lamp, as I had a hand torch instead. I was going to regret leaving my cycle lamp later. Yes, I was slowly getting there. My, my, though – what about all the papers and maps accumulated, which together were approximately the size of a family Bible? I had to bite the bullet and reduce and lighten the load. Decision time: that's it, no more. We cyclists know the weight of both cycle and bag to be transported. It's all dependent on one's physical fitness and stamina. The bottom line is that you are the driving force. Too much weight can have an adverse effect. I intended to fully enjoy my cycling.

Details of what I carried

On bike:
Rear lamp, water bottles (2), cycle pump, rear bags (2), mirror, computer milometer, handlebar bag.

On person:
Cycle top (waterproof), underpants, cycling shoes, cycle vest, cycle shorts, bottom pants, socks, hard hat, cycling gloves, American Express travellers' cheques (dollars), British monies, visas for Pakistan and India, CTC membership card, CTC travel insurance certificate, Sental help card, Royal Bank of Scotland credit card help line number.

Around neck:
Passport, photocopies of visas, credit cards, health cards, EEC E111 form, £10 English money for Turkey visa, injection medical card, driving licence, BT phone card.

Medical kit:
Multivitamin tablets, sterile dressings (2), syringe needles, Paludrine tablets, fungicidal cream, surgical tape, pre-injection swabs, Imodium capsules (for diarrhoea), chlorine tablets, chest antibiotics, first aid kit, plasters.

Left rear bag:
Madison (com tool), four-inch shifting spanner, puncture repair kit, Zeval pump (spare seals), compass, hand torch, mending kit, tyres (2) 700x35 spares, plastic gloves, cycle lubricant, waterproof mail tags, sunglasses, party poppers.

Right rear bag:
Windproof survival sheet, underpants, waterproof shoe covers, towel, cycle vest, socks (one pair), waterproof bottoms, cycle lock and chain, maps for 10 routes.

Front handlebar bag:
Allen keys, ear plugs, pencil, Vaseline, sun block cream, comb, dust mask, electric razor, H_2O iodine tablets, spare glasses, BA nuts and bolts, plastic ties, log book, pen, toothpaste, TCP cream, Dettol, universal sink plug, plastic razor, camera and film, cycle gloves, De Railleur gear cable, brake straddle wire, Philips small screwdriver.

Final checks and goodbyes

The countdown was on with just days to go. I had regained my cycling fitness throughout the winter and April was a fairly good month weather-wise. This allowed me extra training prior to the off.

I held a family party in the 'local' to say our farewells. I had also advised Gill of all our assets and what to do in the worst case. Gill would be my one and only UK contact. We agreed that if I reached Singapore, she would come out for a holiday. One thing was worrying me: Gill was due to go to hospital for an operation on her left foot. My two daughters, Karen and Alison, assured me they would look after Gill's every need. This put my mind at rest.

The last thing I did was to make a will. I looked upon it as a laugh and saw it as keeping the family paperwork up to date. I also had my last medical check with Dr Beaven. As he checked my chest he laughed and said, 'you are OK – ready to go.' I was apprehensive, as I'm slightly asthmatic. How much of the world I'd see depended on me.

Great Britain

Orkney

John O'Groats
Helmsdale
Inverness
Blair Atholl
Edinburgh
Berwick-upon-Tweed
Sunderland
Selby
Grantham
Chipping Ongar
Dover
Folkestone

1st May - 10th May 1995

John O'Groats to Helmsdale

On May 1, 1995, I intended to catch the short sea route boat from Burwick in the Orkney Islands to John O'Groats; the start of my world tour. Did I sleep the night before? You know, I can't remember - I was on cloud nine. Packed and ready to go. When I say packed, for some inexplicable reason at the last moment I changed my cycle bags from two panniers to a single seat bag. I had ridden with a single bag on previous occasions. I was to regret this change of bags.

On the morning of May 1, I was surprisingly calm as I ate my breakfast with Gill. Again, we talked over all the job aspects she would cover while I was away.

Time to go. I said my fondest farewells, gave Gill a big kiss and an extra big hug. I could see a small tear in the corner of her eye. I quoted the usual words: 'Don't worry, everything will be all right.' We waved to each other until distance dulled the image.

I was on the ferry to John O'Groats; the weather was cloudy with showers, but surprisingly not cold. As the ferry docked, I glanced back at Orkney. My mind was flooded with thoughts as, clank, the gangway hit the deck. I grabbed Blue Goose, walked the plank and landed on John O'Groats. No photographers at the famous spot where everyone stands for their photo call on completing the 'end to end'. Never mind, Mac, it's too early in the season for tourists. I gave a quick glancing check over Blue Goose. All okay. I was under way, the rain cooling my hot brow. I started to sing the words of Willie Nelson's song, which I find very appropriate at the start of a cycle trip.

On the road again,
I just can't wait to get on the road again,
Going places that I've never been,
Seeing things that I may never see again.

I'd cycled approximately two hundred yards down the road - my God, what was that? A bus passed me with the luggage doors still open. That was too close for comfort. The driver stopped the bus further down the road, closed the luggage sides, looked at me sheepishly and drove off. My first close shave of the trip had come very quickly. (During the trip I did learn that we all have a built-in sixth sense - self-preservation.)

It still rained. So what? I was under way, the signpost read Wick; I decided against my wet weather gear. The weather abated to showers. On reaching Wick, the rain stopped and the sun shone.

The first three days of a cycle trip I always find the hardest, as with the first twenty miles of the day. Today was no exception. The Blue

Goose did not handle well - the balance was wrong. I soon concluded the problem was the single heavy seat bag. I over-corrected going round a corner. The weight in my bags soon became very apparent and the need to travel lighter a must. Don't overload the donkey.

For those of us who have had the joy of cycling 'end to end', the great Berriedale hill is imprinted on the mind. This was my fifth time on the hill. In my log of the day I referred to it as both gut and butt busting. I was nearing the hill top on the south side, pushing Blue Goose - what a leg and stamina tester - when an 'end to end' passed me with a smile on his face, being pulled along by his back-up truck. That's one way up, I thought, although it's not safe. I reached the top of the hill and sat down on a big stone on the side of the road, knackered.

A car pulled up alongside me. 'What are you doing, Mac?' I looked up and saw friends from Toab in Orkney, Les and Arnie Foubister. My matter-of-fact reply made them smile - 'My first day of cycling the world, Les.' My water bottle by now needed replenishing. Arnie, Les's wife, handed me a bottle of Pepsi. My God - fuel - nectar of the gods. Help when I really needed it. They wished me well as they waved goodbye. Many thanks, Les and Arnie.

The afternoon turned out to be extremely hot. I was not acclimatised to this weather. People ask me how do I know when to stop? My reply is short and sweet - you stop when your body tells you to.

Helmsdale. That's it. Stop here. I found a B&B lodge, £15 for the night. It was clean and homely. I was hungry. The landlady directed me to a café/restaurant, La Mirage, where a fish and chip meal was £5. What a meal - possibly one of the best of my trip. The café was out of character for the area, with a décor like a film set. Fed and watered, I returned to my B&B.

It was imprinting itself on my mind: must travel light, must travel light. On request, Blue Goose was garaged for the night and safe. I had my bags in the room. What should I do? I emptied the lot on the bedroom floor and just looked. What a heap. I carried a spare plastic bag. The plan? To reduce my bag contents. But what? Here goes: hand soap, wool, rain hat, a pack of travel tissues, sun hat with shade flap, air pillow, spare bike bottoms, shirt (off bike), two pairs of socks, swimming trunks, flip flop sandals, bottom bracket extractor, candle, waterproof matches, one puncture repair outfit, party poppers, bottle can opener, insect repellent. I know what you're saying - I can hear you now. What's he carrying party poppers for? The answer - to ward off dogs. I concluded that if I required any of the above, I could purchase it en route. I tied the bag, penned on my address and requested mine host to leave the bag for collection. 'No problem,' was her reply. Many thanks Highland shop, Berriedale. I was ready for my bed and slept like a log.

Helmsdale to Inverness

I was up early and breakfast was first class. I thanked mine host, bagged up Blue Goose and checked it over - all systems go. Yes, it did handle lighter. The weather was mixed as I headed for Inverness. I was feeling happy.

My happy feeling was to change suddenly as I came across two dead deer on the roadside. What beautiful animals. Seeing dead animals on the road I find quite upsetting. During my trip I was to see many more - birds, insects, bees - unfortunately, the list would fill this page. I ask myself the question - is this the price we pay for faster transportation? My opinion is that it's not worth it; we'll see the day that we'll regret it. Animal conservation on the roads is a must. Kill the speed, not wildlife.

Inverness was drawing closer; the miles were clocking up, but the wind and rain made it a hard ride. I needed shelter and a fir tree beside the road saved the day. Within half-an-hour the rain had eased. The Black Isle road was busy. Every car and lorry that passed gave me a shower. I was so wet I was getting cold. Inverness bridge, thank God. Hello, Inverness - it's nice to see you. I turned right at the roundabout, the road was wet and muddy. 'Take care, Mac.' Too late. I fell off my bike. Damn. I dragged both myself and Blue Goose on to the grass verge and did a quick damage check. My shoulder hurt, and the handbrake lever was knocked up the handlebar. You are one lucky man. Normally the roundabout is full of vehicles, but not today. I concluded that someone somewhere loves me - thanks.

I realigned the brake lever, feeling a bit sorry for myself, remounted Blue Goose and found the road into town. Let that be a warning to you, Mac Petrie - take care. I soon found a B&B and a safe garage for the Goose. After a hot shower and a good meal, I hit the sack. What a day.

Inverness to Blair Atholl

I overslept, and in the morning my shoulder was stiff and slightly discoloured as a result of the fall yesterday. Breakfast was good. I soon bagged up Blue Goose and was on my way. Today I ride the mighty A9. My water bottle was full and I'd also bought apples for a snack.

I cycled through the morning traffic of Inverness and joined the A9. The weather was fine. I soon found the right gear to help me climb the steep, undulating hill out of Inverness.

The hills from Inverness to Aviemore are leg testers. They sort out the men from the boys; stamina is tested to the full. The beautiful mountain scenery is legendary. At times I would stop for a photo call and to behold the beauty, breathtaking at times. Aviemore is an excellent stopping place; good food and lodge - all services offered.

The route to Blair Atholl from Aviemore is again a picturesque ride. The wind was in my face. It both helps and hinders - keeps you cool at the same time as slowing you down.

The A9 is not an easy road to ride; the traffic is so heavy. Also, I found it most annoying that the three feet of road between the edge and the first white line had been spoilt by relaying the road surface. The original road was great to cycle on - a smooth finish from the white line to the edge. Please, Mr Highlands and Islands Road Department, return the roads to their former rideable state, thanks.

I find it good for the soul to have a little moan now and then; one feels one has achieved something.

Blair Atholl - a great name for a house. I love the name. There was a B&B so I pulled in for the night. I could think of no better relaxing place to be in the early spring; the sun and the first flash of green on both the hills and the trees. The views stay impressed on my mind. Must remember to return next year with Gill - same time of year, if possible.

Blair Atholl to Edinburgh

Day four. Time flies, as the saying goes. I ate a filling breakfast, topped up my water level - my back teeth felt as though they were under water - and filled my water bottle. I bagged up Blue Goose, gave a quick visual check on the mechanics and a squirt of oil on the chain. I was ready for the road.

Edinburgh. Will I reach it today? The weather was fine, face wind - always is when cycling! Blue Goose is not balancing correctly. I will ask Gill tonight to forward my rear pannier bags to Folkestone. She must send them now so they arrive at the post office before me.

Cycling from Blair Atholl to Edinburgh calls for good navigation. As you leave the idyllic surroundings, all your senses are soon fully tested as you launch yourself back on to the main A9 road to Perth. Traffic? This is one busy road; the stunning scenery makes up for the modern speeding cars and lorries.

A sad moment occurred when cycling on a lonely part of the road. I came upon a wire fence with the wooden post broken off; two colourful flower wreaths hung from the wooden post and marks on the road conveyed the tale. I got off my bike and stood in silent homage. One can but wonder who the victim was.

I could see it in the distance - the Forth Road Bridge. Just crossing the bridge gives me a psychological boost. I stopped to view the surroundings, the countryside and the sea. It was breathtaking.

The ride to the bridge had been fairly tough. Stop Mac, said my body. I decided to stop at the hotel at the bridge. I parked Blue Goose in my room, which was handy as we were both in need of a good clean. I was also in need of sustenance after all that work; I had a pint of beer. From my room I had a good view of the bridge. As the lights of the bridge and the car headlights flickered, so did my eyes. Good night.

Edinburgh to Berwick-upon-Tweed

I was up early, ate a good Scottish breakfast, filled my water bottle, topped up my water level until my back teeth were awash, bagged up the Goose and gave the chain a shot of oil. I viewed the road from the hotel. Just look at that traffic. Then it dawned on me - Edinburgh rush hour. I pushed out and joined the ritual - hydrocarbon fumes saturated the morning air. What a way to get a fix.

I was soon cycling through Edinburgh, my favourite city; the first city to cycle through on my trip. The streets were busy with traffic and people heading to work. All systems were on red alert.

I was soon out of the city limits, cycling through farming country again. The Goose was flying along and I felt good. My body now had that cycle fit feeling. Fields were showing the first flush of green, cattle were grazing and contented, barley was showing its first green flash of crop. Spring was fully in the air, the weather was again sunny and warm and I was enjoying my cycle. I was also making good time.

Berwick - there it was and all the shops were open. I felt the pangs of hunger. Why not? It's what your body tells you. I did enjoy sitting in the spring sunshine eating a large ice cream.

I had no problem finding a B&B and garaged Blue Goose. Phoned Gill - all OK. What a good day. Night night.

Berwick-upon-Tweed to Sunderland

The folk in the B&B were first class. I had an excellent breakfast and good advice on my day's travel. I attended to my personal needs, thanked mine hosts, bagged up Blue Goose, pumped air into the rear tyre and gave the chain a shot of oil. All systems go. I waved to the folk and was on my way.

Sunderland today. Would I make it? I rejoined the route south. The weather was good, spring in the air, but I was feeling the effects of sunburn on my legs and arms. Mile followed mile. I was happy. I passed the morning singing my full repertoire of songs. What a lucky week to choose to go cycling the length of Britain. Spring - is there any better time to travel? I don't think so. After a long, hard winter, everything you look at is of interest. Two butterflies and one swallow don't make a summer, as the saying goes, but they made my day.

Man, this A1 road is busy today. As I cycled past a closed main farm gate, a big pickup truck stopped, a burly farmer got out and from the open back a massive dog leapt. What a size. I quickened my pace automatically. The dog ran faster, following me. The farmer was shouting his all to Ben, with a few other words thrown in. Ben never looked back. As the dog closed on me, I thought I'd lose at least an arm or a leg. Neither - Ben ran straight past me.

Darting in and out of the busy car lanes, Ben carried on down the road. Cars were taking avoiding action, the farmer still shouted. With that, a pheasant arose in full cry. The last I saw of Ben was dashing across a field. The farmer was still waving and shouting but the distance from the farmer to the dog was so great, his shouting was inaudible. We see something new every day.

Sunderland. My honest opinion - I did not like it. Most of the B&Bs were full. My accommodation was a hotel - posh in name only. I've got a moan. Many hotels I stayed in were not, in my opinion, up to the star standard they displayed. I sometimes wonder what galaxy the stars come from. Dirty rooms, dust, dirty showers, paint, decoration, food. Is it the labour cost, or lack of supervisory knowledge or training? B&B in ordinary folks' homes in most cases is first class.

Shut up, Mac Petrie, don't moan. You're tired - go to bed. OK.

Sunderland to Selby

Again the sun was shining. As I looked out of the window, the roads were quiet. I topped up my water levels, bagged up the Goose, checked out the mechanics and oiled the gear change. I wanted to beat the morning rush hour traffic. This I did. I intended to stop for breakfast further down the road.

Cycling was good. The roads were well signposted; I went through a mixture of built up areas and open land. Stopping at a roadside café, I consumed a fairly large breakfast. Grand. That'll last me well into the afternoon. Cycling through York I had a close encounter. A car came down the wrong side of the street. We both pulled up at the last possible moment, my front wheel to his bumper. He wound down the window and said sheepishly, 'I'm lost.' You're a lucky man, Mac.

Selby. This is my kind of town. Do try the mushy peas and the fish and chips - they're out of this world. People are so friendly, happy and obliging. I always think the town was built with a lot of thought; the large, open square gives a panoramic view.

Selby to Grantham (Travel Lodge)

My B&B last night was excellent; the breakfast of a very high standard. As I wrote my daily log last night I didn't realise I had completed my first 100-mile run of the trip yesterday. Well done, Mac. Some say self-praise is no recommendation, but it gives you a lift. I remember the first time I cycled 100 miles, from Bettyhill to Beauly. As the 100 miles came up on my cat-eye computer, I looked about. No one there. I let out a big Highland cry. Well, some people do react differently to others. Have you ridden 100 miles in a day?

I drank four cups of tea during breakfast and my liquid level was high, ready to meet the day. As I fitted the bags to Blue Goose, I made a mental note that it was in need of a clean.

The sun was warming the early morning air and the traffic was light. It would build up during the morning - it always does. Considering I completed my first 100-mile day yesterday, I was not stiff. My energy level was high. All systems go.

Mile followed mile. As I cycled through towns and villages, flags were flying; there were street parties and bunting danced in the day breeze. There was music and dancing. I stopped and asked the obvious - what's going on? - to be told, fifty years since VE Day. I felt I wanted to stop and join in the celebration, as it was also part of my life. I remember the troops coming home from the war, parties in the street, singing, dancing - food appeared as if by magic. Memories not to be forgotten. For some reason, I felt down. I think it was the bad memories. 'Come on, Mac - lift out of it.' It was the Inner Man speaking to me. Remember I spoke about him earlier? Second opinions do help.

The day found me between Stamford and Grantham. B&Bs were few and far between. I was ready for a stop. Travel Lodge. Why not? I pulled off the road and booked in no problem. Blue Goose was allowed in my room. I fully recommend the lodges. In future, I will use them again. They're clean, with good food. The room was quiet. I filled in my daily log. Can't keep the eyes open. Good night.

Grantham (Travel Lodge) to Chipping Ongar

As usual, I was up early. I had slept like a log, as the saying goes.

Breakfast was plentiful and everything was clean. I increased my liquid level, neat tea; I had my fix. I bagged up Blue Goose, checked the tyres, two shots of oil - yes, I did clean all my gear last night. All systems go. What a week. The sun was shining for me again.

I launched us both on to the A1 road. There is always traffic on the roads. No, I don't like cycling on the A1. As I reached the turning for Cambridge and left the A1, I don't think the traffic was less. I stopped and checked my map and decided to cycle to Royston. I found a need to stop and check my map at regular intervals today. My navigational skills were being tested, but I was enjoying the ride. By lunchtime my cat eye computer had logged up sixty miles. It put a smile on my face.

I bought my usual sandwiches and Pepsi for lunch. The afternoon soon passed as I cycled the country roads. I find the flat roads of England good to cycle on. I pushed on and was soon entering Chipping Ongar

I found B&B in the local pub, the King's Arms. The Goose was garaged and I had the key. I completed my end-of-day chores and showered - heaven. Good night.

Chipping Ongar to Dover/Folkestone

I was hungry last night. The pub pizza filed a void. Checking my cat eye computer, I had logged 104 miles. No wonder I slept.

I was awake at 0700 hours and was soon downstairs devouring an excellent breakfast and drank my usual cups of tea, back teeth afloat. I checked out and bagged up the Goose and pushed out into the morning air. The weather was overcast, but mild.

What did the map say? Follow the A128 to Tilbury. I made good time, no hills, and the traffic was fair. If I have a comment to make at this time, Tilbury is poorly signposted, for someone new in the area.

I caught the ferry from Tilbury across the River Thames to Gravesend. It cost £1.80 for the Blue Goose and me. In my opinion, an excellent ferry service.

I followed the main road to Sittingbourne and picked up the A2 to Dover. A most enjoyable cycle ride, I must admit. Kent is aptly named 'Garden of England'. The last time I rode this route cherries were in season. I love cherries, but it's the wrong time of year.

Dover - what an interesting town; the sea, cross channel ferries, a good shopping centre, it has the lot. A place to sit and watch the world go by. I bought myself a cup of tea and fancy cake and did just that.

'Come on, Mac, off your butt - enough of that daydreaming.' Folkestone. That Inner Man won't let me rest. Oh well, let's go.

Folkestone, here we come. The road from Dover to Folkestone is very hilly. What a pull. The last few miles of the day seemed never ending. As I rode the last hill, there was Folkestone, spread out below me. I sat back on the Goose and rode for town.

I must be on the right road. There were B&Bs everywhere, spoilt for choice. I'm glad to say I made the correct choice. Blue Goose was housed in a large garage, the over-large Alsatian dog eyed me and smiled. I was accepted, thankfully.

Part of my master plan was to stay in Folkestone for two nights, which I had already booked at the B&B. I was looking forward to the rest. The landlady of the house directed me to a first class restaurant. I also enquired where I could wash my cycle clothes. 'I'll do that,' she said. I duly gave her all my cycle clothes.

The evening meal was top class. If you can't spoil yourself now and again, when can you? A glass of white wine tasted very good, so I had another glass. I wandered back to my lodge in a very relaxed mood. As I lay on the bed I contemplated my trip up until now. I also rang Gill - it was great to hear her voice. I was one contented and happy man. Sleep came easily. Good night.

Folkestone

Morning tea - along with the bacon, egg, mushroom and sausage - were first class. As I left the dining room I was presented with all my cycling clothes washed clean and pressed. I thanked the lady of the house. What excellent service. The Inner Man said, 'you're spoilt, Mac.' For the first time, I had to agree.

I sat down in my room to digest my breakfast and made a mental note of the list of things I needed to do today.

Post office, pannier bags, medical supplies - I had not taken my medical bag with me because of the weight factor. I posted it ten days ago, before setting off, to be collected at Folkestone post office.

Blue Goose. When I came off my bike in Inverness, the brake cables must have been damaged as they were stiff to operate.

I also had to pre-book my passage to Boulogne in France.

The landlady directed me to the various places. The weather was again fine. Can't understand it - don't it rain around here?

I removed the handlebar bag and emptied all the contents out of the seat bag but left it fixed to the Goose.

As I left the house, the dog nudged me and offered me his paw. I shook his hand. Good morning. Without the bags, the Goose flew down the road. I intended to spend the day exploring Folkestone. First stop, the post office. Yes, my bags had arrived. That was the good news. The bad news was that my medical bag had not arrived. Damn. I fitted the panniers, went back inside the post office and redirected my handlebar bag home to Orkney. I decided to call back later in the day, to see if my medical bag had arrived.

Cycling on, I found the bike repair shop as directed by the landlady. Yes, they could repair the problem with the brakes if I left it there for a few hours. On request they also pointed me to my next port of call, to book the Channel crossing to Boulogne. This was painless with the aid of my flexible friend. The ticket was booked for tomorrow at 11.15am. The cost - £22. I walked back into town. I must have looked a real tourist in my cycle gear, like a rider without a horse.

My medical bag was nagging on my mind as I ate my lunch of fish and chips. What would I do if it wasn't there? I had until 0930 the following day to make up my mind. My mind was like a computer full of alternatives, but no answers.

On my second cup of tea, whilst gazing out to a blank, open sea, the answer filled my mind. If it's not there tomorrow morning before catching the boat, then I'll ask the post office to send the medical bag back home to Orkney. I'll phone Gill and tell her to re-direct it to the post office in Ankara, Turkey. Sounds feasible. I'll enquire at the post office.

Calling back to the cycle repair shop, yes - your bike is repaired. I read the amount on the bill and gave a big cough. Sorry, I said, a chip stuck in my throat. What a cost! It's the way of life these days. I paid the man, thanked him and was on my way to the post office.

Yes, the Goose handled as it should. No, my medical bag hadn't arrived. I explained my problem to the post office desk man, and the solution. The guy was very understanding and said to speak to him in the morning. I thanked him for his help.

Where had the day gone? I cycled back to the B&B. It had been a busy day and I still had to clean Blue Goose, which I did in the garage. I was still not satisfied bagging all my gear. I also balanced the bags. It will be strange for a few days to find where everything is packed.

The Goose looked altogether better. I was soon riding down the road - what a difference to the handling. I was one satisfied man; all systems go for tomorrow. I rang Gill to give her an update on events, and to say what to do if my medical bag didn't arrive tomorrow. It was nice to hear her voice. I sat back on the bed and rested.

Thinking back on my trip, I did enjoy it. The weather made it. First week of May and sun most days. What did I learn? I had tried an experiment cycling through both Scotland and England. Was I ever on my own at any one moment on the road? The answer is for two minutes in Scotland. This conveys the amount of traffic on our roads. There is a need for change and one of my conclusions is that lorries over a certain tonnage should travel on the roads at night. This would relieve the congestion. I speak of A/B roads. As you know, cyclists cannot ride on motorways.

One lorry passed me on the road with sheet ropes on the rear just blowing in the breeze. I only realised this as a rope narrowly missed my face. This next one is a warning to others - any cyclists from 2-80 years old. Be aware of the air pressure generated by lorries passing from the rear; air pressure can rocket you forward, also generating a side pressure. This is enough to knock any weary cyclist off his or her bike. A lorry passing on the opposite side of the road can virtually stop you riding, exerting enough pressure to knock you off the bike. My conclusion is that this knowledge should be added to the lorry drivers' test. They should know the damage they can inflict on other road users.

There, I've had my little moan. Look at the time - I'm starving. I was soon in the Black Bull sitting down to a pint and an evening meal. It was really excellent food. I had another pint. Big day tomorrow. As I made my way back to the B&B I opened the door with the key. The dog sniffed and let me pass. I wonder if he was checking if I was sober? He did smile, didn't he? I took no rocking. Good night.

France

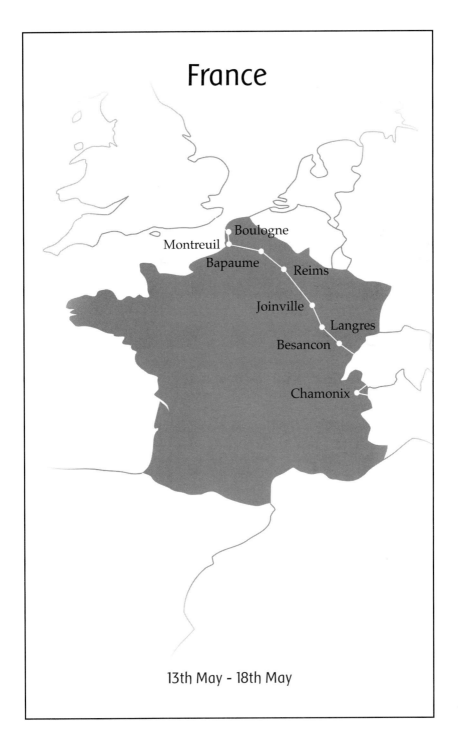

13th May - 18th May

13

Folkestone to Boulogne

I was awake extra early feeling slightly apprehensive, and yet excited. I ate a hearty English breakfast but cut back on my liquid intake. I don't want to be running to the bog on the boat all the time, do I?

I bagged up the Goose, thanked the landlady for all her kindness and shook hands with the Alsatian dog. They say they're very intelligent. Did I hear him say, 'call again' as I rode away? Maybe I did.

What time was the boat? 11.15am. Good. That gives me time to check with the post office again, to see if my medical bag had arrived.

The post office was opening as I arrived and the man himself was at the desk. Any luck? 'I'm sorry, sir, nothing as yet,' was his reply. I gave him my return address and paid the postage. I emphasised the need to have the bag. 'I'll do my best,' said the man. I thanked him and was soon on my way to the boat.

The weather was overcast, slightly windy, with pockets of rain. The forecast was gales, increasing to force 6 in the English Channel. It didn't worry me. Usually I'm a good sailor.

I arrived at the port in good time and checked in my ticket and passport. I was handed a boarding pass and awaited my call to board. Blue Goose had handled well on my short morning run. I removed my handlebar bag as it had my goodies in it - camera, etc. It was light to carry.

Finding myself a seat with a view, I waited in relaxed mode for the off. In a very short time we were under way. I changed my Scottish money to francs; the exchange rate was fairly good. I soon found myself a cuppa and a bite to eat. The boat trip was OK - a few bounces and dives but nothing to worry about. I tried to remember all the dos and don'ts regarding France. Yes! The most important one - only cycle on the right-hand side of the road.

As the boat docked, I said, 'welcome to Boulogne, France, Mac Petrie.' It was raining.

Boulogne to Montreuil

The drivers were called to the car deck. I followed and replaced my bag on the handlebar and untied the rope. I was ready for the off. No, I was not the first off, but the last. The hydrocarbon fumes made me retch. I gasped down the fresh air when I reached the end of the gangplank.

As I cycled through Boulogne harbour I stopped to take some photos. The wind was fairly strong and it had been raining. I checked my route and pushed off. My mind was over-active, the Inner Man was also shouting, 'stay on the right-hand side of the road.' That's all I need. Don't nag.

My navigation was poor and within two miles I was back where I started. In other words, I had chased myself up my own butt. As I set off again I did wonder if the hydrocarbon fumes had left me on a high. That I will never know. On checking the map, I could see where I'd gone wrong.

I was on the right route this time and the rain had stopped. Blue Goose handled like a dream. What a difference the correct balance makes. It made me wonder how on earth I cycled the length of Britain as I did. One learns something every day.

It was late afternoon and I'd cycled approximately twenty-five miles. An hotel loomed in the distance. I checked in. Yes, I could leave the Goose in the lounge; it was safe, no problem. I paid the bill with my visa.

The weather had turned cold and I was also cold. I carried out all my chores, and showered. The room was what I would call fair; the most important thing was that the bed was clean. As I lay on the bed I checked my route, wrote my log and fell asleep. Good night. No food, silly boy - you know today's food is the fuel of tomorrow.

Montreuil to Bapaume

'Come on, move,' said the Inner Man. He does get on my nerves sometimes. Time, 0700 hours. I checked the weather through the misty window. It was cloudy but dry, and it looked cold. I finished my morning ritual and looked in the mirror. He'll do, I thought. He smiled back. I was hungry. Breakfast was continental, just fine - though there was a slight language problem explaining tea without milk or sugar. Sorry I spoke! I made sure I drank my cycling fill.

I bagged up the Goose and squirted a shot of oil on the chain. I wound some white tape on the right handlebar to remind me to cycle on the right.

Today I enjoyed cycling. There weren't many hedges, just like home in Orkney. Trees sometimes followed the roadside, obviously hand planted - I think they're poplar trees. Fields were larger than I'd imagined and the land was well farmed.

Roads? So far, not as good as Britain's. The traffic was light to moderate. I found it good cycling country; one could really knock up the miles.

I concluded that France was geared up for credit cards, no need for money. Winter had not gone to sleep as yet; it was still on the cold side - roll on spring. I stopped en route at a supermarket and bought my lunch and an afternoon bite. I was still hungry from last night.

My body started to look for a B&B. I checked my cat eye computer; it read 90 miles. That's a good day's work. A hotel came into sight; it looked tidy. Good night.

Bapaume to Reims

I woke this morning thinking about Gill. I was unable to contact her last night, and no wonder. I rang my daughter Alison - she told me Gill had been called into hospital at short notice for an operation on her foot. The operation was today. Through telepathy I wished her well.

I was now getting used to fitting the rear panniers. The Goose was ready, the continental breakfast was fine. I tried French coffee in a small cup, black with two spoons of sugar. 'Bonjour,' I said. Now Mac, don't overdo it.

I was soon on the Goose heading for Reims, on the right-hand side of the road. The countryside was beautiful; the weather sunny, but cold.

I cast my mind back to last night; the meal was not what I would call good. At best, it was fair. I did manage to do my washing and it was dry this morning. As for the shower operation, one needs to be a member of Mensa to work out how to operate the darn things. 'You do go on - shut up and ride.' You know who said that.

I was more understanding of the roads. One thing ahead of Britain was the fact that all the roads were well signposted. Well done. I did find roundabouts slightly confusing on the first few days, but soon settled into the way of the road.

As I cycled Gill was again on my mind. I would phone again tonight. Feed the Inner Man. I was hungry. I stopped at a roadside café and bought a cheese roll and a Coke for lunch. The day was on the cool to cold side, surprisingly not as warm as my trip through Britain. You don't drink out of your water bottle as often in the cooler weather.

The roads were good, the countryside flat. I passed quite a number of war graveyards. Makes one feel sad, irrespective of who, or which side, is buried there. What a waste of young life.

It was no time before Reims was visible in the distance. I checked my cat eye computer - 90 miles. Balladins Hotel appeared as if by magic. I checked in both myself and Blue Goose. 'You can keep your bike in the room,' said the receptionist. I thanked her and booked the restaurant for later in the evening.

After completing my chores I showered and felt human again. The big job of the night was to clean Blue Goose. No, I didn't make or leave a mess, but I did use half a toilet roll.

Once I had eaten I felt tired; it was the best meal so far. Phoned my daughter Alison. Yes, Gill had had her operation and all was well - she should be home in two days. As I relaxed, tiredness swept over me like a wave. I retired to bed early. Good night.

Reims to Joinville

I have no alarm clock other than my Timex watch; a great piece of engineering. I was ready to go. 'Early to bed, early to rise,' is a true saying.

At breakfast this morning the waiter understood my plea for tea. I stopped my liquid intake when it was at a high level at the back teeth. Weather-wise, the wind was strong to gale force and it was raining; a day for the wet gear. I always think wet gear restricts one's movements on the bike. As I took off it was also damn cold. My god, what a morning.

It was hard-going making headway against the wind. I congratulated myself on the cycle through Reims yesterday. As the wind decreased, the rain increased. I wear glasses; a problem in weather like this. This morning I cycled through both Chalon-sur-Marne and Vitry-Le-Francois. Gill has a saying that irrespective of where one is on holiday, all places look alike when it's raining. I would say it was true. I must ring her tomorrow - she is due home from hospital.

Stopping for lunch, I bought two salad rolls and a Coke. Despite the weather I was knocking up the miles. St Dizier came and went. The rain was unbelievable. The sign post said 'Joinville'. I checked the cat eye - 85 wet miles - further than I thought I'd cycle today in these conditions.

'Enough is enough,' said the Inner Man. At that moment, a hotel appeared down the street. It usually only happens in films. I checked in both the Goose and myself. I was cold and wet. After I checked in I found there was no form of heating in the room. That don't happen in films. Damn. The shower arrangement, however, was not too complicated. I was soon out of my wet gear, soaking up the heat in the shower. Limbs defrosted, one at a time. I changed into dry gear and felt human again. It pays dividends to put all items of clothing in plastic bags before placing them in the panniers.

For my evening meal I had a bowl of hot soup and a salad. It was early evening. To keep warm, I jumped into bed. I studied my basic French format sheet. The TV came on at the first attempt. My, what luck, it was Clint Eastwood in a spaghetti western. Good night, folks.

I was up early, feeling fine and rested. I didn't have to look through the window, I could hear the wind and rain. I opened the curtains - it said it all. The young green leaves were being blown off the trees; what damage.

Yes, it did enter my mind to give the day a miss, but no, I would cycle today. I checked my wet gear - it was dry. It had drip-dried overnight, because I had hung it up.

Slowly, I ate my breakfast, hoping against hope that the weather would change, or at least that the rain would stop. No such luck. The third cup of tea filled me with go. Before bagging up the Goose, I checked that all my gear was in plastic bags, even my log book.

I oiled the chain outside the hotel - 'no oil on the carpet, please.' Quite right. As I pushed out and mounted, a high-sided lorry passed at speed. You guessed it, I was as wet as a drowned rat. You know, I'm starting to have a love/hate relationship with lorries. That wetting set the pattern for the day: wet, wet, wet.

As I cycled out of town, three young men passed me at speed, lifting their hands in acknowledgement. I wished them the best of luck in my mind. They were soon out of sight.

Cycling was a struggle; the wind was side to face, and strong. I was glad I'd made the decision to cycle today - the wet miles were slowly mounting. I pulled over in Chaumont for lunch - two rolls and a Coke.

My glasses became a problem, so I removed them and cycled on. The world did look different; I didn't have spots before my eyes. It was mid-afternoon. I stopped and put my glasses on - what did that road sign say in the distance? Langres. The wind and rain had made me tired. I intended to pull off the road early. My cat eye said 50 wet miles.

As I cycled down the road looking for a lodge, I caught up with the three young cyclists that passed me this morning; they were surprised to see me. They looked wet and fed up. Was this a case of the tortoise and the hare?

I soon spotted a hotel. 'Yes, we have rooms and room for your bike.' I checked in. It must be knocking up the pennies on the visa. So, what? Life's what you make it.

The room was clean and the bed looked inviting. There was a bath, but no shower. My cycle jacket had kept my body dry. I soon ran the bath and the water was hot. I loaded it with all the soap goodies, stripped off and hung up my wet gear. Yes, there was a heater in the room, and it worked.

I sank slowly into the hot bath; right up to the arm pits, as they say. I can only describe it as wet bliss.

The food was excellent, although I was wary of what I ate. My stomach last night was not altogether right and I had suffered the dreaded runs this morning. I did take the appropriate stomach tablet this morning, and tonight, before dinner. It's one of those problems of life, what one eats in strange countries. I keep well away from shellfish and fish; I speak from experience, one can easily get caught. I rang Gill. Everything was OK, she said. I was ready for my bed. Good night.

Langres to Besancon

The Goose was bagged up; it stood in the room, panting, ready to go for a run. I ate my normal breakfast. I cannot speak French. I find it's best to talk little, only convey one's wants. Pigeon French and sign language will get you there. 'Tea,' I said. 'Tea,' said the waiter. (One must teach English essentials also!) He smiled, I smiled.

The weather was mixed - rain, fog, thunderstorms and a head wind. I had what one would call a crap hand. The weather pattern across France had been approximately ten days of rain, whereas across Scotland and England I had ten days of sunshine.

I pushed off into the rain. My cat eye computer was playing up. I stopped and fixed it; man, was I wet. It was running out of my butt. The morning passed uneventfully, when 'bang' - just like a rifle being fired. Blue Goose was all over the road. I managed to stop; lucky we were all in the perpendicular position. No, it wasn't a puncture; a spoke had broken. I looked up and repeated one of my many sayings: 'why me, lord?'

The rear wheel had practically collapsed; I couldn't believe it. I do remember while I was cycling 'end to end', a spoke broke in the rear wheel. On closer inspection, the wheel had buckled. I remounted with care. Yes, I could make slow headway. Besancon was only a few miles down the road, by my reckoning. Yes, it duly appeared.

The first two hotels I tried looked at me like I was a very wet tramp. A shake of the head said it all. It was early afternoon; who knows? Out of the blue a young woman approached me. 'You looking for a hotel?' she said, pointing down the road. I nodded and thanked her. She nodded back and smiled. One can also teach the French sign language. No time for jokes, my problem is serious. I walked down the road in the direction the lass had pointed. There it was, Balladins Hotel. I was so relieved.

'Yes,' said the receptionist, 'we have a room. You can leave your bike in the room.' I also told him of my problem with the broken spoke. He glanced at his watch. 'Too late now,' he said. 'See me tomorrow morning. I will ring a taxi to take you where the wheel can be repaired.' I thanked him. It then dawned on me I'd better book the hotel for tomorrow also. 'No problem,' said the young receptionist with a smile.

Under the circumstances, I was happy with progress. I had not noticed I was wet through to the bone and Blue Goose was in a sad state. I removed all the bags and set about cleaning it. I also removed the offending rear wheel, tyre and tube, and cleaned the wheel for tomorrow.

On the rear frame of the wheel was fitted two spare spokes. I decided to take them with me in case they didn't have a spare. I stood back and surveyed my afternoon's work. I was chuffed. I had used nearly a roll of toilet paper as a cleaning aid but I had left no mess. I now felt more relaxed.

Ringing reception, I booked an evening meal and showered. I hung up my wet clothes, sat back and rested. I'll take no rocking tonight.

Besancon - a rest day

I slept well last night. There was no rush, so I showered. It sent life surging through my body. I ate breakfast at a leisurely pace.

I was lucky; the young receptionist was the same one from yesterday. 'One moment, please. I will ring a taxi.' I returned to my room for the spokes and wheel. By the time I arrived back the taxi was there. The receptionist spoke to the driver, who in turn smiled at me in acknowledgement. I smiled back. We were under way; the distance to the repair shop was about five miles.

What a complex. I'd never seen so many cycles and accessories under one roof. It was more like Aladdin's cave. The taxi driver led me to a work stand within the complex. He spoke to a young man, whom I took to be the cycle repair man. Yes, I was right first time. In no time the fitter rigged the wheel on a frame, replaced the offending spoke (using my spare) and balanced the wheel. He smiled and handed me the wheel together with the bill and pointed me over to the till. I paid the man and gave a tip to the fitter that brought a smile to his face.

Soon we were in the taxi and heading back to the hotel. I shook hands with the driver, thanked him and paid the bill, giving him a tip that made him smile.

Back in my room I read the bill from the repair shop. The letterhead said 'Roberts Cycles, Peugeot'. All I can say is thanks to everyone who helped me.

Weather: the sun was breaking through the patchy cloud. I spent the rest of the afternoon refitting the tyre, tube and wheel, washing the dirt out of my clothes (they would dry by morning), repacking my panniers and checking the plastic bags were sealed.

Blue Goose looked like new. I was sure the wheel would be OK. Throughout my trip, I never had spoke problems again. I had a pain in the gut. What had I eaten? I shat through a gnat's eye and felt better. To be on the safe side, I took another tablet. I hope that's a one-off.

Lying back on the bed, I studied the maps of Switzerland. With luck, I would pass over the border tomorrow. So, farewell France; I enjoyed it. The only time I felt sad was passing the many graves of both world wars; what a damn waste of life. The war touched most people's lives. I liken France to the biggest cosmopolitan graveyard in the world.

Roll on tomorrow: new places, new faces, new country. Reminder - must ring Gill tonight.

Switzerland

Lausanne

Martigny

20th May - 21st May

I checked my watch by pressing the illumination button: 0500 hours. Go back to sleep, it's too early. But my mind was in gear; I was raring to go. I planned that, with luck, I'd be in Switzerland today.

As I lay in bed I felt fully rested. I checked my watch again – 0700 hours. The Goose was bagged ready and I ate breakfast in record time. Yes, I had my morning fix of tea. The weather was fine; it was nice to see the sun. There was a slight side to rear wind. In no time I was back on the road, the Goose handling well – even better than before. I did rebalance the pannier bags, which might have been the answer.

I noticed a reduction in the amount of traffic on the road. I was still in France. I enjoyed cycling through St Gorgon Main. I by-passed Pontarlier but stopped at Jougne for a late lunch; two rolls and a Coke. This was my last stop in France before passing over the border into Switzerland.

I passed the border marker at approximately 1500 hours. Cheerio France – hello Switzerland.

I was feeling fine. Inwardly, I smiled to myself; I'd achieved something I'd always wanted to do. At the first chance I changed my French francs into Swiss francs. My American Express cheques also came in handy.

The countryside started to change; fields were turning into mountains. I could see the Alps in the distance; were they French or Swiss? I don't know.

I had to work hard but my legs were working well. The rest yesterday did me the world of good. The sun was shining. I can't remember saying that over the last ten days.

Cycling along merrily singing, I came alongside a big herd of cows. I stopped near the road edge. Each cow had a bell tied round its neck. Every step they made the bells would ring. It fascinated me. The musical notes sounded into the afternoon mountain air. You could shut your eyes and imagine you were at the last night of the Proms, with the orchestra warming up (or was it the 'Swiss Cow Polka'?).

I was making good headway and cycled through Pompaplas and Cossonay. My next stop would be, by my reckoning on the map, Lausanne. In the distance I could see it. I glanced at the cat eye computer – 90 miles. I don't know if that's exactly true, as I did have problems with it earlier on.

I felt elated as I rode for town. It was Saturday night and I'd had a good day. The hotel in view read 'Novotel Hotel, Lausanne'. 'Go on, stop there,' said the Inner Man. I did just that. 'Good evening,' I said.
'Could I check in for one night, and could you garage my bike?' 'Yes sir,'

was the reply. 'Your bike will be in the manager's office for tonight; it will be safe there.'

Thanking the receptionist, I made for my room on the fourth floor. It was of a good standard. I pulled back the curtain and my! - what a view. Lake Leman, with the Alps in the background.

I couldn't wait to get in the shower. I stripped off and turned it on; it was a power shower. I thoroughly enjoyed the experience; my skin felt as if it had had a massage.

If I have a gripe, it was the food. I'd only give them mid-marks for trying, although I had a glass of wine, which I enjoyed.

On returning to my room, the last rays of light were passing. Inwardly, I was a happy man. I felt I'd achieved a great deal today.

I rang Gill. She was keeping fine and all was OK. I told her where I was – Switzerland. 'Where's that?' she said, with a laugh. I do miss her (and her home cooking).

I filled out my log and lay on the bed. Swiss dreams – good night.

Lausanne to Martigny

I slept well last night; it must be the Swiss mountain air. Sunday morning, the same the world over, is quiet and slow; folk change down a life gear.

I ate an early breakfast: what a choice of food – far superior to last night's evening meal. I gorged into the fruit and drank my fill of orange juice, topped off with tea.

The receptionist repatriated Blue Goose from the manager's office. I thanked him, bagged up and oiled the chain outside on the road. Visual check and tyre pressure OK – we were under way.

Weather, dare I say it, was fine and sunny; traffic was sparse. I followed Lac Leman and it was scenery to behold. I kept stopping to take photos.

Sunday morning cyclists began to appear, all dressed in racing gear. What a great sight. Some passed me like jet fighters. I was plodding slowly on, like an overloaded bomber.

I cycled through Vevey, Montreux and Agil. All too soon I left Lac Leman behind. I made a stop for an early cup of tea and a cake and enjoyed the view, watching the world go by.

The cycling was by no means easy. What a pull and a walk – my stamina was tested to the limit of endurance.

Motorbikes started to pass either way; what a great, powerful sound the engines make. Long ago there was a brotherly affinity between cyclists and motorcyclists. I concluded it must be the two wheels and the open air.

It was mid-afternoon when I saw Martigny, which sparkled like a jewel in the spring sunshine. Should I stop, or go on? 'Go on, Mac,' the Inner Man piped up. I checked my map and hit the right road. These mountains just go up and up. I called on my water bottle; I was sweating profusely. I stopped on the mountain road.

Martigny was stretched out below me, with mountains on either side. What a subject for a painting. I noticed that there were no safety barriers on the mountain roadsides. One false move on the edge and you were a gonner. The road levelled out at the top of the mountain. The remains of winter snow were still to be seen on the roadsides. It was strange to see snow.

I cycled on up the Col de la Forclaz and glanced at my watch; 1530 hours. My cat eye showed 58 miles. I'd been approximately ten hours in the saddle and was now feeling the exertion of the day. The altitude also has an effect on one's stamina. I must admit, I was feeling tired.

I pushed on, wondering if I had done the correct thing to keep on cycling. Five miles down the road, would you believe, was an Alpine hotel. I checked in there and then. 'Yes, we have a room. Yes, we will garage your bike.' I smiled and thanked the receptionist as she gave me the key.

What luck. The interior immediately caught my eye – all pine wood. Even my bedroom was covered in pine. I completed all my evening chores. I'd booked an evening meal when I checked in and I showered, washing away all the road dirt and sweat of the day.

The evening meal was by far the best yet; roast chicken and ice cream. I was one happy man. I was washed, fed and watered.

Sleep was not far away – it must be the Swiss mountain air. They buy it in tins in America. Good night.

Italy

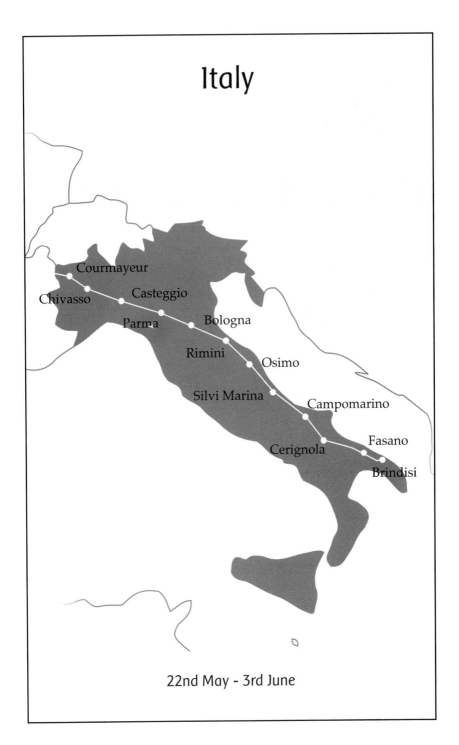

Courmayeur
Chivasso
Casteggio
Parma
Bologna
Rimini
Osimo
Silvi Marina
Campomarino
Cerignola
Fasano
Brindisi

22nd May - 3rd June

Martigny to Vallorcine
Vallorcine to Chamonix
Chamonix to Courmayeur

This is going to be a strange day. Why? I'll be cycling from Switzerland to France and into Italy, all in one day. So be it. Take it as it comes, as the saying goes.

My breakfast was as good as the main meal last night. I was spoilt, there was even a choice of tea bags. The standard of food in this hotel is, in my opinion, first class. My gripe is – if they can do it, why can't other establishments?

The Goose was bagged up waiting. I oiled the chain on the road – it makes it easier to change gear.

Weather was blue skies and sunshine; what wonderful views. I don't think I'd seen the like. It was slow-going; so many photo calls. I was aware of one thing; it was cold on the hands and feet.

I cycled most of the morning in the snow belt just taking my time. It was approximately twenty miles to Chamonix.

After passing through Vallorcine on the Swiss border, I was back in France. I stopped for a morning break; a roll and Coke. I was on my way to Chamonix. I looked across the country – what scenery. That was some mountain. Then it dawned on me – it must be Mont Blanc. I was heading downhill. The town down below must be Chamonix.

I must say the backdrop of Chamonix, set against the mountain, was worth every drop of sweat of the trip – that's how impressed I was. What also intrigued me were the many coloured hang gliders, hovering like great dinosaurs over Mont Blanc, just as if painted on the sky, balancing on the thermals. To my mind, hang gliding over Mont Blanc must be the ultimate; it was both scenic and graceful.

I sat at a table in a roadside café and ordered pizza and a glass of white wine. I don't know when I've felt more relaxed. I had wined and dined – what a life.

I found the bus station and bought tickets for the 'tunnel bus' for Blue Goose and me. The time of departure was 1730 hours. It went under Mont Blanc to Courmayeur in Italy. Most of the afternoon I spent drinking in the scenery; it was a most enjoyable stay. I made a mental note to bring Gill on holiday here in early spring next year. I also changed my Swiss francs to Italian lire.

When the tunnel bus arrived, the Goose and I were transported under Mont Blanc to Courmayeur. I cycled along the road and came across self-contained flats. On enquiring, yes, they were B&B. I paid the man and had a lodge for the night.

I bought my breakfast from a late night shop. The flats were very serviceable. I did all my chores, showered and ate my evening meal in a restaurant (yes, it was pizza).

My flat was on a hillside, overlooking other houses below. I enjoyed the view, not the noise; some tempers were raging to the smoking gun point. I was tired – good night.

Courmayeur to Chivasso

Cheerio Switzerland, hello Italy. It's strange, but I never had the same euphoric feeling in Italy as I felt when entering Switzerland. I can't explain it.

I was awake early. The unfamiliar sounds of the town had woken me a few times during the night. I ate my fast-food breakfast and drank orange juice and tea until my back teeth alarmed on high level. Blue Goose was in the garage below. I bagged up, did my usual visual check and was on the road early.

I felt really rested. There were no changes to the road regulations. I checked the tourist book this morning. Road traffic was busy, just the same the world over on Monday morning. I'd say the standard of driving was good and the roads I cycled on were well-maintained.

Hills were plentiful, both up and down. I was suffering from the Alps. As I cycled along I thought of the family. Gill – what did you say last night? Yes, it's my daughter Alison's driving test today. I tried some positive telepathy – 'Alison, I will you to pass your driving test.' I also have a daughter Karen, and a son, Stuart.

Blue Goose was waltzing along, mile followed mile. I forgot to say that the weather was again fine – sunshine and blue skies.

The countryside and the fields did not have the expanse of France, with smaller, well-maintained farms. I did see a hooded crow, as we would see in Orkney. I also heard the first cry of spring – a cuckoo! I've not heard a cuckoo for years. I stopped and listened.

I cycled past Aosta, Chatillon and St Vincent, and pulled off the road for a bite to eat at Pont-St-Martin. I sat at a pavement side table, ordered my usual and watched the world go by.

Late in the afternoon, I passed Ivrea. The standard of road was not as good. It was a minor road – that accounted for the change. I cycled down the road to Chivasso.

The Inner Man said, 'enough is enough, Mac – look for a hotel.' I didn't have to wait long. It said 'The Ritz – four star.' I did wonder if the stars came from the same galaxy as some of the other hotels. Now, Mac, don't be cynical.

'Yes, we have a room, and we can garage your bike.' I pushed Blue

Goose into a lock-up garage. There wasn't a lot of room. What car is that? I smiled to myself – it was a Rolls Royce. My, I thought, we are posh tonight.

The hotel was reasonably priced and my room was a high standard. I completed all my chores, showered and felt ever so good. My cat eye said 90 miles. Good going, if I say so myself.

The evening meal was, no, I'm not going to say, Italian. I also had a pint of chilled beer. I was one contented man. I wrote my log and rang Gill. All was well on the home front. She missed me; I missed her. And Alison had passed her driving test. That was good news. My mind was uncluttered and free. Good night.

Chivasso to Casteggio

I did sleep well last night, it was so quiet. I was up early as usual and breakfast was plentiful – all the choice of food one would want to see at a table. I smiled at the waiter – tea? – no problem. I drank my third cup to my usual level.

The receptionist opened the garage door and there was Blue Goose, alongside the Roller. If I were offered the choice I would still take Blue Goose; I was the pal in need, it was the pal indeed, or words to that effect.

Weather – you guessed it – sunny with blue skies. I gave all the final visual checks and was under way. I had now left the Alps, and after a few miles the undulating roads changed to flat, straight roads. I by-passed Torino and headed for Asti. For the first time, I could feel the heat from the sun. I always think a little sun has a calming effect.

Asti was picturesque and I was blessed with all my needs, a roll and a drink, whilst sitting at a pavement café, watching the world go by. I learned to judge a town by its residents and the way people go about their business. In a car you pass the world by; on a bike the world moves with you.

In no time I was back on the road. The fields were wet; I mean, they were holding a lot of water. The smell was a bit overwhelming, to say the least. What a noise. I'd heard that sound before, in Hong Kong and the New Territories. Bull frogs, that's what it was. I wonder if it was the bull frog polka?

It was a grand sunny afternoon as I cycled through Alessandria. The next thing I knew I was flying through the air, cursing in both Welsh and Orcadian. I had been knocked over by a car as I cycled by the entrance of a petrol station. He just drove straight out on to the main road and knocked me off my bike. There was a young teenage girl sitting next to him; I don't think he saw me.

I picked myself up very slowly. My knee was hurting and I was bleeding badly. I jumped up and down in a temper, cursing profusely. My hard hat and cycle gloves had saved the day, but Blue Goose was in a heap. There was a broken pedal and the brake lever was pushed up the handlebar. The young car driver was standing there with a sweaty red face, shaking. As luck would have it, a passing policeman had witnessed the accident and he was giving the guy some stick.

The road was blocked and irate Italians seemed to be everywhere. Horns were sounding, but I was oblivious to it all; I was busy checking over Blue Goose and myself.

I bandaged my bleeding knee. I was sore in different places but didn't think I had any broken bones. I uplifted Blue Goose and moved it so that cars could pass. The policeman was speaking in fast Italian to me. I couldn't understand; I just shrugged and spread the palms of my hands. He nodded sympathetically. I checked Blue Goose again. Surprisingly, with the bags on the rear it had rolled over, so the damage was limited. I also checked the wheels, front and rear; there were no broken spokes and the wheels were not buckled.

With that, another police car drew up, blue light flashing. Two police officers got out and some very quick Italian words were passing between them. The car driver just stood there, head down, an 'I done it' expression on his face.

An hour must have passed by now. I had straightened the brake lever and the pedal was not bent, although a piece had broken away. In my opinion, Blue Goose was fit to ride. I was expecting the shakes to start with the shock, but there wasn't a tremor.

The police who arrived in the second car spoke to me in perfect English – they said they were tourist police. They asked me to repeat my story; the driver looked forlorn. By now, tempers had cooled.

The tourist police wanted me to go to hospital. With a smile, I declined. They then spoke about charging the driver. He said I had twenty-four hours; in that time I could bring charges against him. I'm sure the driver could understand our conversation.

I looked at him; he was a beaten man. 'No,' I said to the policeman, 'I don't want to bring charges against him.' I told the policeman that, in my opinion, I was fit to ride the bike.

I thanked the police, and shook hands with them, and the driver. I saw the look on his face change to one of relief. I'm sure I made his day, although he had not made mine. The first thought I had when I was knocked over was, damn – that's my world trip over.

I was back on Blue Goose. I stopped to straighten the handlebars and with this done I carried on, my mind full of the day's happenings.

My hard hat and gloves had played a big part in saving me from injury. I rode another thirty miles that afternoon, passing through Tortona and Voghera until I reached Casteggio. I found a hotel – how many stars it had, I didn't notice. When I had bedded the Goose down, I showered, dressed my knee, lay on the bed and fell asleep under the hotel stars. Good night.

Casteggio to Parma

As I woke and made a move, my knee, shoulder and right ankle hurt. I stretched in pain; I was paying the price for my accident. Man, I was feeling sorry for myself before I even got out of bed. 'Come on,' said the Inner Man, 'move your butt.' With those words of encouragement, I made a concerted effort. I was on my feet, hunched up in pain as I stood there, not daring to walk.

How old was I? Sixty. This morning I felt ninety. Gritting my teeth, I did some positive arm and leg movements and felt more supple. I dressed my knee with a shot of neat TCP – I must keep it clean. Shit or bust, I must keep infection out.

At breakfast I must have smelled like a chemist's shop. The waitress gave me a funny look when she delivered the pot of tea. 'Go on, you must eat.' I had no appetite – I hadn't eaten last night either. Emptying the pot of tea was a good start and I soon downed a load of fruit. 'Well done, Mac' said the Inner Man.

Collecting the Goose from the garage I bagged up. Making the ultimate effort, I mounted; we were on our way. I had also taken aspirin, to ease the pain. After an hour, I did feel better, and more supple.

The weather was sunny with blue skies. Blue Goose took over and did the hard work, or so it seemed. I cycled within myself, not pushing too hard. Towns came and went: Broni, Stadelie, Castel San Giovanni. It's strange, no two towns look the same; they all have their individuality. They all have that certain magic that catches the eye and you wonder what it would be like to live there. It's a funny old world.

Piacenza was a sizeable town; I cycled through slowly, but positively. By the time I reached Fiorenzuola D'Arda I was in need of a rest; my Inner Man was shouting for sustenance. Today I had a change of menu; two Parma ham rolls and a pot of tea. The rest was as good as a siesta; the passing world made me forget my aches and pains.

Blue Goose flew the afternoon away. I just held on and enjoyed myself. I found the Italian road signs not up to the standard of the French ones.

In the late afternoon, I reached the outskirts of Parma and carried on until a motel caught my eye. 'Yes, we have a room with all facilities, and you can take your bike in.'

Across the road was a supermarket where I bought my evening meal and my breakfast for the following day. I also bought apples – I'm very partial to an apple.

On checking my cat eye, I had completed 72 miles today. I was one surprised and happy, tired man. Filling the bath with hot water, I slowly slid in and washed the road grime away. I dressed my damaged knee; some of the bruising was showing through and I looked like a yellow and blue minstrel.

On completing my log I felt tired and went to bed early. No, I did not ring the police. Also, I must not tell Gill about the accident or she would want me home. It was one of those days you want to forget. Good night.

Parma to Bologna

The alarm call of nature sounded. What did it say? High water level. I was lying in a pain-free position and slowly I stretched and lowered my legs to the ground, levering my body to a sitting position on the bed. I was feeling better than yesterday. Last night, I slept like a log.

My joints were still a little stiff, and the bruises were turning to black and blue. Through a chink in the curtain, the sun was dawning on a new day. I felt better; more like my old self. I tucked into my takeaway breakfast. No tea – but I filled up with orange juice to my normal cycling liquid level.

The Goose was sitting there waiting, bags fitted, raring to go. Traffic passing the motel was fairly sparse. Outside, I gave the chain two shots of oil and we were on the road. As the saying goes, 'another day, another dollar.'

It was my intention not to go too far today; there was a need not to push the wounded donkey too much. Checking the map, the city of Bologna was within my distance. I enjoyed the apples I bought last night; I found them a good hunger pang filler during the day's ride. I intended to buy more.

Reggio nell'Emilia town was big, busy and well-designed; the modern architecture blending in with the older buildings. Rubiera was what I would call a rural town.

A change of weather was on the way – I could see cloud building on the horizon. The town of Modena soon appeared. It was early for lunch. So what? When you're hungry – eat. I asked the question when the waitress came – 'do you have a pot of tea?' 'Yes, tea,' with a nod of the head. It was my day. I ordered two rolls and tea. Sitting back in a relaxed mood, I ate and drank contentedly.

The weather forecast was not far out; within an hour-and-a-half it was raining. I stopped and dressed in my wet gear. Soon I was on the outskirts of Bologna. It was late afternoon. What a shambolic road system – or was it me? I had a problem finding my way and got lost a few times; it was a navigational nightmare.

It rained heavily – so heavily I sheltered in a covered bus stop. It was big enough to hold both of us. The rain never eased. I took advantage of the time and cleaned Blue Goose, I also did running repairs on my brakes. Hilarity passed me by in the shape of a guy on a bike with an umbrella in one hand and the handlebar in the other. A few minutes later another guy passed on a motor scooter. I would estimate his weight to be around thirty stone. On the scooter's floor pan sat a very contented dog. I laughed again, although it didn't look safe.

Hotels? I tried six with the same answer – 'sorry, we're full.' They always say it with a smile. I couldn't believe it. I asked a receptionist what was the problem with all the hotels full. She pointed out that there was a festival on. Her advice was priceless – 'try again tomorrow.'

That remark brought a smile to my face, but I was fed up, far from home and wet, and still no hotel. 'Keep trying,' said the Inner Man. I came to a hotel on the city limits – four star, it said. In I went. Yes, we have a room and garage for the bike – but only a double room for you. There's always a catch. I sometimes wonder if it's a sales pitch. That I would never know.

I accepted the room and booked a meal. On completing my chores I rang Gill. Her foot was getting better, I'm glad to say. Not many miles, but a busy day. The shower was first class. I was knackered. Good night.

Bologna to Rimini

I did sleep well last night and felt so good when I got out of bed. I always find early morning the best part of the day; I feel fresh and in a good mood. My joints were slightly painful, but nothing to write home about. Rest, as they say, is a healer. Breakfast was first class. I consumed enough to last me the day; tea level alarmed after the fourth cup.

Rain was but a memory, sunshine streamed through the bedroom window. Studying the map I could see I was off course. I wanted the Rimini road. I always find it better to ask directions when lost.

When I said that rest is a healer, I've only had two days' rest all trip. Due respects to myself. My body soon tells me my fitness limits – I must fit in some rest days on rainy or windy days.

I bagged up the Goose, topped up the tyres with air and gave the chain two shots of oil. I set off, but my navigation was off line. I stopped and asked directions to the Rimini road. An English-speaking Italian soon told me which way to go.

I was off, the roads were flat and Blue Goose was flying. While cycling, I thought of the standard of the hotel I stopped at last night. Yes, it was expensive. Don't over-count the stars where I stay in future; two star is good enough for me. I'll put this one down to necessity.

Yesterday's mileage was 65; in the circumstances I was one happy man. I estimated Rimini was approximately 90 miles. We will let the cat eye decide tonight.

En route, cyclists became more frequent – the speed with which they approached and passed me made me think I was on stop, or go slow.

It was flat country. We passed through a few towns: Castel San Pietro, Imola and Facnza. I could smell the sea in the wafting breeze. By midday, I was making good progress – just flying. I enjoyed surveying the towns as I passed through, although some were little more than villages. They looked prosperous, judging by the houses and the cars, and the folk were well-dressed. Maybe the EU has raised the standard of living? I know it has in Ireland.

I was not so self-pitying today. Forget about that accident, Mac; it's all in the past. Cycling through Forli shopping centre, or market street, I decided to stop for a bite to eat. Eat when you're hungry, drink when you're dry; why not? What a hustle and bustle of folk. When you sit back and look at human nature, are we any different from ants? I sometimes wonder.

After I'd eaten I had to answer the call of nature. What a pain in the butt. It's not easy leaving both the Goose and the bags unattended. I overcame the problem by chaining the Goose to the railing outside the café and fitting the lock. You must keep a close watch on yourself and your belongings in this day and age.

Soon I was back on the road. A grand sight was a cycling club passing me by, all the colours of the rainbow – heads down, butts up, going hell for leather, all trying to reach there before they left.

Cesena was a fair size of a town and the roads were well-marked. I was through it in no time. Savignano Sul Rubicone and Santarcangelo di Romagna were what I'd call villages in the tourist belt. They were very prosperous and expensive-looking places to live.

The road passed through these small villages, then – there it is – I could see the sea. The last time I saw it was in Boulogne, France.

I live near the sea in Orkney; it's an everyday occurrence just to look at it. As I turned the corner, there was Rimini. I was feeling good.

When I checked the cat eye, it was reading 80 miles.

The first thing was to look for a hotel or a room. I was in luck: two-star, a room on a side street near the sea front. It had all the facilities and a garage to house Blue Goose. I booked the room for two nights. I would need to buy my own breakfast and main meal; no problem.

The shower was one of those walk-in types. When you turn on the water the whole bathroom gets wet. What a damn mess - water everywhere. I dressed in my best clean clothes and glanced in the mirror. What a scruffy-looking guy. I can't help it, I was born that way.

I was ready for a meal and twenty yards down the road I was in among the restaurants. Why are they queuing at that one? Then it dawned on me – it has the best food. I joined the queue and it was well worth it; by far the best pizza I've tasted. I'll be back tomorrow night for another one.

Time flies. With that meal filling my tum, I was tired. Soon I was back in my room. I lay on the bed and fell asleep. Good night.

Rimini (rest day)

I really enjoyed it. The sun was shining, I cleaned Blue Goose and washed all my cycle gear. I was going to go for a swim in my pants, but when I saw the water, it was so dirty I couldn't believe it. The water at home is pristine clean.

I sun-bathed on the beach and drank Coke. I'll see you tomorrow morning. As they say, have a good rest day.

Rimini to Osimo

Rest days always pass too quickly, as mine did yesterday. I find on a rest day one can catch up with one's washing and bike cleaning. The room was adequate for my needs, and was reasonably priced considering it was located in a central position in Rimini. Some years ago, Gill and I had a holiday in Rimini. Never in my wildest dreams did I imagine I would one day cycle here.

I'm feeling well-rested and my knee is healing. I've removed the bandage. Let Mother Nature heal the rest.

As usual I was up early, bagged up the Goose, ate my supermarket breakfast and even had a cup of tea. Yesterday I bought tea bags. I checked both my water bottles. By the forecast, it could be a hot day.

My plan today was to cycle south on the coastal road. The weather was fine and sunny. I was raring to go as I pushed off into the southbound traffic. Rimini was busy even in the early morning; I think its central position makes it so.

My, what a grand morning. The rest has been like a regeneration. I feel full of beans - or should I say pizza?

The coastal terrain was well-blessed with hill upon hill. The view relaxed my mind, and I could see the sea. As morning progressed I cycled through a number of coastal towns: Pesaro, Fano, Marotta. Each town had its own unique feature as well as a sea background, boats, fishing boats and a feeling of community spirit. It would be good to live in any of them. I stopped for photo calls frequently.

Hills on hills, but my legs were holding out, no problem. In fact, I said, give me a hill I can't climb (big-head). The water bottle was being used frequently; I was sweating profusely in the heat. My safety hard hat doubled as a sun hat. Without it I'd be in trouble – it keeps the head cool.

As I cycled through Senigallia, I decided to stop. My, what a pretty place. Pulling into the nearest café, I ordered my usual, roll and tea, then sat back and gazed at the sea. What a relaxing pastime. I did have a frown on my face, though – one of concern. What contaminates the water of the Adriatic? Is it human-generated flotsam? It's not unlike the North Sea; both seas are used as dustbins. One day we will reap what we have sown.

I had relaxed too deeply and was in pensive mood. 'You can't put the world to rights today; snap out of it,' said the Inner Man.

I drank two slugs of water. The sun was burning my legs and arms. Keep the throat well lubricated.

In no time I was back on the road. Again today, many cyclists passed me by in both directions. Passing through the town of Falconara Marittima, I found it very similar to the other coastal towns I'd passed through this morning; colourful and attractive to live in, or visit on holiday.

No, I'm not going to say that again – show me a hill I can't climb. This afternoon has been a hill-climbing lesson on how to climb in the relaxed position, yet still pedal positively. And if a hill goes up, then it comes down again.

I by-passed Ancona, although I did intend to make it a night stop. I cycled on to Osimo, a small town just off the coast. On reaching Osimo I'd done enough cycling for the day. I found a reasonably-priced lodge, with a clean and tidy room. They also garaged the Goose. I purchased my evening meal and breakfast for the morning. I was tired. Good night.

What a sleep I had last night. I checked the cat eye before writing my daily log. I had completed 80 hot, sweaty, hilly miles. No wonder I slept.

My carry-out breakfast was fine. You only purchase and eat what you want, not what someone else wants you to eat.

I checked the map route for the day. My plan was to head straight down route SS16, coastal road. It's nice to wake up with no stiffness and no pain.

Blue Goose was bagged up, chain oiled, tyres checked. Mechanically, the chain must be kept supple and in good working condition; it's oil-dependent.

The weather was cloudy with patchy sunshine; not as warm as yesterday. Don't talk so much – move out. This I did. We were on the road, heading south.

Town cycling was the name of the game today; it sharpens all the senses. The first towns came and went: Porto San Giorgio and Grottammare. They were typical of the other coastal towns; very picturesque and tourist-inviting. Grand places for a stay.

The roads today were soon becoming problematical. Typical town roads, they had been dug up so many times for drains or cable trenches – you name it. When filled back up they have never been filled to the original road level. Invariably, when cycling over a trench there was an almighty thump. Even the road's inner edges were broken away and the cambers were way out. These roads, in my opinion, were not safe to cycle on.

When you get an almighty thump on a trench, it's not unlike a kick in the butt and a bump on the back. My wrists and shoulders were aching, as I had to hang on tightly to the handlebars. I only hope one of you Italian council men reads this and takes action.

The concentration needed to hold on to the Goose became tiring. You cannot relax – you get all tensed up waiting for the next bump.

The morning soon passed and I was in need of a snack. I decided to pull into the next town. I was not enjoying my cycling. The town of San Benedetto del Tronto soon appeared. What a grand name, I thought – but what a name for the children to have to write in school.

I pulled up at a café, ordered rolls and tea and sat back enjoying myself. You know, I can't ever remember cycling like this today. The state of the roads have made it damned uncomfortable. The weather stayed cloudy. No sweat, like yesterday, only butt pain.

All too soon I was back on the track – I won't call it a road – and I was suffering. I'm glad to say the towns of Porto Di Gascol, Alba Adriatica and Giulianova, came and went. I was concentrating so much on keeping the

Goose upright, I could not relax and see the sights. Another town went by – Roseto degli Abruzzi – the name was as long as the town. It was too early to pull off the road. 'Stay with it, Mac,' said the Inner Man. With all the effort to correct the balance of the Goose, it had rubbed the inside of my leg against the seat. I was uncomfortable. I cycled through Pineto, a small village, with some very prosperous-looking and costly houses.

Silvi Marina – I liked the way it slipped off the tongue. I'll stop here tonight. I soon found a room in a small, family-run hotel. Yes, they could put the bike in the garage. I most wanted a shower. It was hot, and I soon lost the pain of the day, except the inside of my leg had rubbed raw. I gave it a quick flush with TCP to prevent infection.

The room was clean and the bed looked inviting. No, I must eat. I soon found a takeaway and had my fill. I'm tired – must be the TCP fumes. Good night.

Silvi Marina to Campomarino

As usual, I was up early. I completed my morning rituals and it was good to feel so well-rested. The seat burn on my inner thigh looked angry and raw. I slapped a copious amount of Vaseline on the burn, and on my butt. Don't laugh – try it. It's a sure way of getting a pain-free cycle, and it keeps you clean.

I enjoyed my bought-in breakfast, and the yellow-label tea bags. I drank my tea watching the world go by through the bedroom window. Bagged up the Goose, and gave it a maintenance check – it only needed oil on the chain.

It was the end of May. Time waits for no man on a bike.

To maintain your position on a bike is all-important. The Goose and I are as one. You must adjust all aspects of the bike to yourself. Don't make big moves, only small ones at a time. My arms never over-reached the handlebars and my hands slotted in the brake hoods. My butt had moulded the Brookes leather saddle to my shape, my legs exerted pressure where and when required. It's essential not to over-stretch or strain yourself. Man and bike become a working, mechanical team. Together this equals progress and mileage.

Days like yesterday spoil the equation. After checking the map I decided to follow the SS16 coastal road. There weren't as many towns – it should make cycling more pain-free today. The weather forecast was rain, showers and thunderstorms.

I expected a build-up of traffic as I'd be passing Pescara, which is on the main link road between the Adriatic coast and Roma. My plan was to by-pass Pescara, if my navigational skills were up to it. 'Move it, Mac,' said the Inner Man. I pushed off, heading still further south. All systems go – everything felt sound.

There was a build-up of traffic as I approached Pescara. I soon found the by-pass road. Back on the main route the traffic level returned to normal. So far this morning I'd only passed though one town, Montesilvano al Mare. So far so good. The Goose started to fly. I hung on, enjoying the ride; the Vaseline had done the job.

Rain clouds started to build up; I hoped they would keep away. It was later in the day before it rained, thankfully. As I cycled I had a view of the sea. It made me feel happy.

Starting to sing, I had a choral hour. I sang all the songs in my repertoire. People I cycled past looked and smiled. I really enjoyed the singing. It is said that a smiling, singing man is happy.

I was entering another town, Francavilla al Mare. I would call it a small village on the coast. Italy is full of these picturesque hamlets.

Rain wafted in slowly off the sea. I stopped and changed into my wet gear. Before too long, it belted down.

Torino di Sangro Marino soon came into view. It was early afternoon and I in need of a snack. One thing is for sure – in Italy there is no problem finding a café. I was soon sheltering with tea and a cake; most enjoyable. The thunderstorm broke when I was sitting in the café. I sat it out with two cups of tea.

The rain eased. I was on the bike again and heading south. I stopped and changed out of my wet gear. That's better – more freedom.

The town of Termoli came and went. What a difference in a day; I was thoroughly enjoying my cycle. Campomarino came into view in the late afternoon. I had no choice of hotel – I only found one. The receptionist said that they had a room and could put the bike in a garage. 'Food?' I asked. 'No food,' said the receptionist. I checked in. The room looked clean. I showered and changed into dry clothes. I wrote my log and lay on the bed – the bed collapsed with a clatter. Watch this space. Good night.

Campomarino to Cerignola

The good news – the bed held up all night. I put it down to my building skills. Yes, I'd say I was rested and my gear was dry. Complaints? Did I complain? No, I slept with them. Who would listen?

I ate my breakfast – one apple I had in my bag – and water.

I was on the road early and there were no problems with the Goose. The roads were in good condition and the Goose moved as if it had a mission in life. As it flew down some hills I held on. I was happy with progress. My mileage for the month of May was 2,000.

Again today I plan to follow the SS16 coastal road south. My, it's some length of road. I've been travelling on it for days, but I'm not complaining.

Cycling through a small village, I came across a supermarket. The very thing. I parked and chained the Goose and once inside the shop I was spoiled for choice. I purchased my needs (don't forget the apples). Outside the shop were a table and chair, so I sat down and had a feast. I was like a squirrel – I stored the apples in my pannier bags.

I was soon on the Goose again. Mile followed mile and I could feel the heat of the sun. I sweated on a few hills – not a town in sight – and it made my day.

Late afternoon I came across a big market town, Forria. No, I did not stop – I was still full from my morning meal.

Some travel books say that the north is more populated than the south. I tend to agree. The south was farming country, but how anyone can work this land I don't know. Even in the early spring it was dry and sun-baked.

I enjoyed cycling through both the north and south of Italy. If only people would smile. They never seemed happy, as if they were always looking for something. What, I don't know. 'You are some miserable critter,' said the Inner Man.

Later, I was approaching the town of Cerignola. I decided to call it a day. I neared a hotel, it didn't have that 'too expensive' look. I checked in. 'Would you garage my bicycle, please?' 'No,' said the young male receptionist, 'we don't accommodate bicycles,' in an officious tone. I've got one here, I thought to myself. I told him of my travels and the fact that this was the first hotel that had refused to accommodate my bike for the night. I wore an aggravated, hurt and annoyed look. By his expression I could see I had slightly swayed him. My next salvo brought him to his knees, as they say: 'I want to see the manager.' His eyes opened wide. 'Yes,' he said, 'we will garage your bike.'

I turned on my heel and went to my room. I smiled to myself. 'Don't feel annoyed – you won the day.' The hotel was clean and tidy; my room had all the facilities. The shower was excellent and the food first class. I had a glass of white wine to finish the day.

I wrote my log – 75 miles today. I was pleased. I looked under my bed; it had four legs – it looked safe. I made a mental note that Blue Goose needed a clean. I intended to do this in the next day or two.

I rang Gill and she said her foot was healing well. 'When are you coming home?' she asked. I laughed and said that I loved and missed her. With Gill on my mind I lay back on the bed and closed my eyes. Good night.

My ritual in the morning does not change often and my pre-checks to the Goose are a neccessary part of it. Although I'm doing something I've dreamed about for years, it's not unlike work. Repetitive as work is, cycling every day can sometimes feel the same. The only difference with cycling is that I don't know how far I'll go today, or if I'll find a lodge and food – and I do see new places and faces.

I had bagged up the Goose ready to move out when the owner or manager of the hotel stopped for a chat. He showed an interest in cycling and inspected the Goose, asking various questions. The over-officious receptionist looked on, head bowed sheepishly. 'Let that be a lesson to you, my Italian friend,' I said to myself as I rode away.

The weather was sunny. If it stays like this, it will be hot this afternoon. My cycle route today will take me on a new road, the SS98, joining the SS16 at the town of Bari.

I was on my way. The further south you go on the Italian roads, the flatter they get. Within the first hour the wind increased in velocity. Blowing from the north it was in my back – this doesn't happen often. The Blue Goose just flew along, I only steered. The driving force was the wind, plus my effort.

Towns and villages were few and far between. I could see the town of Andria in the distance. I also saw Corato. I joined the SS16 route south at the town of Modugno and decided I would silence all my hunger and thirst pangs. Soon I was sitting in a roadside café; tea and cake did the trick. I couldn't believe the miles I'd covered this morning – cycling was effortless.

Soon I was back on the road. I didn't want to 'miss the wind', as yachtsmen say. I by-passed the town of Bari. It must be a busy port, as the traffic increased over the next twenty miles.

I could see the sea. The SS16 followed the flat country roads. Today, road safety was paramount; I needed that sixth sense. The back wind, if anything, increased in velocity. I stopped for a top-up, bringing my liquid level back to normal. I've been hitting the water bottle hard, as they say.

I'd missed some meals over the last few days, and that makes a difference to your stamina. The wind was still fresh, so I took advantage and cycled into the evening.

I entered the town of Fasano. The Inner Man said, 'enough is enough.' Availability of hotels – only one. I was given directions and found it. It seemed very quiet. I asked if they had a room. 'Yes,' said the receptionist. 'We don't open for the season until tomorrow, but if you want a room I'll let you have one. We do not have food, but if you hurry there's a café over the road. You can park your bike in your room.' I didn't have to ask – that makes a change. I was in. The shower was electric – I soon found out how to work it.

I was soon at the door of the café. 'Sorry, sir – we are closing – but we have ice cream and beer.' I bought two ice creams and two beers. I was one tired man. I remembered the apples in my panniers. Yes, I had two. I wrote my log and checked the cat eye. I gave out an impressive 'YES!' – a real physical reaction. I had completed 131 miles today. I was elated; the adrenaline was flowing and I was on a high. It was the most miles I'd ever done in a day.

I lay on the bed. What a day for a daydream! Good night.

Fasano to Brindisi

Sleep came quickly last night, although I woke to the wing beats and buzz of a mosquito. I glanced at my watch – 0200 hours. I dread the noise in my ear, and my efforts to stop the dive-bomber were to no avail. In desperation, I sloshed some TCP on my face and ears. I slept until morning.

I was out of bed early as usual, with some lumps on my arms and face I did not have last night. I washed, shaved, and touched the lumps and bumps with TCP. I put them down to mosquitoes and bed bugs.

Breakfast was non-existent. After celebrating my record personal mileage last night I had eaten two ice creams and two apples and drunk two small bottles of beer. I was hungry.

I bagged up the Goose, oiled the chain and launched myself out into the traffic of the SS16 road to Brindisi. The weather was fine and sunny, unlike yesterday. Traffic was light for the first ten miles, then it increased as I approached Brindisi. It must be the rush hour.

On the outskirts of Brindisi I checked my cat eye – 20 miles. It was still early morning. I was suffering from hunger pangs; my stomach thought my throat was cut.

Out of the blue on the outskirts of the town, a shipping booking office appeared. I immediately took advantage. I parked and chained the Goose to the cycle stand.

Behind the counter was a young lass. 'Yes, I can speak English,' she said. I was in luck. Could I book a ticket, single, from Brindisi to Igoumenitsa in Greece? I would like a cabin and I also have a bicycle. She uttered the universal words: 'no problem.' Well, I was booked as quickly as that, as I handed her my flexible friend.

The boat was due to sail at midnight. She directed me through Brindisi down to the harbour. I thanked the lass and was under way. It all happened so quickly and it was only 1100 hours.

By 1130 hours, I had cycled through Brindisi and found the harbour. What do I do now? 'Nothing but wait,' said the Inner Man.

In other words, a rest day. I was starving, the hunger pangs in my stomach were rioting. I had to eat to suppress the hunger.

The weather stayed fine; you could feel the heat from the sun. Cycling though the town I soon found the harbour and the ship's berth. The town was full of backpackers, tourists, cyclists, not unlike myself; the one way to describe what I saw was a 'jam pot' of people from all walks of life and from all over the world.

A pavement café. I parked the Goose against the wall, ordered a sizeable pizza, which was most enjoyable, and some ice cream, washed down with a cup of tea. Where did it all go? One satisfied customer – I cleared the plate in front of me.

It's a great pastime just watching people go by. A Mercedes car pulled up outside the café. Out of the car stepped an immaculately-dressed, middle-aged man, plus two well-dressed men who were acting over-observant. The three men sat at a table, but only the middle-aged man ate. What a fuss the waiters made of him, running and attending to his every need, whilst the other two men sat in silence observing the area.

In my opinion, he was the mayor, the police chief, or a mafia boss. 'Mac,' said the Inner Man, 'you have been watching too many gangster films.'

Exploring the town and window shopping passed a few hours. It was a very prosperous town, was my conclusion.

Saturday afternoon is the same the world over. What folk about. Ships came and went, unloading and loading their human cargo. Through observation I concluded that Italian youth are born posers. Their actions were hilarious to behold; the name of the game to impress one another.

I met a young Belgian lad who spoke good English. He said he was also awaiting the boat to Greece. His name was Derek and he told me his intention was to backpack the world. We passed the time away, talking. Pointing to the backpack, I said with a smile that it looked heavy. He assured me it was. He opened the pack and produced some heavy books. These were travel books and it was his intention to edit and update them on his world travels. We planned to meet in Pakistan.

Stretching and yawning, I'd seen enough of the world going by. You can have too much of a good thing. Looking at my watch the time was 2200 hours. There was a movement on the back loading ramp of the ship – action at last.

Ship loading at home is an accepted part of life; an everyday occurrence. What I was about to see brought a smile to my face. It was like an ad lib stage show. I'll do my best to describe the farce.

The ship was aft the loading ramp, open on to a large car park. Cars, lorries, motorcyclists, camper vans, cyclists, all waited to be devoured by the ship. Suddenly the lights of the loading deck and the ship's ramp lights announced the start of the loading. Standing on the ramp was a boat's official; a purser or a loading master. He was an imposing-looking man, dressed in white shorts and a short-sleeved shirt. He was smoking a big grandee cigar that enveloped him in smoke. His weight was in the region of twenty-five stone.

His ramp-loading act began with a series of arm gestures, pointing in turn to a car or lorry, motorcyclist or camper van; they all duly disappeared into the mouth of the ship. When two or three cars came to the ramp without his direction, he would wave his arms and shout, then jump up and down on the spot in his obvious temper. Sweating profusely and billowing cigar smoke, this guy was a hard act to follow. Funny – he had no applause for his act.

He pointed at me at long last. The Goose and I were up and over the ramp in a flash.

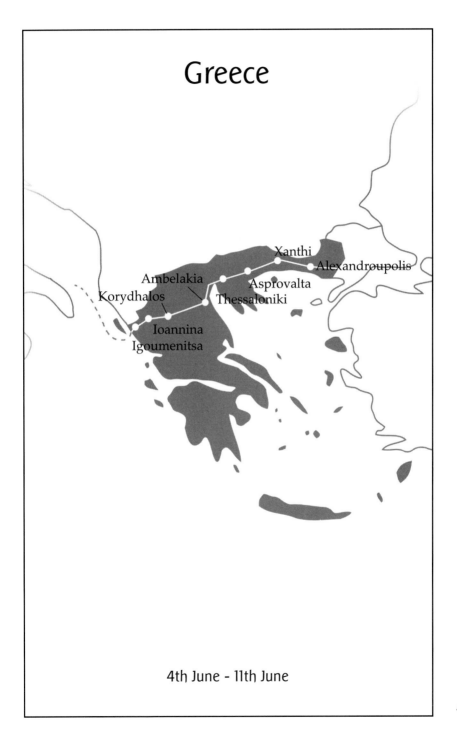

Greece

Xanthi
Alexandroupolis
Ambelakia
Korydhalos
Asprovalta
Thessaloniki
Ioannina
Igoumenitsa

4th June - 11th June

47

The ship's tannoy system announced the time – 0600 hours - and wished the passengers good morning. My brain was far from receptive. The announcement also rumbled on about unloading in Corfu. What was this guy on about? Man, you have disturbed one comfortable passenger form his bunk. As I dressed, the last night's happenings flashed through my mind.

Blue Goose was hitched to the ship's rail on the car deck. The ship left Brindisi at midnight; my cabin was comfortable with shower and bunk. My meal in the ship's restaurant last night was excellent.

As I reached the outside deck, the early rays of the morning sun made me blink. I asked a fellow passenger, 'where are we?' 'Corfu, mate,' was his reply. If I'd known we would be stopping at Corfu, I might have considered cycling around the island for, say, three or four days.

It was not to be. Staying on deck, I watched the activities of unloading passengers and freight. From my vantage point on deck, the view of Corfu was excellent. I had never visited the island.

We were soon under way, heading for Igoumenitsa, docking at 0730 hours. Glancing at my watch, it was one hour slow. I reset it. Greece is approximately two hours ahead of UK time.

I untied Blue Goose from the car deck, fitted the bags and pushed it down the ship's ramp. After all the formalities, we were ready to roll, as they say. Stopping to look once more at the ship, I thought of asking someone to take a photo as a memento. A willing passenger obliged, taking a photo of all three of us; the boat, the Goose and myself.

Two buses were on the pier; their destination, Athens. It was Sunday morning and the sun was shining. One final check of the Goose. Yes, I oiled the chain. The map said E92 road; all roads were signposted from the pier. Hello Greece! We were under way.

Very soon I noticed a crowd of ladies walking down the street in their best attire, all heading towards the church. The colour and splendour of their clothes made me think instantly of a film set.

All too soon Igoumenitsa was but a dream. Hills on hills became a reality all too quickly. Soon the hills had changed to mountains; the cycling skill in granny gear was the only way to make forward progress. The off-bike rest period changed to one of walking. I had to re-think my natural instinctive reactions.

The heat of the day was overpowering. I was hitting the water bottle. My hard hat was again keeping me cool.

Soon I was passing through villages, or small towns: Vrousina and Soulopoulon. Stopping, I bought apples, and some Coke to supplement my water. I was consuming copious amounts of water; sweat was dripping from my brow.

Photo calls became a part of the day; in five hours I had taken more pictures than in all the days I was in France.

Klimatia was the largest town so far. Cars were few and far between and no other cyclists passed. It was late afternoon as one tired, leg-weary, sweat-drenched man cycled into Ioannina. 'Call it a day,' said the Inner Man. I didn't need a second telling. I found a hotel and booked in both the Goose and myself. Good night.

Ioannina to Korydhalos

As usual, my eyes opened with the light of dawn. Is it the animal instinct in us? With all the walking on the hills yesterday, I had visions of leg stiffness today as my feet hit the floor. I did press-ups. There was no stiffness and I was pain-free. That's fifty per cent of the team fit to travel.

The standard of food in the hotel was good; my breakfast was most enjoyable. On paying the receptionist last night for my room, he told me if I paid by credit card it would cost twenty per cent more than paying by cash.

On checking the map, the route I intended to cycle was very mountainous, over the roof of Greece. It would be strenuous cycling for the next three or four days, calling on all my reserves of strength.

Bagging up the Goose, I oiled the chain and checked the brake blocks and the brake operation. I pushed off into the line of traffic heading down the E92. It was Monday morning, the sun was shining and I was feeling completely happy with life, even here in the traffic rush hour. It's the same the world over – not a smiling face to be seen.

On leaving town, the traffic eased but the hills tested my legs. There are twenty-one gears on the Goose; I was using the bottom three plus the 'granny gear', which is the lowest. Photo calls were numerous; the sun rays painted pictures on the beautiful landscape.

Hills turned to mountains. Up and up I went, cycling and walking. I was certainly cycling fit, but walking fitness is different. Soon, however, I was into the way of it. The water bottle levels were dropping too fast. On the side of the road were strategically placed water fountains. I know what you're going to say. Yes, I did drink out of the fountains, with no bad reaction.

The village of Mazia was built to view the surrounding landscape. The colours blended in unobtrusively with nature.

Cycling up hills or mountains can be intimidating to some folk. I sometimes use the psychological strategy of don't look up the hill or mountain you are going to climb; just cycle, change gear and run on autopilot.

Down hill at times was hard on the hands and the brakes. The weight factor, if you let it take command, would propel you down at speeds in excess of forty miles an hour. One false move and you're off the road.

The roads were of a good standard although the signposts were few and far between. I never saw any animals. I passed through the mountain villages of Voutonasi and Metsovon. Stopping at a café I ate my usual – tea, and is it cake? It tasted good, anyway.

I was feeling good; the sun in the afternoon was hot. I was congratulating myself on the day's progress, and my ability to climb the hills and mountains, when there it stood: the granddaddy of all mountains. I looked at it with my psychological eye. 'Go for it, Mac,' said the Inner Man. Changing down through the gears, I was under way.

The work load was demanding; all my strength and stamina reserves were called upon. I cycled, walked, rested, cursed, spat and drank my water to quench the inner demand. Sweat ran off me, dripping on to my knees as I peddled. Soon, I was in autopilot; I had broken the pain barrier. The road flattened out. Glancing at the signpost, it said: height 1,690m. I was on top of the world. The strange thing was the strength of the wind – it was blowing a gale. But it was in my back so I didn't mind; it was cooling. I rode down hill at a great rate of knots. My hands felt the pain and the strain as I cycled into Korydhalos. I looked for a hotel for one tired man. Good night.

Korydhalos to Ambelakia

In the pure air, I slept like a mountain goat. Talk about goats – I saw two herds yesterday. Glancing out of my bedroom window, it was soon apparent I was in the mountains. I reckoned I should be out of the mountains by the late afternoon.

The hotel is family-run, spotlessly clean and the food is first class. After checking the map, I saw that the E92 was still my route today. If I can reach Larisa I'll be one happy man. The sun was shining with some cloud in the sky. I bagged up the Goose, oiled the chain, pushed off and joined the E92.

Mental notes for the day: change my money to drachma and purchase some vitamin tablets. When cycling long distances continually, I do take vitamin tablets. I'm a firm believer that nutrients leach out of the body when cycling day after day.

The hills today were manageable – not like the mountains of yesterday. There was a need to cut back on photo calls; they were interfering with my cycling rhythm. The beautiful scenery was like a magnet to me; the mountains and surrounding country glistening in the first flush of spring growth.

It's surprising how sometimes you can laugh on the road. Today was no exception. A young guy at the wheel of a car turned a corner to reveal a girl's legs protruding out of the passenger window. What a way to keep cool.

Cycling through Kalabaka, drinking in the sights of the small town, suddenly I hit a hole in the road. It stopped my momentum dead. What a body shock. It was like hitting a brick wall at thirty miles per hour. Somehow I managed to balance and hold the Goose upright. I wasn't sure if I'd dislocated my neck or broken my wrist, but that's how it felt. Hello – what's this hole at the back of my front teeth? My tongue investigated. I had lost a filling, and, what's more, I'd swallowed it. Let that be a warning to you, Mac. Don't daydream while cycling through towns.

I changed money and bought vitamin tablets and apples on the way through Trikkala. The roads started to flatten out, the hills were fewer, and the miles were mounting up. The Goose was on autopilot. My legs were having a rest; I was enjoying my cycling.

The road sign said 'Larisa'. My, this was today's objective. It was quite a big town. Taking advantage as I cycled past a café, I stopped and ate a meal of Greek salad.

It's a funny old world. This morning I was spoilt for hotels, but in the late afternoon there was none to be seen. Cursing myself, I realised I should have stopped in Larisa. I checked my map. The nearest small town was twenty miles down the road. As I cycled on there was a sort of picnic park. Cars could stop and there was a guy selling food. Through sign language he understood what I wanted and pointed up the mountain. I checked my map. Yes, there was a mountain village. All the time, this guy was swiping at flies with an over-sized fly swatter, trying but failing to keep flies from the food.

My decision: twenty miles down the road, or three miles up the mountain? The choice was made – mountain village. Well, to climb three miles at the end of the day, virtually straight up, was not an easy task. Today, I reckoned I had consumed four litres of water. The sign post said 'Ambelakia'. What a beautiful Greek mountain village. It made me forget my aches and pains. Through the old sign language I indicated I was in need of a night's lodgings and was directed to a house. I tapped on the door. Yes, there was a room for me and the Goose. Sweet mountain dreams. Good night.

Ambelakia to Thessaloniki

The harsh calls of a mountain crow were as good as an alarm clock.
I don't know what it was saying, but it rang the alarm bells in my
subconscious. Opening my eyes, I glanced out of the window. It was a
sunny day. I smiled. What a wonderful view of the mountains. I was
living a 'taste of Greece'; a quiet mountain life.

Last night I was lucky to secure the lodge. Mine host spoke English,
which made life easier for me. The inside of the house impressed me;
highly polished pine covered the floors, walls and ceilings, and the
doors were craftsman-made. Shoes had to be left in the hall, but slippers
were provided; goats' hair soft slip-ons.

There was no evening meal, but breakfast was provided. After my
shower I walked through the village. What stunning views – it really
impressed me. Old ladies in black walked slowly and deliberately about
their village way of life. Village houses, the square and the church,
looked as if they had all grown up together. The church bell rang,
or rather clanked. It must be cracked. What a feeling to cherish – it
enveloped me. The atmosphere was one to treasure. Greek mountain life
in the raw.

Time for breakfast. As I opened my bedroom door, on the outside
was a 'good luck' key fastened to the door. I took a photograph. For
my breakfast there was tea, goats' cheese and biscuits. I ate slowly,
savouring the nourishing taste. I was starving.

All too soon, I had to leave the mountain village. I bagged up the
Goose, oiled the chain and shook hands with mine host. My map said
join the E92; my proposed destination, Thessaloniki.

What a way to start the day. Three miles down hill was heavy on
the hands, working the brakes all the time. After the jolt from the hole
in the road yesterday I could still feel a pain in my neck and wrist. No
toothache, I'm glad to say.

Turning a corner on the way down the hill, I stopped to take a
photo. There, halfway across the road was a tortoise. I'd never seen one
in the wild before. It's said that if a black cat passes you, it's good luck.
What about a tortoise? I don't know.

At the bottom of the hill I turned right and was back on route E92.
The roads were surprisingly traffic-free. Cycling was easy on the flat
roads and the Goose was flying. 'Hold on, Mac,' said the Inner Man. The
first village I cycled through today was Platamon and I kept my eyes on
the road. Once bitten, twice shy. I kept glancing at the sea; it made me

one happy man.

Following the coast was most enjoyable; the scenery was so different, though not so photogenic. This was cycling at its best and the morning passed in a flash.

The sun beat down. I was lowering the water level at an alarming rate. Skala Leptokaria was on the horizon. As I entered the town a café loomed up. Stopping, I soon ordered a meal; Greek salad, with extra goats' cheese and olives, followed by tea. I did enjoy the meal. The waiter filled my water bottles on request. I thanked him as he uttered the famous words, 'no problem.'

I soon passed through Skala Leptokaria. These small towns to me were seaside villages. I felt happy and, for now, my hunger pangs had been suppressed. Flat coastal roads resulted in mile upon mile building up. Methoni was again a pretty seaside village. The Goose was flying. As I entered Thessaloniki, I made a mental note to stop.

I was spoilt for hotels and made my choice. 'Yes, we have a room for both you and your bike; also an evening meal.' I checked in and ordered my meal. The room had all facilities. I showered off the day's sweat and felt human. Lying back on the bed I checked the miles for yesterday – 86; today, it was 88. Good night.

Thessaloniki to Asprovalta

As I opened my eyes, my mind slotted into gear. 'Move it, Mac,' said the Inner Man. In less than two shakes of a lamb's tail, as they say, I was on my feet and dressed.

A glance out of the window confirmed that the weather was fine: calm sea and no wind. Thoughtfully, I cast my mind back to the miles I had completed in Greece. The mountains were by far the most demanding of my stamina to date. I decided that a rest day was called for soon. There was a need to catch up on my personal chores and clean the Goose.

Again, I ate goats' cheese and biscuits for breakfast, followed by tea. No wonder I can cycle up mountains like a goat. It must be the cheese. I bagged up the Goose and we were off. Today's plan was to follow the E90, cutting across the headland, leaving the sea to follow the shoreline of two lakes, then picking up the sea again at Asprovalta.

As I pushed off, the traffic was by far the busiest I'd seen it in Greece. I put it down to the rush hour. It was all of an hour before it eased.

The morning's cycle turned out to be on flat roads, no hills, and the mountains were but a distant, hazy view. I cycled through the small hamlets of Langadhikia and Nea-Madhitos. As I cycled, my mind filled with thoughts of Turkey. Within days, I should be crossing the border. It's an unknown entity to me; one can but wonder.

It was picturesque cycling beside the two inland lakes; the road followed the edge of both. They seemed to me void of one thing: wildlife. Yes, I did see some birds, but only a handful. The reasons for this I don't really know.

Soon I was cycling through the village of Rentina. Taking advantage, I called a tea stop. I sat as usual at an outside table and ordered tea and cake – it was like honey to a bee. The town was very quiet. No one was rushing about. I could see that life was taken at a leisurely pace. As a stranger and in my cycling gear, I must have stuck out like a sore thumb.

It was mid-afternoon when I cycled into Asprovalta; 1430 to be precise – that's what my log says. My first impression was that it was a quaint seaside town, as pretty as a picture. The old saying entered my mind, 'that's where I'll hang my hat,' – and that's just what I did.

I found a hotel and in an instant was inside. 'Yes, we have a room for both you and your bike.' I was checked in for two nights, the Goose was allowed the same room as myself.

The room was complete with all necessary facilities. There were no evening meals, but they served breakfast; that suited me fine. On checking the cat eye I had completed 53 miles today. I was one happy man. I felt relaxed already – it was like being on holiday.

Asprovalta – rest day

I know what you're thinking: what does he do on a rest day? Well, read this space.

I enquired if there was a laundrette nearby and the receptionist directed me to one across from the hotel. I was in luck. Soon I had washed all my dirt and sweat-filled clothes and dried them in the clothes drier. They smelt as fresh as a daisy.

In the afternoon, or what was left of it, I did some window shopping. To my surprise, I bought myself a pair of jeans. They were black, lightweight and very roomy, with an elasticated waist. They would make me more presentable off-bike, and would keep me warm on colder days. I was pleased, to say the least, although I did have the nagging feeling in my mind that I was adding to the weight of the bags.

When I showered that evening, I saw myself in the full-length mirror. What a shock. I was so slim my belly had all but disappeared. I estimated I'd lost two stone. I could but stand and stare.

I was acutely ready for my evening meal. As I glanced down the main road, tables and chairs appeared on the pavements outside restaurants as if by magic. I was spoilt for choice. My fancy of the day was for a pizza. I was soon settled in a comfortable chair with a glass of white wine. I ordered a Greek salad and a medium-sized pizza. There was one person missing. You have it in one – Gill.

With the salad I had extra olives. When I was presented with my pizza, inwardly I said, 'Mac, you guts – you'll never finish that.' You know, I was so annoyed with myself because I did fail to eat my meal, and had a problem sleeping later. I had that bloated feeling.

To top it all, just as I was dozing off to sleep, I was buzzed by a mosquito. Man, I just hate those midges. I thought the best form of defence was attack. I flicked on the lights and attacked with my tee-shirt, but to no avail. I could see more than one. I was some mad. Where's the TCP? I found the bottle and dowsed my face and arms and returned to bed. Yes, I did have some lumps on my arms in the morning.

I reported it to the receptionist on the way to breakfast. He assured me the room would be sprayed today.

Lunchtime came so soon. I ate a light meal, leaving enough room for tonight. On one side of the road running alongside the village was a shingle beach. The sea looked so inviting and I could count on one hand the number of folk on the beach. I wanted to swim. The problem was, who would look after my clothes? I didn't have a swimming costume either. Finding a quiet part of the beach I slipped off my new jeans and was soon in the water in my underpants, keeping a close eye on my clothes with all my worldly goods in them. I so enjoyed the salt water, as well as the swim. I felt so clean.

On leaving the sea I did a quick change, stripping off my wet underpants and slipping on my new jeans. You know, I think it's more relaxing on a bike than sitting out a rest day. All too soon, as they say, good things come to an end. Asprovalta, I'll see you again. One of the most relaxing two-day holidays I've ever had.

On returning to the hotel, I thoroughly cleaned Blue Goose. It looked better for the rest, as I did myself. My mind was in turmoil – what shall I eat tonight? Man, what a choice. As the Americans say, have a nice day. Good night.

Asprovalta to Xanthi

The internal alarm sounded. The reaction was automatic: eyes open and feet hit the floor. The spray must have done the trick; I never saw or heard a mosquito all night, although I did keep my window closed.

Soon I was dressed in my clean cycling clothes, ready to meet the world.

My bags were packed and the Goose looked spick and span. I was fully relaxed. My meal last night was a last minute decision, and not as good as the night before. I ate a steak. But then, I'm not one to complain, am I?

Breakfast was fruit, cheese and biscuits and tea. My water bottles were full – I was also full.

Wheeling the Goose out on to the road, I thanked the receptionist for a good two days' stay. He smiled as I shook his hand and wished him good morning. Well, I made someone's day. It also brought a smile to my face.

The weather was fine, warm and sunny. I oiled the Goose, making a mental note that the oil bottle was nearly empty. My route plan today was quite basic – follow the E90 to Xanthi.

I was under way; route E90, here I come. The traffic was sparse I'm glad to say and the road conditions made for easy cycling. The road followed the coast and the sea was calm. On the land side, I was looking at the first serious efforts to farm the land that I'd seen. I even saw a field of barley about to be harvested. In Orkney, barley has only been sown for five weeks; what a time difference.

In a relaxed mood, I was fully enjoying this morning's cycle. Flat roads in good condition – what more could I ask? The Goose was flying and I was but a passenger.

The first village I passed through this morning was Kerd Hillia, which had a quiet, rural-looking main street. Was it five folk I counted? Mind you, it was early.

I made a mental note that it was Sunday tomorrow and no shops would be open. I'd need to buy apples and water. I was caught out last week when I found all the shops closed. It does help to know the local customs.

The village of Loutra Elevtheron went by. Strange name, but then, in all fairness, the locals would find the village names strange in Orkney.

Cycling along happily, my mood turned to singing. I soon passed an enjoyable hour singing my repertoire of songs, from one-liners to a memory full of song words.

Kavalla is a large, busy town, humming with the hustle and bustle of folk coming and going about their business. Soon my eye fell on a café that over-looked the main street. Sitting there with my cheese and biscuits, washed down by tea, I was happy. Some cars and lorries speed in towns – it's the same world over.

Soon I was under way. The lethargic feeling I had had cycling out of the mountains had disappeared. I was a man with a mission; nothing was going to deter me. With a positive clarity I thought, I am where

I am today, cycling with drive and energy to accomplish the dream. 'Calm down, Mac,' said the Inner Man.

Xanthi. As I entered the town outskirts, I stopped at two hotels; all rooms were taken. My trained eye saw a motel in the distance. I pulled off the road. 'Yes, we have a room for you and your bike.' I blinked when he told me the cost, and reluctantly accepted it.

Again, I bring up the subject of the cost of hotels, or of any accommodation. Unless the price is displayed, they can tell how desperate a person is for accommodation and they can charge what they like. The room was fine; clean with a shower. I was in need of one to cool down. Good night.

Xanthi to Alexandroupolis

When I awoke, my mind changed to think gear. What would be the cost of living in Turkey? The only indication I had were my notes on Turkey. I could but wonder.

My evening meal, a pizza, was up to standard; most enjoyable. Yes, I remembered to purchase water and apples for today. Breakfast was a carry-out – tea from my yellow label tea bags.

I rang Gill last night, it was great to hear her voice. She assured me that she's keeping well. At long last my medical bag turned up; Gill has re-directed it to Ankara, Turkey. I have the phone number to ring when I'm in Ankara. They will then deliver the medical bag to me.

This foreign food fails to satisfy my hunger. What wouldn't I give for a plate of beans on toast? I'm cheap to keep and run.

My route today is the E90. I'll have to sharpen up my senses, especially the sixth sense of survival. I intend to pass through six towns and villages today. If I can reach Alexandroupolis I'll be one happy man. Yesterday the cat eye recorded 85 miles; that's a hard day's work.

The Goose was bagged up, ready to go. I oiled the chain and pushed off. The roads were quiet. It's Sunday – that's a good enough reason. The weather was sunny with a side wind. It keeps you cool, I must admit. The roads were in good condition; the Goose flew the morning away and the villages passed. Vifeika was very quiet, practically deserted. The most picturesque village I passed through was Porto Largo, where the land joins one headland to another, with the sea on either side. Once through the village, the road shoots directly inland to a big town, Komotini.

The apples came in handy, also the water. I took a standing break, enjoying the view of the countryside. The road today was not what I would call straight. Excuse the language, but it was not unlike a dog peeing in the snow – it went everywhere but straight. From Komotini, it again shoots down to the sea, passing through Aratos, Sapai and Mesta. I cycled through the villages without any problems. They all had something to give; each was unique in its own way.

As I cycled towards the sea, I came to the small village of Makri and again took a standing rest. It must be the Sunday afternoon drive; there was a movement of cars towards the seaside, families out for a spring run.

I was feeling the effects of the sun on my arms and face. My nose was peeling and my arms were red with a heat rash. Take care.

The road again followed the sea and farmed land soon became more evident. I bet that land is highly prized.

Soon I was on the outskirts of Alexandroupolis. It was late Sunday afternoon and the sea front was buzzing with youth, all motivated towards one another. My first choice of hotel was full. I found a motel near the sea with a room for the Goose and me. It was clean, with all services. After my shower I went to the beach for a walk. The seawater wasn't fit to wash my clothes, let alone swim. It was pollution at its worst.

I was in need of food and a rest. Good night.

Turkey

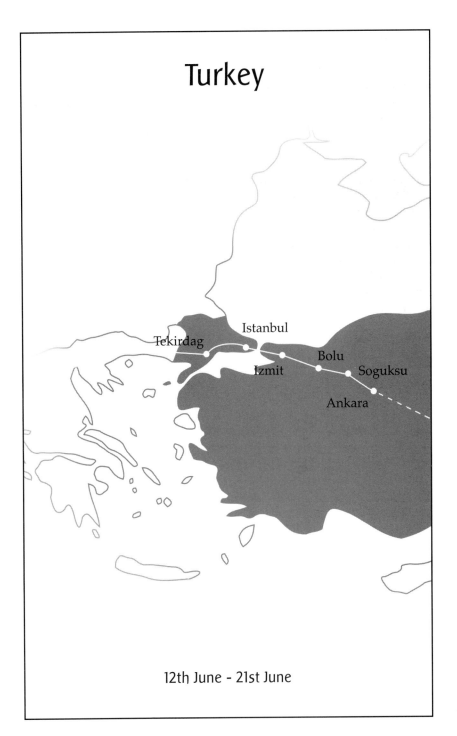

Tekirdag
Istanbul
Izmit
Bolu
Soguksu
Ankara

12th June - 21st June

Rise and shine. Best foot forward. It only takes minutes to dress in one's cycling clothes. Sleep comes easily when you work for it. Yes, I was rested.

The meal last night I purchased at a self-service restaurant. My comment is, it was fair, say no more. My breakfast this morning wasn't great. Let's say it filled a hole. I've had my moan for the day.

My plan today: I should enter Turkey at midday. This morning I'll stay on the E90 until the Turkish border. I'm not sure how the Turks grade their roads. The weather was fine, the Goose was bagged up, all systems go. Move it.

Monday morning traffic. The road was busier than yesterday and the most traffic was on entering town. The road was winding, following the coast, and there was a slight breeze off the sea that kept me cool. The Goose had the bit between the teeth and just flew along. I felt energetic with a spring in my heel. I was cycling the final miles between Greece and Turkey and the traffic was now virtually non-existent. I seemed to be on my own.

Over the last five miles, I became aware of the army's presence. The border crossing soon loomed into view.

Reading the international signs, I joined the small queue marked 'visa'. After filling out the forms I queued again. 'Only English monies,' said the policeman. I put my Scottish ten-pound note away; I was lucky to have an English one. I was annoyed. 'Don't make a fuss, Mac,' said the Inner Man.

An official handed the visa to me, saying that it was valid for only three months. Soon I was across the border and away. Cheerio Greece, hello Turkey. The troops and the police – what firepower and a show of guns at the border crossing.

The first five miles into Turkey the army was to the fore; young soldiers sitting it out – but for what? The traffic remained non-existent for the first ten miles. The road conditions all too soon deteriorated. On each side of the road was a two-metre wide track. Sometimes the track was coated like the road, but mostly it was a rough, loose-stone surface. I weighed up the pros and cons of the road status and decided I could only cycle on the tarmac road.

The need for strong, substantial road cycle wheels soon became evident. Blue Goose fitted that need. My master plan was to by-pass Istanbul. At the last moment I changed my mind. The Inner Man said, 'Mac, but once in your life will you cycle this way.' I joined the four lanes of traffic winding their way like a giant caterpillar towards Istanbul. The heat of day and the hydrocarbon fumes filled my lungs and eyes with highly toxic gases. Again, the sixth sense was on red alert as I joined the bumper to bumper traffic lanes.

I needed accommodation and food – but where? The miles added to miles. I came to a petrol station. They did B&B, or the equivalent. With sign language I asked, 'can I see it?' The guy nodded, 'yes'. I checked it out. This was none of your home comforts, but I accepted.

I showered. The water was cold, but so what? I went down to the so-called shop and bought a few bars of chocolate. The café only sold tea. It was my first cup of Turkish tea. It was good.

On checking my cat eye, I had done 85 hot, smelly, rough miles today. I was tired as I threw back the sheets on the bed. What filth. I covered them back up and lay on the bed in my clothes. The lock on the door was broken. I chained it shut with my cycle lock and fitted the wedge. I tied my bags and shoes to the bed. Good night.

Between Tekirdag and Istanbul

The benefits of sleeping in your clothes is evident. In the morning, after a quick shave and face wash, you're ready for the off.

No breakfast. I topped up my water bottles. The Goose was bagged up and waiting. I retrieved the wedge and my lock and chain. I couldn't wait to get on the road.

I breathed in the fresh air before the cars and lorries ate it all. Within a quarter of an hour of getting up, I was on the road to Istanbul. I didn't know the road number but followed the main stream of traffic.

I soon became aware of the standard of motoring in Turkey. Incessant lorry horns sounded. The drivers must just hold down the horn button while the vehicle is moving. I estimated the noise level must be in the 95 decibel range; my sixth sense was on red high alert.

Stopping in a village shop, I bought fruit, water, cheese and cake – my breakfast. Man, was I hungry. I washed it down with a bottle of Coke. Pangs of hunger were eating my mind.

I had changed money at the border crossing; it should last until Istanbul tomorrow. The route today took me over hills. It became a hard slog, fighting for every mile.

Last night I used the door wedge – it's the simplest and most secure way to stop a door from opening. My cycle lock and chain also double up as a safeguard when a door lock is not secure. I tied my bags and shoes to the bed, as it's been known for bags to be fished out of a bedroom window.

The roads I found to be unsafe. Lorries were top of the pecking order; kings of the road. They had an 'I stop for nothing' attitude. Cars were second, with the old donkey carts and cyclists last. I'm damn sure they would edge you off the road if they could. To quote my log – not a place to bike.

Again it was that time of day. My body tells me when to look out for a lodge, but there wasn't one in sight.

I pulled up at a café and asked; they directed me to a lodge. It looked nothing special. 'Yes, we have a room and you can leave your bike also.' The guy spoke good English. I inspected the room; the bed was clean although the shower was a dump. I was tired. I accepted the room.

Tonight my main meal was apples, chocolate and water. Looking in the shower, the main pipe protruded through the wall and the shower head was missing. The floor was filthy. If I walked in there in bare feet, I would catch some disease. I checked my bag and found two Safeway plastic bags. I put one on each foot and taped them to my legs. I stripped off the rest of my clothes and had a cold shower. What do they call it? Ingenuity.

After the shower I wedged the bedroom door closed as a secondary precaution. The Goose was due for a clean. I cleaned it and it sat there, bagged up, ready for tomorrow. The bed was inviting. I jumped between the sheets. That felt better. Turkish delight? I don't like it. Good night.

Roadside B&B to Istanbul

My eyes opened with the dawn and slight apprehension entered my day. It was going to be a challenge to cycle to and through Istanbul. I calculated the city to be thirty-plus miles away.

Yesterday's mileage was 70 hard, hot, polluted miles. I was getting punishment, but not enough nourishment. My mind was full of thoughts as I dressed. Thankfully, I had no bug bites; must be grateful for no small red lumps.

The Goose was ready to go. I retrieved my door wedge and filled the water bottles. The road was busy: cars and fully-laden lorries, all en route to the city. As I entered the city race, the lorry horns greeted me; my mind was fully programmed with survival senses.

The weather was sunny. There was a slight head wind and heat from the sun; you could see the hydrocarbon fumes shimmering in the dust-laden heat waves above the cars. I was breathing that polluted, toxic air. At least I was removing some of the pollutants.

The name of the morning game was staying calm and alive – holding my line of road. Soon I realised that this kind of cycling was not for the faint-hearted.

Stopping at a small village shop, I purchased my breakfast: goats' cheese, biscuits and cake, washed down with Coke. I also bought apples. As I pushed the Goose up the steps from the shop, my chain caught on the step corner and broke. I carried a spare link and a riveting tool. Soon I was all oil and sweat. I repaired the chain but I had broken the end of the riveting tool. I made a mental note of that.

Back on the road, the outskirts of the city loomed in the distance. Joining the cars and lorries were the city-wise motorcyclists and scooters, all adding together to make a melee of city confusion.

Entering the city centre I dismounted and walked the pavement, pushing the Goose and window shopping as I walked along. I was enjoying the change.

Stopping at a roadside café, I sat in the seat with the best view of the Istanbul world. I ordered a grand pizza meal. It tasted as it looked; delicious. I realised the weight I'd lost. If Gill could see me now she'd say I was as thin as a gypsy's greyhound.

There were tourists from various countries; we westerners stick out like sore thumbs on the streets. What a jumble of folk from all walks of life. It reminded me of a giant human anthill. I bought an ant map of Istanbul to help me on my way.

Soon the harbour appeared. What ships - from ocean-going liners to every conceivable ship one could imagine. The lifeline ferry between east and west across the Bosphorus docked below me. A flow of folk just disappeared into the city.

The bridge joining east and west was a great feat of engineering. I wondered if I could I cycle over it? I still don't know.

After exploring for a few hours I began to tire of city life. I caught the ferry across the Bosphorus to the eastern side. Following my city map, I found tomorrow's route out of the city.

My accommodation was as the previous standard. The receptionist kept on at me to get him into the UK. Another guy from the borders of Iran kept on asking what firms made in the UK. His interest was in turbine blades; he even showed me an example of what he wanted. 'Don't get involved, Mac,' said the Inner Man.

My bed was clean, and I had showered so I was clean too. The Goose was parked on guard against the door. I had eaten a meal in the hotel. I was tired. Good night.

Istanbul to Izmit

Awake early, I carried out all my ablutions. The Goose was ready. I was first down to breakfast; too early for those clowns of last night. The tea was great; I picked at the rest, not knowing what it was. The fruit I enjoyed.

As I pushed the Goose out, I oiled the chain. There were only a few dregs of oil left. My miles yesterday were 35, plus 5 walked miles. I pushed off on to the main road for Ankara. I knew that I wouldn't reach it today or tomorrow. My plan was to ride the day out. It was good forward thinking not to stay in the centre of Istanbul last night. The road was busy with early traffic, with most cars and lorries entering the city.

It took four hard hours to ride myself out of the gravitational pull of the city. Even at the city limits, the lorries sound their horns at all times. I wish I could tell them to stuff their horns where a monkey stuffs his nuts.

The weather today was humid; I was hitting the bottle hard. In the afternoon the sun was so hot I had to cover my arms and legs. The heat was screwing me into the ground.

Hygiene in certain parts of Turkey is non-existent. There are extremes of everything, which, I'm glad to say, we would not accept in the UK. Stopping on the road for tea and cake, I wanted to go to the toilet. It turned out to be a hole in the ground with a bottle of water. It was basic. I filled that basic need. There's a first time for everything, so they say.

The afternoon turned out to be a demanding ride. The lorries were pissing me off, blowing their incessant horns. It made riding over-demanding, like the ground you covered. You fought for it.

The road sign said 'Izmit'. It was late afternoon, I'd given my best and was in need of a rest. Across the road was a restaurant with a lodge. I asked the receptionist if I could see the room. He nodded. The bed and shower were clean, the furniture dust-laden. I accepted the room. I only wanted to sleep there and the price suited my pocket.

'You can bring your bike into the room,' said the fresh-faced youth. At least he could speak English. I also asked about the restaurant. 'Yes, we are open at six o'clock tonight – full range of food and drink,' he said with a smile.

I washed my clothes to rid them of the city dust and dirt. I also cleaned the Goose. I resisted the desire to lay my head on the bed pillow. I knew I'd never get up until morning.

After showering I slipped into my crumpled clean clothes. I was hungry. I filled in the daily log and checked the cat eye; 75 miles. I was pleased with myself. I'd ridden through the biggest cosmopolitan city in the world. 'Well done, Mac,' even if I do say it myself. I think I smiled.

The restaurant was open-air. I drank a glass of white wine and ate a four-course meal. The young receptionist was also the chef and went out of his way to give excellent service. Returning to my room I was full of food and tired. I slipped the wedge in the door and placed the Goose against it. Pulling back the sheets on the bed, the top one was clean, the bottom one not. This was the pits. Again, I slept in my clothes on top of the bed. I was as full as a bug on a rug. Good night.

Izmit to Bolu

As usual I was awake early, and dressed because of my night on top of the sheets. A quick brush of the teeth and swill of the face and I was ready to meet the new day.

Breakfast I decided to buy on the road. The Goose was bagged and ready to go. I retrieved the door wedge, oiled the chain – that's the last of the oil – and pushed off into the line of traffic.

The plan today was for Ankara. At the end of the cycle day, that's where I'd hang my hat. Joining the line of traffic I was greeted with not so friendly horn blasts, all at different pitches. Instantly my survival-programmed brain locked on to my well-being.

The road between Istanbul and Ankara is a busy one, as you'd expect. I should have realised this and headed a different route. Too late, I was committed.

At least one thing was in my favour; the weather was cloudy, killing the direct rays of the sun. Stopping at a small village supermarket I bought my breakfast: cherries, bananas, oranges and Coke.

The farmland was well-cultivated, and I cycled along the edge of a lake. I'm afraid they're not the roads for joy-riding and enjoying the scenery. For most of the day the road was flat, with no hills. That was to change in the later afternoon. I saw the mountain in the distance, but I never dreamed the road would actually run over the top.

What a ride. I fought that mountain for three hours plus. Uphill traffic was mostly lorries, tail to tail. The diesel fumes on the road were pure pollution. I stopped at intervals and walked to the side, away from the road, just to breathe some air. I was exhausted, dirty and sweaty. Halfway up the mountain was a drinking fountain. I drank my fill and showered my head. What a relief, until I re-joined the smoke trail. The injection pumps on most of those lorries must have been adjusted fully open. I had never seen the like. What about the folk living on the side of the hill breathing that pollution all of their short lives?

Reaching the mountain top, there was a hotel set back off the road. It looked a first class place and I checked with reception, 'have you a room?' 'No,' came the reply in perfect English. 'We are full.' Have you ever looked in the eyes of a hotel receptionist when you ask for a room? They dwell over the answer and say it with a smile of accomplishment, 'sorry, we are full.' 'No need to be suspicious,' Mac, said the Inner Man. 'Just because you're dirty, sweaty and exhaling diesel fumes….they do have a standard to maintain.'

I rejoined the line of traffic to my usual horn fanfare and went downhill with care. Halfway down the mountain was another hotel. I turned off the road. It was worth a try. I asked the receptionist for a room. 'Yes, sir – we have a room and a garage for the bicycle.' I was happy. I also booked the restaurant.

The room lay-out was first class and it had a bath. I washed all my dirty clothes and hung them up to dry. I ran the bath, mixing all the scented soaps in the water. It was hot and inviting. Slowly, I slipped in the bath, washing the dirt and sweat away. I was a completely relaxed man.

I must have smelled like a scented sponge as I sat at the restaurant table. My meal and wine were top class. What have I been missing?

The bed was a full king size and looked inviting. I was a renewed man. I filled in my daily log and checked the cat eye; 80 self-polluting miles today. I rang Gill. All was OK. I lay on my bed, exhausted. Good night.

Bolu to Soguksu

I must be getting old. Today, I overslept. My body must have been in need of the rest. I've been on the road a straight nine days.

I ate breakfast this morning and thoroughly enjoyed it. No rush. I bagged up the Goose. No oil – your fault, Mac. I checked out the tyres and pumped air into both, then did a further check on the tyre walls. All was well.

Soon I was back on the road, going downhill at a steady pace. The hill was steep and the tracks on the side were unsafe to cycle on. A lorry passed and pulled up. The driver got out and flagged me down. I stopped. The man came up to me and started to rant and rave and wave his arms about for about five minutes. Maybe I was getting the biggest rollicking of my life for riding on the road? A youth stood by, blank-faced. The driver shook his head and ranted on some more. When he had finished I pointed to the tracks on the roadside and at my tyres, and shook my head, my hand pointing to the track. I never uttered a word. I looked him straight in the eye and offered my hand in friendship. He accepted the gesture and walked away, shaking his head. I do feel that we both learned something in that exchange although I had not spoken a word.

What a start to the day. At the bottom of the mountain I stopped for a photo call; they were now few and far between. Cycling on, the scenery changed from lakes to farmland and woodland; the traffic on the roads was still sparse.

I stopped at a roadside café and bought a cup of tea, or, as the Turks say – 'Cay'. The owner gave me another two cups free, so I've had my fix of caffeine for the day.

Through continental cycling in the heat of the day my arms and trunk were showing signs of heat rash. I decided I would buy some cream when I reached Ankara.

I cycled late into the evening. It was still light and I had started late this morning. The road sign said 'Soguksu National Park'. The roads were unbelievable. The danger of smashing the Goose was ever-present. It turned into a game: use the whole width of the road and dodge the potholes. As one car driver passed me, he held both hands up in a gesture of despair.

Cycling down the road, the light was fading fast. I wondered where I would sleep tonight? As if made to order, a hotel came into view. I stopped and asked for a room. 'Yes,' was the reply, and they could put the Goose in a lock-up garage for which I would be given a key. They also had a restaurant. I booked a meal for the evening. There was plenty of life about. I commented on this to the receptionist who informed me there was a Turkish wedding on that night.

The hotel was named the 'Cam Hotel'. It was three stars. It looked good and it was good. I was soon showered and changed into my clean clothes. After I had walked and eaten I could see the wedding and dancing through the lounge. It entered my mind, 'no sleep tonight'. I smiled. The music was extremely good. I only hope the groom doesn't feel as tired as I do tonight.

The day had been punishing; it must have been that mountain yesterday. It was more a marathon than a cycle. I checked the cat eye; 85 miles today. No wonder I'm tired. Soon my head was on the pillow and I was in the land of nod. Good night.

Soguksu to Ankara

As I awoke it dawned on me; it was a Sunday morning in June. The sun was shining and it was an open road to Ankara. What more can a cyclist ask for?

I thought of the wedding last night and the noise from the music. What noise? I must have slept as if pole-axed. 'Move it,' said the Inner

Man. 'No time to daydream.' I resisted the comfort of the bed and moved my butt.

There was only one other person at breakfast; no sign of the wedding guests. The Turkish tea tasted like a good wine. As I bagged up the Goose and pushed off, I thought how it was a good move to by-pass the main road yesterday and cycle through Soguksu National Park. The hotel was an unexpected bonus.

The nearer I cycled to Ankara, the better the road. The traffic was light. The first twenty miles I felt slightly lethargic. I put it down to a hangover from the mountain marathon.

As I neared Ankara I passed alongside an operational airfield; jet fighters and helicopters were taking off and landing. The obvious security by the armed forces was unbelievable; every few hundred yards, manned picket posts bristled with weaponry.

Traffic built up as I cycled through the city. I was soon to have a near accident. Cycling along, enjoying the view, I looked down and immediately did an emergency stop. In front of my wheel was an open drain; the round cover had been removed. I proceeded with caution thereafter, my mind on red alert.

I stopped near the kerb side where a policeman was standing and wished him good morning. He returned the greeting in good English. I asked him if there were hotels at the airport; he confirmed there were. I also asked him about the removal of the drain covers. He said that at night drug addicts remove the cast iron covers and sell them to buy more drugs.

The afternoon sun was blisteringly hot. I saw a passenger jet aircraft take to the skies and knew I was in the vicinity of the airport. 'Halt!' Being an ex-army man I knew the significance of the command and immediately came to a stop. In English the armed policeman said, 'where are you going?' My reply was that I was going to purchase a flight ticket to Pakistan. 'You can't buy a ticket in the airport, you must go back to Ankara,' he said. 'I'll stop in an airport hotel until tomorrow,' I said. 'No hotels at the airport,' was his reply. His rifle was now at the horizontal, pointing in my direction, the barrel gleaming in the afternoon sunshine.

With a sudden change of voice, he invited me into the guard hut. 'Sit down,' he said. 'I'll phone for a taxi to take you back to Ankara.' I was pissed off, tired, hot, thirsty and far from home. The taxi arrived. I loaded the Goose, placing some rag between the car and my bike frame so as not to scratch the paint. The Goose was tied down to the spare tyre and boot lid and we were under way. Our destination was the tourist hotel in Ankara.

What a ride in the taxi. The driver was a bloody head case; he drove flat out and just flew down the road. There were no seat belts in the car. I was confident I would get out if we crashed, so I never showed I was ready to fill my pants. At the hotel, I paid the driver and he waved and grinned. I stood there with the Goose, then booked into the hotel. 'Yes, you can put the bike downstairs; it will be safe there,' said the receptionist. 'I will check first,' I said. I went down to look and it was indeed safe. I carried the Goose down and chained it to the stair rail, removed my bags and found my room. I was knackered. I fell on the bed and slept. Good evening.

Ankara

For three days I was on hold in Ankara in the hotel 'Tourist'. It was a good class of hotel in the city centre. I also used the hotel for my breakfast and evening meal.

After my Sunday late afternoon snooze, I was awake in the evening rested. I showered and changed my clothes and ate my evening meal in the hotel. I felt human again. In my room I wrote my daily log and studied the travel maps, and the religion and the 'dos and don'ts' whilst travelling through Pakistan.

I phoned Gill to tell her the up-to-date news and my travel plans over the next week or so. She told me all the home news and how her foot was recovering from the recent operation.

I compiled an action list of my wants over the next day or so:
Chain riveting tool and spare chain link.
Small bottle of chain oil.
Air ticket to Pakistan.
Ointment or tablets for my prickly heat rash.
Change money to Pakistani currency.
Phone for my medical bag.
Wash my clothes.
Clean the Goose.
Rest and eat (just as important).
Sightsee and enjoy myself.

If I achieve all the want actions on the list I'll be a happy man.

Ankara (Monday)

I rang the airport carriers about my medical bag. They assured me the bag would be delivered today, and yes, delivery had been paid.

The shops were near the city centre, not far from the hotel. By luck,   69

I found a cycle shop. Yes, they had a chain link tool and a small plastic bottle of oil. That was a good start.

Ankara city centre is not unlike many other cities: all rush, hustle and bustle, people running, children crying. It all adds up to my anthill theory.

Across the road was a chemist's shop. I explained to the shop assistant about my rash. He looked at it. 'Heat rash,' he said. He gave me some tablets. 'These should cure you within days.' I thanked him and paid for the bottle of tablets.

I ate a midday meal washed down with a glass of Turkish tea. I laughed to myself; I'm spending money like water.

On returning to the hotel I found that my medical bag had been delivered. The receptionist handed it to me and I thanked her. My legs were tired of walking. I retired to my room for an afternoon siesta.

Ankara (Tuesday)

What a supply of tablets in my medical bag. There was a need to take tablets prior to entering mosquito-ridden countries. Pakistan being one, I complied with the instructions on the box. My ticket to Pakistan. I asked the receptionist's advice. Within the hour she came back to me and said a taxi would pick me up at the hotel at ten o'clock tomorrow morning, as the ticket office was on the other side of the city. I thanked her. I washed my clothes, Blue Goose and the pannier bags.

Ankara (Wednesday)

As I awoke, my mind was activated to the day's needs. My pannier bags had drip-dried overnight. It was all systems go. I ate a quick breakfast and in no time was in the hotel foyer, waiting for the taxi. It arrived on time. 'Petrie?' said the driver. I sat in the front again, and there were no seat belts. I explained what I wanted to the taxi driver, who spoke good English. 'No problem,' he said, 'the Turkish air ticket office is across the city.' His boot went down on the accelerator and the G-forces slammed me back into the seat. He drove like a man possessed. 'Jesus loves me, yes I know – because this guy is missing everyone else who is driving the same way he is,' I sang to myself.

'There's the Turkish airline office,' said the driver. 'Do you want me to wait?' In my mind's eye I could see the cost of the taxi mounting to the cost of the air ticket. As if by chance, a gap opened by the airline office. The driver parked. 'Just wait for me here,' I said. I jumped out of the taxi and made my way through the door to the ticket office counter.

The sign said 'Turkish airlines'. Damn, I'd landed myself in a queue. There were three folk in front of me. It was my turn. It seemed as if I'd been queuing for an age. 'Sit down, please,' said the girl behind the PC. She looked frightened and ill at ease. The guy who stood by her side looked at me and said, 'she's learning,' with an exasperated smile on his face. He's pissed off for a start, I thought. Why me, Lord?

'You request a single ticket from here to Karachi, Pakistan?' 'Yes, ' I replied, 'today or tomorrow.' 'Late afternoon?' said the guy. 'That's fine,' I said. The girl was hitting the keys of the PC with a brown, nicotine-stained finger. She hit a further button and a ticket popped out. 'Here is your ticket,' she said. I handed her my flexible friend visa card. 'No,' she said, 'cash only.' As I took a deep breath the guy returned. After some muttering and a put-on smile, she accepted my visa card. It was my lucky day, so far.

I was glad to get out into the fresh air. The taxi driver was still there. In no time he had whisked me back to the Tourist Hotel. I paid; he smiled. I had made his day.

It was now midday. It was all go. I packed my gear into the now clean panniers, plus the medical bag, and checked the room in case I'd left anything. I was ready to go.

I paid the hotel and thanked the receptionist for all her help whilst I was there. I slipped her a tip which produced a smile and a flash of her dark eyes. She ordered me a taxi. Within half-an-hour the Goose was loaded and my bags; I was under way to the airport. No police stopped me today. I had my ticket, visa and passport. In what seemed no time the taxi dropped me at the entrance door to the airport. I had enjoyed the taxi ride. It was more of a sightseeing trip; he drove with care and consideration.

Airports – they don't change, do they? The times I've spent waiting. They come up with more excuses for lateness than a school child. The hostesses think they're models: high heels, hats, radios in hand. 'Don't ask me why it's late, I only work here.' The guys walk in twos, sometimes hand-in-hand; I wonder why?

This was another long wait. Within the seven hours I'd been here, I'd checked in the Goose and my bags and had my flight ticket ready. What was to unfold in the departure lounge was real comedy slapstick. It unfolded scene after scene as the day passed on. The lounge was the final destination lounge, with full security checks.

Ankara (airport departure lounge)

The airport lounge held adequate seating; enough to fill a jumbo jet. The lounge was at ground level; a full glass frontage looked over runways and loading facilities. It was a typical modern airport lounge. A single, over-sized glass door allowed both ingress and egress to passengers and airport staff. At the far end of the departure lounge was the security office.

I am one of three passengers patiently awaiting the flight call. All is quiet. A painter arrives outside the lounge's glass door. He tries to open the door and gestures with his free hand. A security man wanders aimlessly from his office and unlocks the glass door. The painter enters, paint tin in one hand, paintbrush in the other. The security man re-locks the door.

Surveying both the walls and the ceiling, the painter walks around the lounge. He stops and opens the paint tin and proceeds to paint patches on the walls and ceiling, standing on the lounge seats to reach the high ceiling. A cigarette dangles precariously from his lower lip as he works; paint fumes fill the lounge area.

Outside the glass door an airport cleaner, with sweeping brush, produces a key from his pocket, opens the glass door, enters and closes the door with his key. He and the painter engage in conversation. At the same time, a white-collar official hand gestures to the painter to open the door. The painter acknowledges his wave, the cleaner unlocks the door. The white-collar official enters; the cleaner closes and locks the door.

The white collar official and the painter survey the walls and ceiling, the official pointing at them with animated gestures. The painter's head goes up and down like Noddy's. The white collar official approaches the cleaner who unlocks the door and carefully locks it again when the official has gone. The motivated cleaner follows his brush with dexterity and style around the lounge floor.

An ingress of passengers now slowly fill the departure lounge. Outside the glass door, an irate white-shirted official, hands full of paper, frantically gestures to anyone to let him in. No notice is taken of him and he departs, his face showing displeasure.

At this point another official with a white shirt and tie, accompanied by a security man, rattles at the door. The security man holds his radio to his mouth. Within minutes, a security man from the office in the lounge opens the door with his key, closing and locking it when the security man and official have entered.

More passengers enter the departure lounge. The painter moves chairs in order to paint the walls. On completion, he replaces the chairs. The cleaner's sweeping brush moves aimlessly around, with no apparent plan.

The tannoy announces flight 182 to Cyprus. A security man appears from the lounge office. He opens the door. All but the original three passengers troop through the door, following the security man. The door is now left open and unattended for approximately half-an-hour. Airport staff come and go unheeded. The security man returns from the aircraft, closing and locking the door from inside the lounge.

An airport official, white-collared, together with a girl secretary, try in vain to enter the lounge. He gestures to anyone, rattles and bangs the door. The cleaner enters the security office and a security man makes his way to the door and opens it halfway, holding it with his leg.

The official reminds me of a bookie on a racecourse. A tic-tac man. Quite an argument rages on, with the security man shutting the door and retreating to his office. The official and the girl beat the retreat.

The painter, who is now resting in one of the lounge chairs, approaches the cleaner, who unlocks the door with his key, carefully locking the door again when the painter has gone.

The cleaner returns to his now tired brushing. Two more officials try to enter the lounge to no avail. All the banging and rattling and gesturing attract no one to come and open the door. The cleaner and the security man take not a blind bit of notice.

A flight crew arrive in the departure lounge, wanting to leave by the glass door. After five minutes a security man arrives, opening the door then closing and locking it when the flight crew have passed through.

The cleaner looks at his watch and hangs on for grim death as the brush dashes around the floor of the lounge, stopping at the door. The cleaner opens it with his key and disappears outside, after locking the door again.

The tannoy announces that flight 123 to Istanbul is now boarding. We three passengers make our way to the glass door. A security man duly arrives, opens the door and points to a plane on the hard standing. As we walked towards the plane, the security man locks the glass door. At that moment a very high-ranking official arrives. He is dressed as a five-star general. He has enough scrambled egg on his hat. He rattles and bangs on the glass door. To see him gesturing in his uniform is, to say the least, comical. He leaves the door, walking away ever so briskly, obviously annoyed.

We board the aircraft, handing our boarding cards to the steward, who, with a gesture of the hand, waves us to the seats. 'Quick, quick,' he says, 'we're late. Sit in any seat.' Thankfully, I sit down, four hours late. I can see the glass door – it is shut as we taxi past.

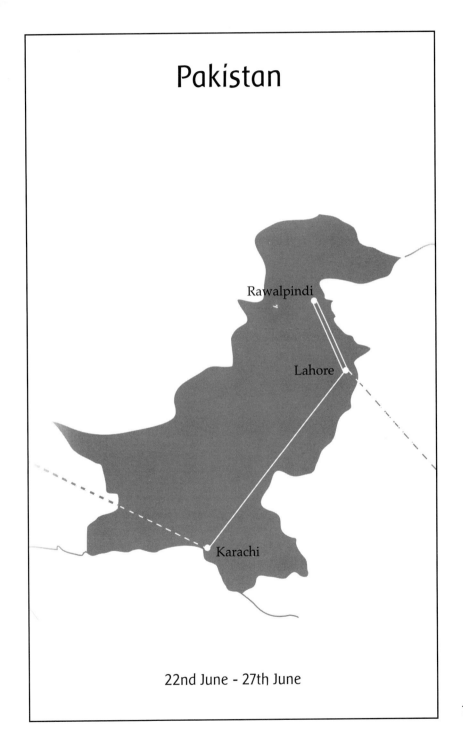

Pakistan

Rawalpindi

Lahore

Karachi

22nd June - 27th June

Relaxing in my seat on the plane, awaiting take off to Istanbul, I shook my head in disbelief at the security antics I'd witnessed in Ankara airport departure lounge. If my flight had not been four hours late, I would not have witnessed the security shambles.

In my opinion, if this is the standard of airport security world-wide, hi-jacks will be a common occurrence.

The flight to Istanbul was short and sweet. On landing, there was a need to transfer to a different departure lounge for the flight to Karachi. I soon found the lounge and passed through security. The lounge was filling up with passengers.

The tannoy sounded: 'Passengers from Ankara, will you please check your baggage prior to boarding the flight to Karachi.' The main door to the loading bay opened; outside were lines and lines of luggage. When you confirmed your luggage to the security man, he marked the bags with white chalk.

We all returned to the departure lounge, awaiting our flight call. There was no toilet in the lounge; anyone needing to go to the toilet had to pass through a security-controlled door. On returning to the lounge, the passenger was searched and one's ticket, visas and passport were re-checked.

I was now getting tired and fed up with airport life. The tannoy sounded: flight 127 to Karachi was now boarding through gate four - 'thank you for flying with Turkish Airlines.' At least we had boarded and sorted out the seating. The in-flight tannoy announced final checks. With that, three security men appeared in the gangway, grabbed a Pakistani male passenger and led him off the plane. The in-flight tannoy announced that one of the passenger's passports was not correct and the flight was now on hold.

Half-an-hour later the guy returned, red-faced, and looking rather annoyed. The air hostess announced, 'fasten your seat belts.' Take off at last. We were on our way to Pakistan.

I lay my head back on the seat and slept soundly, only to be wakened by an air hostess with a smile and dark, expressionless, riveting eyes. 'Breakfast sir,' she said. The usual plastic-wrapped food was placed in front of me. The package was designed to make the customer think there was more food than there really was. Also placed on the table, as the air hostess had said, was a small token gift for flying Turkish Airlines. It contained toiletries. Very acceptable. I would say the flight with Turkish Airlines was on a par with all other airlines I have flown with.

Fasten your seat belts; this was it. Pakistan, Karachi airport – time, 0345 hours.

Karachi

Karachi airport, 0345 hours. This, to me, is an unearthly hour, when the only ones who should be awake are the prostitutes and the moles. I remember working twelve-hour shifts. At this time in the morning, animal instinct automatically shuts one's eyes. It's hard to fight nature.

The lay-out and procedures in airports are usually the same everywhere. Some run themselves, others are run with military efficiency. This was the dead hour; people's heads were down, children cried from being woken from their deep sleep.

Tempers grew shorter by the minute. Yes! Blue Goose and my bags. I retrieved them from the baggage carousel. My rugby training in the scrum came in useful. What a game. Wales v Pakistan. I won. Reunited with my bags and Blue Goose, I now felt complete.

I reassembled the Goose under the stare of many eyes, and joined the queue to change my money to rupees. (Note: always retain the receipt you get with your money, otherwise you can't change your rupees back to dollars.)

I fought my way to the airport exit. There was a still a curtain over the morning lights. I wheeled the Goose down the stairs into the black veil, to be met by a horde of porters and taxi drivers, every one jostling for position. It was like being attacked by a swarm of bluebottle flies. I kept fending them off, using Blue Goose as a battering ram. You had to hold on to your possessions otherwise they would be wrenched out of your hands.

Decision time. My mind was functioning. A hotel in Karachi would be my best plan. I looked at the faces jostling for trade. There was an honest face. As I lifted my hand and made eye contact, he leaped forward, grabbing my bags with a smirk on his face as if to say, 'I won.' Porters and taxi drivers are the same the world over.

They say, the best laid plans of mice and men....This was a true saying. Cycling in Pakistan was to play a secondary role, through no plan or fault of my own. I think about it sometimes and pinch myself. 'Did it really happen to me?' Yes, it did.

The taxi driver spoke good English. Blue Goose was tied to the car boot. 'Watch the paint,' said I, pushing a dirty rag between the car and the frame of the Goose. I was not concerned about the car paint, but the paint on the Goose. My bags were on the back seat; all systems go. 'Karachi Hotel, please.' 'No problem,' came the reply. I had agreed a price after some haggling. I could have made a better deal, but after all, it was the middle of the night and I was tired. The noise of the airport faded as we drove away thankfully.

I checked the watch that my daughter Alison had given me for my trip. It was a Timex with indi-glow function. I pressed the illumination button; 0430 hours. 'What's that?' I asked the taxi driver. A light was flashing us down. 'Police,' said the driver. My door opened and a gun and a light were thrust in my face. 'Passport, visa, money,' said the policeman in a hiss. The whites of his eyes and teeth reflected in the torchlight.

My passport and visa were around my neck; my wallet in my hand. The next thing I knew, the wallet was snatched from my grasp. It quickly became obvious he was more interested in my wallet than my passport. I sat in a daze of bewilderment. Soon I jolted back to reality when the policeman started to extract rupees from my wallet. 'Want your money – the green ones,' he said. At this, the shutters instantly came up. I could see my money going with my credit cards. My world trip was at stake. Action, Mac.

I grabbed my wallet as he dwelt on the last word, 'money'. In my harshest sergeant major's voice, I told him both the money and the wallet belonged to me, and the chief of police was a friend of mine. I would be reporting this incident to him in the morning. 'I have your number,' I told him. This was untrue; I didn't even know if he had a number as it was so dark.

The policeman backed away. I knew I had won the day. I closed the door of the taxi. 'Drive on,' I told the taxi driver, who was trembling. 'Move it – now,' I said, and we drove away. I felt physically tired. I'd only been in Pakistan for half-an-hour and I'd won the day. I looked into the dark morning sky and silently uttered the words, 'why me, Lord?' The taxi driver remarked, 'the police are always doing that.'

Driving through the streets of Karachi, it all looked sinister and unreal, rather like a Hollywood film set. 'Hotel,' said the driver. I unleashed the Goose, together with my baggage. A somewhat bleary-eyed receptionist handed me the key as I filled out the forms. Form filling was now becoming second nature, thank goodness.

The receptionist grabbed my bags and I followed with Blue Goose on my shoulder. No question where the Goose was going; to my room. Believe it or not, I was stepping over sleeping bodies on the floor of the foyer and on the landings. They stirred, not unlike dogs. Some opened bleary eyes to shut them again immediately. What a bloody dive.

If the hotel had stars they are not in this galaxy. The receptionist pushed open the bedroom door and switched on the light. The cockroaches disappeared as if by magic. The sheets were clean. I thanked the guy. No, I was not in the mood to give him a tip. The lock on the door was broken. I slammed in the door wedge and placed the Goose across the door. The noise from the room cooling fan, or as we say south, the air conditioning, was like a BSA Bantam motorbike engine that was being revved constantly. The somewhat ingenious fan pulled or educated air from the outside; the air passed through a wire mesh interwoven with moss. Water percolated down through the moss, which in turn cooled the air.

The toilet had to be seen to be believed. I didn't bother to shower. I'd had a busy day. I scooped two dead cockroaches, plus other unknown species of creepy-crawly bugs off the bed sheets. I decided to sleep in my clothes and with the light on tonight (or was it morning?). I crashed out on top of the bed.

Karachi

I was woken by a noise louder than that from the fan. More noise erupted up from the street; the distinct babble of human voices, shouting. I staggered to the window, where a cloud of red ochre dust enveloped everything. It was just like fog. Buildings were being demolished opposite the hotel. The Inner Man said in a slow, deliberate voice, 'welcome to Karachi, Mac.'

What day is it? I looked at my daily log; Saturday. I decided to stay put and explore Karachi on the Goose. There were no signposts that I could see. What was the name of the hotel? I had written it down on a piece of paper. As if by magic my mind held on to the route, making mental notes of landmarks. The more I saw of Karachi, the less I liked it. I bought some fruit for my breakfast which I ate with gusto. I also bought some for later in the day, and some drink.

I returned to the hotel through the smell, flies, dust and human debris on the streets. Social structure here seemed to be on a knife-edge. Yes, I did wonder if the Pakistani people had a song like the British: *There's no place like home.*

Call it fate if you wish, but the same taxi driver who dropped me off last night was standing at the door of the hotel. We nodded in recognition. Still looking for an honest rupee, he said 'I take you round Karachi to see the sights? Very cheap.' He had a cheeky grin. After some haggling, I said yes. Blue Goose was returned to the hotel room. I was concerned for the Goose and my bags. I chained and locked the Goose and the bags to the bed.

Soon we were off in the taxi. I found the tour of Karachi very informative. 'This is the monument to the founder of Pakistan,' said the driver. 'Also, down the road, our prime minister, Mrs Bhutto, lives.' This proved to be a big complex of buildings surrounded by a rather high wall. Security forces were evident. On he drove until we came to the sea; it made my day. 'All this,' he said, his arm moving across his body with an extensive sweep, 'was houses; the government bull-dozed the lot down.' Now the ground is for sale at exorbitant plot prices. I could but wonder who was robbing whom to make money.

En route, we passed crowds of people, seemingly protestors carrying banners. I noticed the taxi driver looked somewhat disturbed. He said nothing as we drove past. The afternoon was coming to an end all too quickly. It always does when you're enjoying it. The driver stopped and bought a bottle of lemonade and a bar of chocolate.

'Many thanks,' said I, knowing that I was going to pay for this at the end of the day. It was hot sitting in the taxi, so I opened the window as we ate our chocolate. 'Tat, tat, tat, tat.' Yes, I thought I'd heard that noise before; fireworks.

The relaxed face of the driver changed. He looked at me. 'They said there would be trouble. It's gunfire!' he exclaimed. 'Let's go. I would advise you to leave Karachi as soon as you can,' he said in a concerned voice. 'We collect your bags and bike. I will take you to the bus station.' 'Train,' I said. 'That will be full. Far better on the bus.' More and more tat, tat, tat, was to be heard in the distance. Cars passed, driving fast. People ran up and down the streets in confusion.

I paid the hotel, loaded everything into the taxi and we headed down the road to the bus station. As I unloaded the bags and the Goose, the taxi driver said, 'I'll get your ticket. Go up country – it's safest.' He was soon back. 'I got you a ticket to Lahore.' He handed me the ticket. We shook hands. The taxi driver thanked me. I did likewise. He turned on his heel and was gone. I never paid him. 'Thank you,' I said to him, silently.

Karachi to Lahore

Uncontrollable things were happening all too quickly. I stood there with a ticket in my hand thinking, well, I've got a ticket to ride. 'Not funny, Mac', said the Inner Man.

The bus was due to go at 1900 hours. Not a thing moved. A policeman was at the station stopping any bus movement. As he walked by, I asked him if I could cycle out of Karachi up country. 'No,' was the curt reply. 'You can if you wish, but you would very quickly be a dead man. We have a very big problem.'

Shouting and noise with more shooting could be heard in the distance. The policeman moved away quickly. More and more people arrived. Some buses were packed with folk, but still nothing moved. I contemplated my safest move, and concluded that the best bet was the bus. It was Saturday night and, with no ticket, the airport was out of the question.

At last a bus employee started to load the roof with big baggage. I pushed the Goose forward. 'No, no,' he said, gesturing with his hand. Damn it. 'Rupee?' I said. He said a figure; I haggled. I could see this was no time to haggle. I paid the guy. Blue Goose went on the bus roof. I insisted on checking that the ropes were secure. I didn't want the Goose flying off.

I held on to my bags. Night was quickly falling. People mingled around. It was obvious the bus could have been filled many times over. The driver stood at the bus door, waving us on. 'Tickets only,' he kept saying. Each ticket had a seat number printed on it. That's me, right up front. I stuffed the bags in the overhead rack. What a relief to sit down. We were off, but we didn't move far. The police stopped us for a check.

'Stop here,' said the policeman. 'It's not safe to travel.' Another two hours passed. The police and army were everywhere; gunfire and shouting could still be heard.

A policeman waved us on. 'Come on,' I said, under my breath. 'Get out of this crazy town.' We were under way. The bus was packed with a mixed bunch of folk. I was sitting in a very uncomfortable front seat with no safety hand rail. I soon gained first-hand experience of bus rally driving. Strapped to the door handle of the bus was a ten-gallon water tank with a common drinking ladle with a long handle. After seeing some of the passengers drinking out of the ladle, I decided to stick to my bottle of lemonade. I would only drink the water in an emergency.

Sitting directly behind me was a woman of the night. Her dress was immaculate, as was the make-up on her face, plus the fact she wore more gold than could be found in the Welsh mountains. She also wore a set smile; her manicured, decorated nails and hands moved elegantly.

Also on the bus were six young Muslim men; very well-dressed and talkative. I had talked to them whilst waiting for the bus in Karachi. For the first 50 miles, the seat next to the woman of the night was empty. A male passenger stood in the bus aisle rather than sit next to her; the reason being, I was told, his Muslim faith.

We were stopped at various times by the police, who entered the bus and checked the passengers. One policeman with a sub-machine gun made a joke at my expense. With the gun pointing at my face he loudly stated he would see I was looked after. The bus passengers all laughed. What did I call him? Under my breath, 'dick-head, sir.' At one of the stops the driver approached me after a quick discussion among the male passengers, not in my tongue. 'Do you mind sitting next to the woman?' he asked 'Not a bit,' was my reply. The passenger who had been standing sat in my seat uttering a big sigh.

I sat next to the woman, who smiled and in a rather deep, contralto voice, said 'where's your wife?' My reply was short and sweet and true. 'At home,' I said. She smiled again, exposing a row of immaculate white teeth. Her eyes expressed a look of contentment. I relaxed back in my seat. She laid her head on my shoulder. My, what a fragrant smell; I was in a bed of roses.

Male passengers talked about me in low tones. They smiled with that look, as if to say, 'you lucky old sod, I wish it was me.' During my prolonged wait in the Karachi bus station, I was never without conversation. A doctor, who talked to me for an hour, stated that some of the young men had approached him and said they also wanted to speak to me. I let it be known through the doctor that I would be pleased to speak to anyone on the bus. I moved to the middle seat, which had been vacated. I was not without conversation for the rest of the journey.

The questions came thick and fast. Where was I going? Where did I come from? I was also asked my opinion on what I saw, and my opinion on many political things. True to form, I could hold a conversation on many subjects. It passed the time and I found it very interesting.

The young Muslims on the bus also spoke to me. They were full of questions on all aspects of life. When the bus stopped for us to have a bite to eat, I sat with the group. We talked and laughed; they were very friendly.

The young travellers made much merriment of me sitting with the woman of the night. As the miles went by, each one sat in turn with me to talk; some simply to try out their English. Again, international sign language saved the day quite often.

I was tired and only managing to cat-nap. A dust storm stopped our progress. The headlights were useless; we were forced to stop. What a black-out when the wind got up with the storm.

When the storm eased, we were again under way. There were many passing cars, lorries, donkeys or bikes. The driver blew his horn incessantly. This action annoyed me immensely, remembering the same habit of the Turkish lorry drivers. Again, the bus was the dominant beast of the road. Often the road was nothing more than a dirt track, dust everywhere.

The bus was driven flat out at all times, swaying and jumping. There were many emergency stops, making it difficult to hang on. What an experience. In one way I was glad not to be riding these roads on my bike. News spread very quickly that 20 people had been killed in Karachi last night, with the trouble still continuing. I was glad to be out of that city.

As we approached Lahore it was dark. There was discussion about whether there could be trouble there too. I was but a western straw blowing in the wind. One young Muslim sat next to me. 'Where are you stopping tonight?' he asked. I just shrugged my shoulders. 'I don't know,' was my reply. 'You could stay with us,' he said.

Through conversation I now knew the young Muslims were fundamentalists, Mujahedin; very religious. I put my thoughts on overdrive, contemplating all aspects. 'You know what you're doing, Mac?' asked the Inner Man. 'Yes,' was my reply.

'Many thanks for the offer,' I said. 'I'll come with you.' A male passenger on the bus seemed quite concerned that I had chosen to go with the group; he put doubts in my mind.

The bus stopped. Blue Goose was handed down to me from the roof. We all stood in a group by the roadside. Lights of passing vehicles illuminated what seemed to me to be a battlefield, not a road. Dust filled our eyes and mouths whenever vehicles passed; the grit grinding between the teeth and drying out the throat. 'This way.' At least one of the guys knew the route, thankfully. We approached and stopped at a well-illuminated closed gate, surrounded by a high, chain link fence. The armed security guard checked us through, stopping at me. After some fast talking and smiles, I was let through with the others. I was assured my Goose and bags were completely safe in this area.

'You can sleep here.' It was a clean bed in a dormitory with others already sleeping. I hung my monies and passport round my neck. My head was full of different thoughts as I lay on the bed but I was a tired man. I crashed out. Good night.

Lahore

I was awake at first light. A guy came in and talked. He told me to follow him to meet my friends. I grabbed the Goose; the bags were still fitted from last night. I was led into a very large complex to be greeted by my friends. I instantly felt more relaxed.

The building I was in was not unlike a gymnasium with a large floor space. Various groups of people were gathered, talking and laughing. Breakfast was offered. I ate with the communal group, not forgetting to eat only with my right hand. Don't ask what I ate; I was thankful.

I was allowed to leave the Goose in the building against the wall. Around the inside periphery of the wall were straw mats and pillows. This building was an all-purpose dormitory cum meeting room.

The call of nature brought me to the outside toilets; all but one was a hole in the ground. At the far end were some showers. Both the toilets and the showers were clean. I returned to the Goose and found my wonder towel in my bag. Gill had bought it for me. Soon I was showering away the dust from three days in Pakistan. I felt like a new man; I could now face the world.

I was fed, watered and showered. My mind and my eyes were hyperactive. 'Don't rush,' said the Inner Man; 'Remember: slowly, slowly, catches the monkey.'

One thing was foremost in my mind; I was safe and not breaking the law. I knew all about the hostages in Lebanon. At no time did I feel threatened. Speaking to one of the group, I expressed many thanks for the hospitality, but that I had better move on. He looked surprised and said, 'would you like to stay with us for a few days, until the troubles are over?' It seemed a logical idea, to let things cool down. I said thank you; I would stay for a day or two.

'Our group is visiting the city this afternoon; would you like to come?' 'Yes,' I said, and thanked him. We planned to visit the fort and the mosque. My clothes were in need of a wash; I soon had them hanging from a makeshift line outside. A young gopher, aged about twelve years, came into the complex and said to me, 'you wear women's clothes.' We all laughed. He was looking at my cycle shorts. I explained the difference between cycle clothes and women's clothes. He nodded. I think he understood.

The name of the complex I was in was Mansoorah, as I found out that morning. I was given celebrity treatment; a fully escorted tour of the male hospital ward. One could only say 'shock treatment'. I was introduced to young lads from eight to eighteen, lying in their beds with horrendous wounds. Some had legs, feet, hands or arms missing, plus other mental scars I could not see. Life is life; the full pain of war was everywhere to be seen. One must be prepared to witness these casualties. When you play with fire you can only get burnt, leaving mental scars for life.

My tour of the hospital included the doctor's surgery and the laboratory. I was even taken to the innermost sanctuary to meet the chief administrator. We had a good chat over a cup of tea that tasted like the best house wine.

Mansoorah hospital, he assured me, was run from donations only. This was to my reckoning a great feat, considering modern day costs. The morning passed quickly. I declined to visit the female ward. I'd seen enough for one morning, and anyway, didn't want to miss my city visit this afternoon with the group.

During my stay with the group, I was often asked my opinion during open discussions. It was interesting to hear the different views on many world topics. They were so keen on their quest for knowledge, as if world affairs were not available to them. I likened them to a class of teenagers, with unlimited questions on life in general.

The visit to Lahore city was in the heat of the afternoon. My clothes were not quite dry and one of the group suggested I go as one of them in national dress: loose-fitting white top and loose, baggy trousers. One of the group of similar build to myself offered me a clean set of clothes, which I accepted. Only after he had pressed them carefully with a hot iron did he give them to me. I thanked him and tried them on for size.

They fitted perfectly, as if made for me. The group laughed and sounded their approval, with joyful pats on the back from all as I did a gestured twirl in my Pakistani clothes. With my sun burn, dark eyes and cropped hair, I could pass for a Pakistani.

We caught a bus into Lahore. It was my first sighting of the city. I would say it is more spacious than Karachi, but the cars, lorries and buses formed that never-ending stream of traffic – the same as one would see in any city in the world. The lorry horns played that unfinished, horrendous symphony. There is a need, in my opinion, for someone to invent another method of attracting attention than by noise; it is an abuse of the senses.

Lahore, as Karachi, is not the place to cycle. It's virtually out of the question. The dust was a hazard, and on the road it was every man for himself. Road violation was a way of life. There were also crowds of people on the streets. (You did ask my opinion of Lahore, didn't you?)

I did enjoy walking and talking with the group. It was an interesting experience; one of the highlights of my tour. We did a tour of the city fort. One guy had been there before, so he was the guide. I found it interesting how in those days they devised a system to supply water to every part of the fort by stone ducts.

We also visited the mosque and I found it fascinating, as I'd never been to one before. I was allowed in the entrance hall after removing my shoes. We all had a snack of fruit juice and fruit from a street vendor; I ate with care.

As they say, all good things come to an end. The sightseeing trip was over and we caught taxis back to the camp. I found it interesting to watch one of the group haggling over the cost of the taxis; it's a way of life to these guys. The clothes I wore were cool in the afternoon heat of the day. Sorry – no photo. Next time maybe.

We returned to the Mansoorah hospital. I was now getting an insight into the complicated everyday working structure; slowly the picture was building. Besides the hospital there was also a mosque, and separate schools for girls and boys.

I was asked if I would speak to the senior class of boys, which I agreed to do. They were 15-16 years old. I decided I would try to answer questions on general knowledge and world affairs. For approximately one hour I stood in front of the class and answered their questions. I thoroughly enjoyed it; they obviously enjoyed it also, for at the end of the class they all applauded me and, to a boy, shook my hand. I told them that during the time I was staying at the camp, any one of them could come and ask questions. They smiled and nodded their approval.

One point of interest I forgot to mention; at the end of my tour of the male hospital wards, I was told that the injuries sustained by most of the young men and boys were the result of land mines in Kashmir. This was because of the ongoing conflict there. The management committee of the hospital asked me my view. I stood up and gave a speech on my thoughts.

Late dinner arrived, which was communally eaten by the group. Water was available to drink after the meal. Readings from the Koran were given by one of the group, followed by a prayer. I took no notice. I was asked for my views on religion, however, and answered with thought. One of the groups asked if I would like a person to teach me the ways of the Muslim faith, to which I said no, after thanking him. One guy in the group asked me, 'what is your faith?' To buy thinking time, I answered a question with a question; 'what is your faith?' To which he replied 'Muslim'. I wondered what to reply. The truth, Mac. 'I am a Christian.' I would not and could not deny my faith, irrespective of the circumstance. There was, as it seemed to me, a moment of hush, but conversation soon carried on.

In all honesty, in my life I have never met friendlier people than the group that I was with; they also showed happiness. I was given the name of 'Mr Mac'. The name was used by one and all; even walking down the corridors I would be addressed, 'hello, Mr Mac.'

It had been a long day. Tonight I was to sleep in the main complex, on the straw mat and pillow. It was the communal bed for all. Blue Goose was at my side. The group in my vicinity sat and talked and drank water.

Among the group I had made friends with were a school computer programmer, a cricket player and shopkeepers; people from virtually all walks of life. Some were even on holiday. They all had one thing in common – to give part of their life to the cause of Islam. It is a strong brotherhood.

The news from Karachi was not good; there was an increase in the number of people killed. For reasons of my own, I will not name the friends I made whilst in Lahore. 'Mr Mac,' the question was, 'would you come with us to Kashmir? We want you to report to the world's press what is going on between Pakistan and India.' Ding ding, the alarm bells rang. The Inner Man said, 'take care, Mac.' Not answering straight away, giving myself time to think, I said 'how would I get there?' The reply was, 'you would come with us. We split up tomorrow; three go to Afghanistan, and three plus you to Kashmir. We are awaiting orders.' Things were now adding up in my mind; the comings and goings of personnel. I was in a Muslim transit camp. People going to and from the war fronts. I weighed up all the pros and cons; I even pinched myself. 'Yes, I will go with you,' was my answer. I realised that this could be the biggest or last decision of my life. Deep down I was excited; sleep did not come easily that night. Good night, Mr Mac.

Lahore

With the dawn, the slumbering bodies around the walls of the complex slowly came to life. The arrival of early breakfast motivated the late sleepers. I washed whatever-it-was down with water and prayers were said. The lads told me they would see me in the afternoon as they had to attend a meeting. I grabbed my wonder towel and went for a shower; it made my day.

The bad news from Karachi was that there was still rioting; the good news was that it had not spread to other towns and cities. At any time of the day or night people arrived and departed from the complex. I witnessed a touching scene this morning; a young boy of around 12 years old arrived with his father. They hungrily ate the breakfast leftovers. The lad was all-in exhausted. He dropped on a straw mat and was asleep in no time. His father removed his own jacket and tenderly and lovingly placed it over his son.

Talking to one of the 'staff', I remarked on the construction of the building. He laughed and told me it was an old film studio. He asked if I knew why the red brick walls were laid with every other quarter brick protruding. I admitted that I didn't know why. Delight shone in his eyes as he told me the reason: it's for soundproofing. I thanked him for the information.

One man who arrived yesterday was, like myself, an odd man out. I asked the guy I was talking to what country he thought this man was from. 'Saudi Arabia,' he replied. The Saudi man was all of six feet six – at a guess. He was dressed in a light brown fatigue suit and looked slightly emaciated for his build. I smiled at the thought of him in battle carrying a jerry can in each hand. He was an impressive man. He did not speak to anyone, but we would acknowledge each other by a smile in the eye and a nod of the head. I named him Mr Big-Man.

I had the feeling I had been off the Goose too long. It was a hot morning as usual, and leaving my pannier bags in the complex I decided to explore Lahore on the Goose. Easier said than done. What an experience. The dust and the roads – if you could see them – the cars, lorries and people, all jostling to live and survive. This was another age; British people would not survive in these conditions, let alone live in them. I was glad I'd filled my two water bottles – I was in need of them. I returned to the complex in the later afternoon, exhausted.

I showered after cleaning the dust of the day from the Goose; I also washed some of my clothes. My friends were back from their meeting, all raring to go. Yes, tonight it was all go; three of the group were off to Afghanistan, the other three and myself would leave in the late evening. We were heading for Rawalpindi by bus, leaving from Lahore.

The evening meal was served with the usual water. Mr Big-Man joined us but never once spoke. His features were gaunt-looking, he had a straggly growth of beard, dark smiling eyes and what I would call a prominent nose. I could see this as he sat opposite me. He looked pleased to be with us. As usual, the Koran was read, followed by prayer.

During my cycle today I saw an amazing sight. A young boy of about 5 or 6 years old was sitting on an upturned bucket in front of a metal bench. He was arc-welding two pieces of metal together – no face mask or goggles. I could see the arc eye in his eyes. If I'd attempted to take a photo, the camera would have been taken from me. There are times when desecration is not worth the photo.

The Afghanistan three were ready to go and said their sad farewells. I had grown fond of them. It was emotional and we all hugged; the lads in my group wishing them a safe return.

Rawalpindi

My eyes were heavy when I had the wake-up call. 'Are you packed, Mr Mac?' With a nod of the head I smiled and said, 'ready when you are.'

Whilst packing, rightly or wrongly, I had removed from my medical pack the injection needles and other medical gear. I was surprised what it amounted to. I also included the toiletries bag from Turkish Airlines. 'Here,' I said to one of the boys, 'I want to donate this medical package to the hospital.'

Word travels fast, even late at night. I was surprised to find that pupils I had spoken to were coming up to shake hands and wish me well. I was even approached by a group of pupils requesting that I stay and speak further to them; they had enjoyed the class of questions and answers.

It was time to go. We hugged and wished each other a safe journey. I felt quite euphoric deep down. Mr Big-Man made eye contact and smiled as I did. He returned the hug I gave him. I asked one of the group what was the cost of my stay for bed and food. 'Nothing,' was the reply. He told me that I was the first westerner to be allowed in the Mansoorah complex. I felt honoured as I walked Blue Goose through the security gate; even the guard gave me a wave with his gun.

A taxi was waiting outside on the approach road. I lifted the Goose into the boot with my bags and placed some paper under the frame. As I said before, 'don't scratch the paint.' The other guys were travelling light. Soon we arrived at the bus station and the bus was there. There were problems with the Goose. 'We can't put it on top,' said a bus employee. Money changed hands and there was now no problem, but I was asked to remove the wheels. I removed both wheels and tied the chain; I was afraid of damage.

This will be some bus ride, I thought, with both the wheels and bags in the bus. The Goose was passed back down. 'Could you put the wheels back on?' asked the bus guy. I was now sweating profusely and my temper was on the rise. For ----'s sake. I bit my lip on the second word and found I was bleeding. I replaced the wheels and the Goose went back on top of the bus. I also went on top of the bus to see that it was tied safely; my hands were black with chain oil, even after cleaning them with a cloth.

The bus was now loading passengers. I grabbed my bags. 'Let's go,' I said. The four of us boarded the bus and sat in the back seats. I felt tired. I removed my glasses for some unknown reason and hooked them in the neck of my shirt. It was a bumpy ride. I must have dozed off. The driver executed an emergency stop. Crack! It sounded like a rifle shot through my head. There was blood everywhere.

What happened was that I had dozed off and with the emergency stop my head was propelled forward at a great rate of knots, smashing my nose against the ashtray on the back of the seat in front of me. Blood flowed. I stuffed paper hankies up my nostrils to stem the flow. The pain was excruciating. Looking up, I could see stars on the roof of the bus. 'Why me, Lord?' I said. I also thought – what if my glasses had been on my face; what then?

My eyes are brown but they were now turning black. Sleep eluded me; the pain was constant. What damage I'd done to my nose I didn't know. For weeks after, I could not touch or blow it. Why me? I only wanted to cycle. Was this a sign to keep my nose out? I have often wondered.

The bus arrived in Rawalpindi early in the morning. I must have dozed off to sleep, even after my nose job. The weight of my glasses on the bridge of my nose added to my discomfort. I had stemmed the bleeding and removed the paper nose packing. It must have been swollen because I could now see my nose.

We ate breakfast in the bus station café. Hygiene must be a foreign word; no one in the places I had so far visited understood the meaning of it. I was unable to smell because of my nose, so I shut my eyes and ate. Hunger dulled all my senses. What did I eat? Don't ask; I don't know.

It was interesting times to say the least. No one explained what the plan was or what we would do that day, it just unfolded as it went along. The group called a taxi. We all piled in, the Goose in its customary place in the boot. The taxi worked its way through the maze of streets under the direction of one of the group, stopping at a well-to-do bungalow. This, I was told, was a safe house, and we intended to stop here for the night. In spite of all the door knocking and window tapping, no one appeared. The group fell into discussion and concluded the owners must be away. Tonight we would stay in alternative accommodation.

After a search, one of the group spoke at length on the phone. He returned to give us an update and said there had been a change of plan; only one of the group would now go to Kashmir. The one to go was named; he smiled. We held on to the taxi and drove for what seemed to me for miles, until we came to a stop at the top of a long alleyway with numerous houses. We all got out of the taxi and said farewell with the now customary hug. The three of us who were left were told to return to Lahore and disband. I was to go on my way to India; the other two return to Karachi.

We sat in the taxi, each with his own thoughts. For five minutes it was quiet; no one spoke. Then the group leader spoke up; 'tonight we stay in a hotel and return to Lahore tomorrow.'

Islamabad was not too far away. The taxi was our transport and the journey was full of interest. The north of Pakistan is much more picturesque than the south. We saw the parliament buildings and visited the Faisal Mosque. This, in my opinion, was the grand finale of the day. We removed our shoes and walked through the complex that made up the mosque; crowds of people were also sightseeing. Buses full of folk arrived and departed while I was there. I must have stuck out like a sore thumb, or, should I say, sore nose. The four pyramids, one at each corner, reminded me of rockets.

We were on the Kashmiri border. I stepped over the borderline; the group laughed. In the distance was the green mountain terrain of Kashmir. As I stood and gazed I daydreamed, my mind full of the ifs and buts of Kashmir.

The day soon passed and we returned to Rawalpindi, stopping at a hotel. 'No problem,' as they say. We booked in for the night. We met for an evening meal and celebrated the fact that one of the group at least was on a mission. We drank lemonade and Pepsi; I enjoyed it. That evening we went for a walk and visited the local fun park. We enjoyed each other's company.

Tomorrow's plan was to return by early bus to Lahore. We would all then go our separate ways.

Rawalpindi to Lahore

The return bus journey to Lahore was uneventful. To say the least, we were all a bit subdued. The Goose was on the baggage rack on top of the bus. I had grown accustomed to seeing my nose. 'Don't touch.' It needed a sign.

I found the day trip on the bus far more interesting than the night trip; there was far more to see. I was in good company and enjoyed the ride. When the bus arrived in Lahore, Blue Goose was handed down to me. I straightened the handlebars, checked all the mechanical moving parts, topped up the tyres with air and fitted all the bags. I was ready for the off.

My two remaining friends were now ready to leave; we were going our own ways. We said our sad farewells. Did I see some tears? We hugged each other in turn in our customary way. The lads were returning to Karachi by train; I was cycling into Lahore city. Cycling along I felt alone and slightly miserable; I did so miss the company. My mind soon changed into cycling mode as I dodged the jaywalkers and cars; lorries sounded their horns in out-of-tune notes of welcome.

It was late afternoon; the city centre and crowds were like those in towns and cities everywhere. I found a hotel. Why not, I said to myself. I checked in. 'No Sir,' said the receptionist, 'we will not allow your bike in your room, but you can check with security.' This I did. Security assured me that the Goose would be safe with them. I locked the Goose to the metal fence outside the security office; I also gave the security man a fistful of rupees. I worked out that it was more than he earned in a week. Whenever I passed, he was standing guard near to the Goose; it made me a happy man.

My room was adequate and I was soon showered. I also washed my clothes; they would be dry by morning. I ate my evening meal in the hotel. It was nothing special. I studied my next move; the border crossing and India.

As I lay on the bed, I reminisced about the week's happenings. When I look back at those events, they are like a dream, or watching a film. The need to make day-to-day, demanding decisions in such a short space of time, out of the normal thought patterns of life. Not to go to Kashmir was, in my opinion, an anti-climax; one of life's decisions unfulfilled. Did someone else's decision save my life? The experience filled my mind with lasting memories of friendship, faces and places; and of a world I will never see.

If I was asked the question 'what did you learn from your experiences?' I would answer, 'I learned the true meaning of friendship.'

I concluded, the hand of friendship would conquer all adversity; it's the key to a happy life. Good night, Pakistan.

Lahore

As I awoke, I became aware of the quietness of the room. It was relaxing. My night's sleep had not been disturbed. I glanced out of the window to the security office below. Blue Goose was chained to the fence as I had left it.

I ate breakfast in the hotel. At the next table was a well-dressed Pakistani guy. We talked and he asked the usual questions about where I had travelled and the countries I had cycled. As he was leaving the breakfast room, he called the waiter and said, 'I will pay for his breakfast.' I thanked him.

What a good start to the day, I thought. With that, a white guy sat down at the next table. He was dressed in brown national Indian clothes. When he spoke it was with a strong French accent. Again, the usual questions were exchanged. In quick time he knew about me and I knew about him. He was a young guy in his early twenties. 'So, you intend to cycle to India? he asked. 'Yes,' I said. 'I wouldn't. I'd put it on by-pass; bus it, or train straight through,' he said, with the customary sweep of the hand, as the French do, adding, 'there is nothing there.'

On he went, explaining that he had travelled the world for two years, backpacking. He had been in India for two weeks and was working his way home to France. He said he was so pleased to talk to another white man. We discussed the Karachi problems; the latest news he had heard was that thirty had been killed. We wished each other all the best as we shook hands. I left him drinking black coffee. In my opinion, he was ready for home.

I was reunited with Blue Goose. I bagged up, unlocked the cycle chain and was ready to go. The security guard wished me well and waved goodbye with a big smile on his face. I soon found the road to the Pakistan/India border. My plan was to cross into Amritsar. The cycling hazards are the same everywhere; my mind soon changed gear into red alert. As I neared the border, there was a long line of traffic at a standstill. I reached the border gate after walking as far as I had cycled, only to be told that it was not safe to cross the border owing to problems in Amritsar and Karachi.

Dejectedly, I turned the Goose and headed to the airport in Lahore. What a ride. I enquired about the availability of flights to New Delhi. 'We don't sell tickets here. You need to go to the ticket office for Pakistan Airways in town. Yes, flights are available.' I thought it was my day when the guy paid for my breakfast; now I was not so sure.

The thinking cap was switched on. I concluded that if I cycled into town and back, I would need to stop another night in Pakistan. Taxi! 'Yes, Sir, Pakistan Airways. I know where that is,' he said. He put the bike in the boot. I was under way, my mind still active; I was remembering the same situation in Turkey. 'Airways office,' said the driver. 'I will meet you here in one hour.'

I bagged up the Goose. The office was on the ground floor and it was like a doctor's surgery. Each one in turn went to the desk when called to the next room. A young guy appeared and pointed to the door. I pointed to the Goose. 'It is safe here,' he said. There was doubt in my mind so I chained the Goose to the chair. Waiting people stared with blank, expressionless faces; only the young guy smiled. I was at the desk. 'Single ticket to New Delhi please, with bike.' 'We will check. Please sit and wait. Do you pay by cash or credit card? 'Travellers' cheque,' said I. 'No problem,' he said. 'The flight is late afternoon.' I accepted the flight followed by the ticket. I was halfway there.

Lahore airport

I unchained the Goose from the chair and glanced at my watch. I had ten minutes left before the taxi returned. Where did I say I'd meet him? Was I lost? No, there he was, good man. I lashed the Goose to the boot as I said, 'airport check-in please. Watch the paint.'

Soon we were at the airport. I paid the taxi man, plus a tip. It must have been enough, it brought a smile to his face. I wheeled the Goose through the door to the airport check-in. 'I don't think we can take the bike,' said the clerk. 'Who said we could?' I was taken aback by the question. I thought quickly, exaggerating. 'The boss man at the ticket office,' I said, 'he had rings on his arm.' It worked, I could see it in his face. 'The bike and the bags go on,' he said. 'I need to check your hand luggage.' That was my handlebar bag. 'Open it up – what is inside?' said the guy. I was now pissed off. I felt like saying, 'the kitchen sink.' I bit my lip instead. I opened the bag and he had a good look, a bemused look on his face as he rummaged through the contents. Stamping the bag, he said this would allow me to pass through customs.

The tannoy announced the boarding of flight 196 to New Delhi. I made for the boarding gate - it felt good to be going – only to be stopped by a security guy who said I did not have a stamp on the bag that hung around my neck. 'Go back to the check-in for a stamp.' I waited in the queue just fizzing. The guy checked and stamped the bag and I was allowed on the plane. The tannoy sounded flight 196 to New Delhi was on hold for half-an-hour. I concluded that airport officialdom was hyper-bureaucracy gone crazy. The Inner Man said, 'did they load the Blue Goose?' 'Don't you start,' I said.

I sank back in the aircraft seat and smiled. What do I really think of Pakistan? It was in its democratic infancy, like a child with stunted growth. Only time will tell. Modern arms such as the rifle and rocket launcher can be bought cheap by underprivileged people in the second-hand markets for a few rupees. Irrespective of which countries they come from, the suppliers should face life in prison or be shot. Like alcohol and drugs, guns are democratic destroyers.

Goodbye my Muslim friends, I did so enjoy your company.

'Fasten your seat belts for take off.' New Delhi, India, here I come.

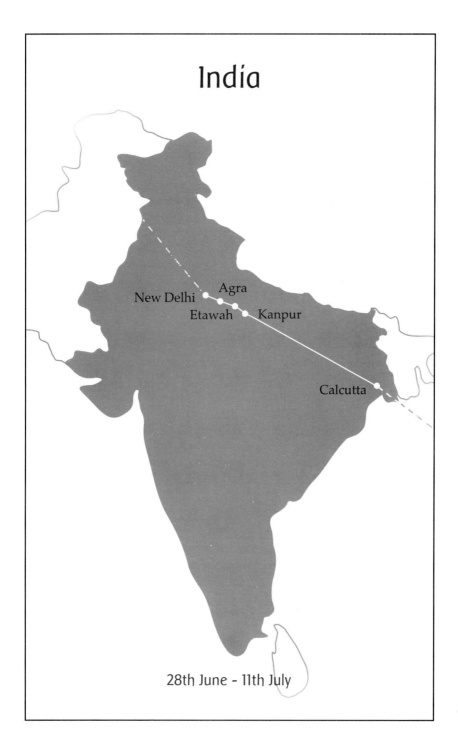

India

New Delhi
Agra
Etawah
Kanpur
Calcutta

28th June - 11th July

I must say that I enjoyed the flight between Lahore and New Delhi, which took one hour, forty minutes. I had a grand view through the aircraft window of Pakistan and India. It seemed in no time we were landing. Walking through New Delhi airport, I checked the flight number on the luggage carousel. There was the Blue Goose and my baggage. I bagged up and made for the exit. Wheeling the Goose to the lift, an American voice said, 'where are you going, fella?' 'To cycle India,' was my reply. 'Rather you than me,' he said. In my opinion, the most dangerous ride will be in the States. I nodded thanks. A real Job's comforter, I thought.

The lift was too small for the Goose, so I walked up the steps carrying the bags and the Goose. Why not? The Goose had carried me this far. Oh my God – when I stepped out of the airport entrance, the taxi drivers and porters attacked like a swarm of bees. I retreated in haste. I'd forgotten to change my money to Indian rupees. I duly changed my money. Again, I kept the receipt for when I leave the country.

In anticipation I made my exit from the airport. The baying, hounding taxi drivers descended on me like I was a film star; I broke through their ranks, using the Goose as a battering ram. As if by chance, a smartly-dressed Indian wearing a turban stepped up to me. 'Excuse me, if you want a hotel, there's one two miles down the road to Delhi. Cycle 500 yards down the road and turn left.' I thanked him as I broke free through the remainder of the mob.

I was cycling in India; I felt great. My dreams had become reality without a prayer. 'On the road again; just can't wait to get on the road again,' I sang as I swiftly covered the two miles. There it was; I could see it in the distance: Hotel Centaur. As I entered the lobby, I could see this was going to cost me money. The receptionist welcomed me. I booked in for two nights; I was in need of a rest. Pakistan was both physically and mentally demanding. The Blue Goose was housed in the security office.

I placed my bags in my room. It was first class. There was also a full-size bath; I'd try that for size later. I walked around the hotel; it was very impressive. 'Hair cut sir?' Why not. I must have looked a scruff as I sat in the chair. 'How do you want it?' asked the guy. 'Just cut it all off,' I said after seeing myself in the mirror. The barber smiled. When he had finished I smiled at my refection; I looked just like a Buddhist monk with my dark glasses and sunburnt face. I shrugged. What the hell? No one knows me.

Wandering around reception I came across a tourist officer with a map of India spread out in front of him. I glanced at the map. 'Are you travelling our country, Sir?' I must have looked a real scruff in my cycling clothes. They were clean but not pressed. 'Cycling,' said I. 'What route?' he asked. I showed him. 'Well, Sir, we don't under any circumstances allow you to cycle in the state of Bihar. That's the state before Calcutta. It's not safe for a lone rider. Religious problems – they are Buddhists.' I felt like saying 'where the hell can I cycle then?' If Buddhists were a problem, at least I looked like one.

I returned to my room full of thought. The bath soon distracted me. I ran the water and mixed in the soaps. It was bliss. Was it ten days since I'd bathed? I also washed all my clothes. I looked at myself in the mirror. Is that you, Mac? I looked and smelled like a scented, half-starved spring chicken.

That night I ate in the hotel restaurant. What a meal: tomato soup, chicken, chips and veg, followed by a bottle of chilled lager. Food, glorious food. I slept like a king. Good night.

New Delhi – rest day

My second day in Delhi I classed as a rest day and thoroughly enjoyed it. The hotel ran a bus service into the city every hour. Delhi is a busy place, people everywhere. I'd rather be on the road, it's less exhausting. I also enjoyed the hotel facilities. The heat I find oppressive at times; the temperature yesterday was 38 degrees at midday; today it's 40 degrees. This class of hotel can spoil your conception of B&B. Big hotels for single travellers can be lonely.

I rang Gill. She gave me a row for not ringing sooner. 'Where are you?' she asked. 'India,' was my reply. 'Don't leave it so long before ringing next time,' she said. It was great to hear her voice; she assured me all was well. Gill was on my mind as I retired for the night. Good night.

New Delhi, on the road to Agra

I was up at the crack of dawn and ate a full, enjoyable breakfast. I topped up both water bottles, bagged up the Goose, checked the tyre pressures and oiled the chain. I thanked security for looking after the Goose. The security man indicated he wanted to give it a test ride. This he did, with a big smile of approval.

I was on the road to Agra; the time, 0530 hours. The route passed through Delhi and I was lost many times, even after studying the map. The best way to make progress was to stop and ask, as road signs were non-existent. The roads were quiet. I found the Agra road; I was on my way. The sun was a ball of fire as it rose over the horizon, painting the whole countryside in a yellow pastel wash. Even the sun failed to burn away the early morning pollution. As the temperature of the day increased, the water in my bottles became almost tea hot. I needed to supplement my drinking water on many a day with Pepsi or the other popular drink, 'Thumbs Up'; I think it was a product of Coke. I still have an acquired taste for Pepsi.

The roads were now crowded with people on foot, or cycling like myself. Some would make my day by acknowledging me with a cheery 'good morning'. Again, my hard hat became my double saviour against accidents and the sun's rays. The heat in the afternoon was so intense it screwed me into the ground.

The Goose started to sway. Wowee, hold on, Mac. What's wrong? A puncture. Well, that's the first, so don't moan. By the time I removed the tyre and repaired the puncture, a dozen or so people were standing around watching and discussing my actions. It was now 1300 hours; the temperature of the day was peaking. I was swathed in a bath of sweat; at least when cycling you create a cooling breeze. A lorry stopped on the road, the driver jumped from the cab dragging a dirty old bed cover, climbed under the lorry, lay on the cover and went to sleep. I was to find that this was the order of the day around noon.

My handbrakes on the Goose were red hot, as were all its metal parts. My nose bridge was still sore, and peeling in the sun. I must protect my nose somehow, I thought. Vaseline; it was my saviour. I applied a liberal amount, and even it turned to thin liquid in the heat of the day. I kept my arms and legs covered otherwise I'd pay the price with sunburn. No words to describe the landscape other than dry, parched, arid land with some trees.

The dominant lorry was here, as in Turkey and Pakistan, the tiger of the road. At its roar of 95-plus decibels on the horn, everything moved out of its way. Lorries were loaded to twice the load limit and objects stuck out from the sides. Road safety was obviously unheard of. I was quick to learn to vacate the road on the blast of a horn from the rear.

The roads were built with what I would call a cart track on either side, for cyclists, pedestrians and ox carts. When a lorry wanted to use it, however, you instantly vacated the track. I forgot to say I was now cycling on the left hand side; it's the same for Pakistan. What one would call the good old British tradition. I had a close call. A lorry was overtaking another lorry coming towards me. I was the one expected to leave the road. In other words, the lorry said, 'move your butt, this road is mine.' To say the least, it was annoying, but when in Rome....Who am I to change the ways of the world?

I cycled up to a motel partly under construction. The sign said 'open'. I rode to reception. 'Yes, we have a room.' What an unexpected find. 'We also serve food,' said the receptionist. I was allowed to park the Goose in the main hall; I chained it to a chair. It was cooling to get out of the sun and the room shades were drawn. 'We have a small problem,' said the receptionist, 'the power supply is not constant today. When the power supply shuts down, we need to reset it in the main reception.' 'Thank you,' I said.

As I switched on the cooling fan it took off like a Spitfire engine with a broken prop. The speed was adjustable so I slowed it down. An air conditioning unit protruded from the wall. The switch said 'press to start'. I followed the instruction with my index finger. It started. Jesus loves me, yes I know. As the fan reached its full rev limit – or when the shit hits the fan for want of another expression – a mass of creepy crawlies was dislodged from the fan blades all over my bed. Some were dead, others were still alive. I stemmed the moving mass with a spare pillow from the bed, rendering them all dead and harmless. The once-clean sheet now took on a different look; together with the underside of the pillow they looked like a Picasso. I reset the power supply five times that evening. I was wary of the creepy-crawlies, but that initial fan start had dislodged all of them.

The view from the room was excellent, better than the norm; farmland and rice fields, with unfamiliar birds and water buffalo. The evening meal was good and the dining room quiet; only two Asian families were there apart from myself. Fed and watered I rested in my room to keep cool.

From the time I started to take malaria tablets in Turkey, I had not felt myself. It's hard to explain; my mouth was always dry, like blotting paper and I was continually sipping water. My right arm was swelling up; I put it down to water retention and kept it covered from the sun. If it was the tablets, I intended to stop taking them completely on leaving India.

As I lay on the bed, my everyday repetitive chores went through my mind in turn. Had I forgotten anything? The oil on the derailleur chain cogs was to make gear-changing easier. Every fourth day I cleaned the Goose; that's just good housekeeping. My cycle seat was now well and truly shaped to my butt. Hygiene in that area is paramount. If you develop pain while cycling, remember that continual vibrations and bumps are also transmitted through your wrists, arms and shoulders as you go along. Washing both yourself and your clothes is a daily necessity, as is checking the trueness of the front and rear wheels and the state of the tyres and air pressure. My mind fluttered to a halt. Surely I had forgotten something? I closed my eyes, counting the creepy-crawlies. Good night.

The road to Agra

No, I didn't have nightmares about creepy-crawlies; in fact, I slept so well I was late getting up. I enjoyed breakfast, bagged up the Goose and checked the time; 0600 hours. Late, my boy – but only by half-an-hour.

Would I make Agra today? I asked myself as I mounted the Goose. At least I was on the correct road, not like the problems of yesterday morning. I was soon following the Indian way of road cycling. My arm was no better; it was swollen but not painful. I still think it's water retention.

'Good morning.' I said it thrice in as many miles. The roadsides were well trodden. As I slowly cycled along dodging jaywalkers, lorries welcomed me with their tuneful horn blasts. Young Indian boys raced up the road with all the exuberance of youth. The morning sun soon had me reaching for my water bottle; the heat even melted the mind. 'Yes, it is hot for this time of year,' said a cyclist, joining me as I went along. We talked about everyday things. He said he was a solicitor and he was dressed in a summer suit, a briefcase strapped to the Indian-made bomber bike.

I was saddened by the sight of two brown dancing bears being led down the road fastened by a rope around their muzzles. I wished I could turn them loose. I also passed an Indian elephant dressed in its finery; what a majestic beast. I began to think I was cycling through a safari park. Later in the afternoon, as I cycled up to an old, but still impressive, ruined building, I was confronted on the road by a pack of baboons; they partially blocked the road. I rode through them with a certain amount of apprehension. The next moment they were but a memory. That's the beauty of cycling; new faces and places at every turn.

'Agra' – that's what it said on the signpost. Bikes, pedestrians, taxis, cars and lorries all increased in number the nearer we got to the city. No, I don't want to stay in a tourist hotel. I decided to seek out an Indian hotel on the periphery. I cycled on the by-pass road and soon came to a hotel. 'Yes, we have room for you and your bike, sir,' the receptionist said with a smile. The hotel's décor looked just fair, but I was only interested in the bed. The porter took my bags, and I carried the Goose. As he opened the bedroom door, the crickets high-jumped everywhere as if in the Olympics. The porter made short work of them with a well-aimed fly swat; the dead and dying covered the carpet. 'I'll come back and clean up, sir,' said the porter, pocketing his tip.

The room had all facilities; there was even a kettle and some cups. I had my own tea bags. The Taj Mahal is one of the seven wonders of the world. I'll see it tomorrow.

I was hungry, and crossed the busy road to the shop opposite. I bought paper-wrapped biscuits and a bottle of Pepsi. When I opened the biscuits, I noticed the sell-by date was two years ago. I ate them – at least they'd been wrapped. I know what you're saying: 'what did they taste like?' Musty sawdust, washed down with Pepsi and tea. There was a knock on the bedroom door. When I opened it, a woman and two workmen stood there. 'I hope you don't mind, sir,' she said, her eyelashes vibrating with over-loaded mascara; they shook as if they had St Vitus' dance. Come on, get to the point, I said to myself. 'You see, Sir, the crickets come in through the air vents at this time of year. We need to cover the vents with mesh; the job will take two hours.' 'Carry on,' I said, with a wave of the hand while I reclined on the bed. How do they say it? No rest for the wicked. Good night.

Agra

I was late getting out of bed. I ate some breakfast and drank tea until my back teeth were awash. There was a need to carry a high level of liquid to meet the day's demands.

The Taj Mahal was an hour on the Goose from the hotel. I left the pannier bags in my room. Cycling through a town or city in India is like cycling continuously through a flock of sheep. You bump and are bumped; it is a case of every sheep for himself.

The hard-sell merchants stood in rows at the entrance to the Taj Mahal. They'd sell sand to an Arab, as the saying goes. They were self-trained in the most up-to-date techniques of selling unwanted gifts to a gullible public. No, I didn't buy anything. I'd have to carry it, that's my excuse.

Yes, I was impressed and it was well worth an extra day's stay-over. What can I say about the Taj Mahal that hasn't been said before? A wonder of the world to see, touch and smell and hear the tourists babbling like sheep as they wander in wonder around the splendid marble structures.

A monument to his wife. I ask myself – where did he get the money to build such a fine monument? What if he had spent the money on his loyal subjects – would the social and economic structure be more stable than it is now? I don't know; I'm only surmising. But we would have had only six wonders of the world, not seven; the economy of the area would have been possibly poorer.

I moved through Agra with my eyes fully open, wondering about life. What would a westerner do if he lived here? Possibly go crazy, I thought. It had been a worthwhile day. I needed to change money to rupees. I waited in a bank for over an hour to change my American Express money. I saw three different guys and filled in three forms before I had my Indian rupees.

One tip on handling or accepting Indian bank notes: check that the notes are not worn through; by that I mean dirty or torn, with holes ripped in them. The Indian shopkeeper will not accept damaged bank notes, as I was to learn to my cost, but they play a game of passing them, or, as we would say, passing the buck.

By the time I got back to the hotel I was knackered. I was also hungry. As the porter passed me, I asked if there was a restaurant. 'Yes, Sir.' Good, I thought. In for a penny, in for a pound. After waiting patiently, hunger pangs ripped the last pieces of flesh from the inside of my rib cage. The chicken dinner eventually arrived; two legs and a wing, plus rice covered in veg. I dug in the fork; it was like a lucky dip, everything was hidden in the rice. I reckoned, not being facetious, someone must have run the meat off the chicken before they caught it; the meat from the two legs and the wing amounted to half a mouthful. I was far from full but felt too exhausted to scavenge amongst the rice. No thanks, I don't want a sweet. I couldn't face it. Tea? Yes, thank you. I walked to the shop opposite the hotel and bought a packet of biscuits and a Pepsi. I returned to my room to find that no one had cleaned the workmen's mess from yesterday. I opened the biscuits and flipped off the top of the Pepsi. I looked at the sell-by date; things were getting better – only one year out of date. The Pepsi masked the taste of the biscuits. After eating them I felt full. 'Agra Cadabra,' I said before crashing out. Good night.

Agra to Etawah

The hotel I was staying in was situated on the main by-pass road; the traffic was busy at all times of the day and night. I was on the road early after doing all my morning chores; the time was 0530 hours. I launched myself into the traffic. 'Beep, beep – up you too!' An over-loaded lorry was too near for comfort. His load stuck out at either side; close.

The sun rose on time. I often wonder who pays him to work every day? It was only 0700 hours, but the sun's rays penetrated all aspects of life. If I were home, I'd say it was a scorcher of a day.

For miles I cycled through row after row of trees. I found this a good shelter from the sun. Today I met some interesting people. When

I stop for a Pepsi, invariably a crowd gathers. Today was no exception. I stopped on the roadside and bought a Pepsi, sitting down at the table to watch the world go by. 'Hello there!' A hand was thrust my way. I returned the greeting and shook the hand. As the guy sat down he told me he was a retired headmaster. His speech was slow and deliberate, as you might expect in films. People appeared as if from nowhere; to his peers, he was 'king of the walk'. I enjoyed our conversation; he highlighted all the problems in present-day India. He asked in a forthright way if I thought the world would know of India's problems. I assured him that, in my opinion, the world would know. When I made a move to go, all faces smiled on cue. I returned the smile and was on my way.

India was a country of extremes; village life was basic and raw, while city life was another planet. When I chanced to stop in the rural villages, children would look at me with wonder in their eyes; possibly I was the first westerner they had ever seen? Cyclists joined me and chattered as I rode along, others passed by as if they wanted to race. Traffic was scarce today for some reason. I passed two overturned over-loaded lorries. There is a limit to what you can load on a lorry; if you flaunt it, you pay the price. Small, three-wheeled taxis were numerous, and the village buses were loaded to the gunwales with their precious human cargo.

'How far you cycling?' The question caught me by surprise; I must have been daydreaming. I looked to see I'd been joined by a smart young man on a bike. 'I'm cycling to the nearest hotel,' I replied. He said he was going to Etawah and there was a town hotel there. As we cycled together it was good to talk. He asked questions on questions and I managed one or two myself. 'What do you do?' I asked. 'I'm in college, studying English – my finals are next year,' he said. I wished him all the best with his studies. As we entered Etawah, I offered to buy him a Pepsi. He declined the offer and remarked that a drink at the town water pump was far cheaper than Pepsi. He drank and waited for me. I followed the same actions as he, holding the water in my mouth and then spitting it out; I was afraid to swallow. We smiled and shook hands; he thanked me for speaking to him. 'It's not often I get the chance to try out my English,' he said. 'The hotel is 500 yards down the road on the right.' With that, he was gone. I soon found the hotel and checked in, and the Goose was allowed in my room. It was clean and basic, with a shower and toilet. 'What do you want for 150 rupees?' said the Inner Man.

Must feed the Inner Man I said, patting my now concave belly. I walked the main street and bought apples, plums, cookies and a bottle of Pepsi for dinner. What I did learn early on was not to walk around strange towns or cities at night; one is quickly courting trouble. I ate my dinner and completed all my chores. Good night.

Etawah, the road to Kanpur

I was awake early; I needed to take my daily dose of Paladrine tablets. My arm was still swollen with water retention. I looked in the mirror – I'm sure the sunburn on my face and arms was darker than the local folk. My cat eye computer recorded 80 miles yesterday in the sunshine. This was to my mind a good mileage; the recorded temperature was 40 degrees.

I was soon on the road. My! Cycling through Etawah early in the morning, my education on the life and habits of the town was filled to overflowing. Sleepy-eyed local folk were sweeping their shops and house fronts; the dust enveloped the brush drivers. People slept outside on low wooden beds, all curled up in the land of dreams, not wishing to open their eyes to the day. Some were stooping in the road, carrying out their daily chores, cleaning their teeth. Holy cows ate from refuse piles on the roadside; their droppings were evident. Some shopkeepers were unloading goods from lorries into their shops. I felt I was an intruder. I looked on in fascination; it would make conversation in many a home or café. It was what I would call a happening.

Traffic was slow to build up although the roads were full of folk going about their business. The heat of the sun was unbelievable; my cat eye was unreadable; the letters and numbers had liquidised in the glass face. I was particular about drinking the water; I added iodine drinking tablets to all the water I drank in India. What did the water taste like? Sour wine. My mouth was still blotting paper dry and I continuously sipped the water bottle without relief.

I'd been on the road from 0600 hours this morning; it was now 1500 hours. I had completed 65 miles and the heat was relentless. I was feeling jaded, to put it mildly. I cycled into a fairly large village; people thronged the roads and pavements – the shimmering heat rose off them as if they were cooking. 'Where do you stop for today, Mac?' I said to myself. I began the relentless task of asking folk, 'any hotels?'. Some just looked at me dully – maybe they thought I was dull? I felt a tug on my sleeve. 'Follow me,' said a man. I followed like a lamb, pushing through the crowds until we came to an old church building. He pointed, I looked. When I turned he had gone. I didn't even have time to thank him.

I entered the building through an old wooden door into a courtyard, to be met by a man with his hands together as if in prayer, nodding his head. I smiled and said 'room?'. He nodded and led me to a bare room with a none too clean mattress. 'This is all we have to offer,' he said. 'We might have a chair and a sheet later.' He turned on his heel and was gone, never to be seen again. I surveyed the room; no lock, metal bars on the window, a tap with water in the corner. I decided it was better than nothing at this time of day.

I thought this place must be an old fort or prison. I looked on the map for the name of the village between Etawah and Kanpur, but it didn't seem to exist. I was hungry. I must eat. I had seen market stalls and shops on the way in, outside the building. I was soon checking out the food stalls. I had palmed my money, so as not to have to open my wallet in the crowd. One soon learns. The street was packed with folk like working ants. 'Three apples, please.' They were slightly bruised, but they were the best on show. As I was paying I was aware of a young man next to me taking notice of what I was doing. In perfect English he quoted a price – more than the one offered by the man who had served me.

The alarm bells rang. What's going on here? Take care, Mac. At the next shop I asked for six plums and the same guy appeared. 'This is also my shop,' he said, and quoted a price for the plums. That's expensive, I thought. He grinned; I scowled. I looked around the shop and asked the guy behind the counter the cost of some biscuits. He gave me a price. The young guy was still there. 'This is also my shop,' he repeated, and quoted me more for the biscuits. Ding, ding! I was being taken for a ride by this rogue. I looked him straight in the eyes. 'I don't like you,' I said. The guy tried to back away; I saw fear in his eyes. 'You're trying to cheat me. For your cheek, I don't want your goods.' He vanished, never to be seen again. The shopkeeper pleaded with me to buy the goods at his price. I relented. I also bought two bottles of Pepsi – one to be kept for breakfast.

I retired to my cell. A clean sheet was on the bed and a chair had been provided. There was no lock on the door. I wedged it closed and put the Goose across it; I would know by the clatter if anyone attempted to come in. I hit the switch on the overhead cooling fan. It played its remorseless tune, 'klunk, klick, klunk, klick'. I can stick it – can you? I ate my dinner and kept some for the morning. I lay on the clean sheet; the mattress must have been made of tarmac. I slept in my clothes. Good night.

Kanpur

I was out of bed early, well-rested. I ate my breakfast; at least it was food. My arm was still swollen. I bagged up the Goose and removed the door wedge. I was out and on my way to Kanpur. The streets were deserted; only an old man with a dog was shuffling along and cows rummaged in the plastic bags outside the shops. Vehicles were few and far between.

I looked at my watch. It was 0530 hours; the sun as programmed rose in the sky. It was never that close at home, I thought. Yesterday the temperature reached 41 degrees. It will reach it today, too, by the feel of it. Today, for fully two minutes I was cycling on my own. I looked on this as an event; there was no other traffic to be seen on the road.

I enjoyed my cycling today; cyclists outnumbered all else on the road. I dreamed we cyclists should rule the roads. With that, a lorry blasted his way past, his horns sounding like a mobile ghetto-blaster at full voice. We followed our usual dispersal tactics. My conclusion was you want the CTC (Cyclist Touring Club) to work for your cause. I'd topped up my water bottles from the tap this morning and added the iodine tablets. My mouth was dry as usual; not a nice feeling. The Goose flew along, the miles passing fast. As I neared Kanpur, the traffic noticeably slowed us down; cars, lorries, taxis and scooters were all fighting their corners to enter town.

It was every man for himself. The road disappeared. There were no traffic lights, only a policeman with a long cane, or you could say a big stick; he stood on the pavement and got agitated if someone stopped. He would soon whip them on. It was crazy. There were no signposts. Which way do I go? I was feeling hot and bothered to say the least. These townies can have their town. I'm a country boy; I yearn for peace and quiet.

It was 1500 hours. There was no breeze in town and the sun was relentless. I was in need of shade. Hotel India loomed up; I could see the sign in the distance. I fought my way across the road, the Goose acting as a human ram. I was exhausted but I made it; I was in a bath of sweat. 'Yes, we have a room – the bike can stay in the foyer.' I chained the Goose to the stair rail and carried all my bags to my room. I'd stopped at worse – at least the bed was clean. I crashed out in a bath of sweat, exhausted. Even my sleep was deep in sweat.

When I awoke, the bed was soaking wet and it was early evening. I showered under the cold water tap; it only produced fairly hot water. I reluctantly ate my Paladin tablet. I think my swollen arm has reduced in size. I did the pinch test on the fatty areas of my body. I'm sorry to report there were none. Damn, I was thin; I must eat. I was now determined. I dressed and looked as local as the locals. I walked with the crowds. Local eating dives were scattered all around. They all looked the same; uninviting. I was on the road to the railway station.

'You must eat,' said the Inner Man. OK, don't nag.

I sat at a somewhat dirty table. The poor guy who was serving was lost for words; he kept wringing his hands in nervous agitation. I got up and looked at the communal cooking pots all steaming on the fire. I pointed to three items: rice, boiled eggs (I held up six fingers) and veg – don't ask me what it was. I also pointed to a soft drink, holding up two fingers. Dinner is served. The boiled eggs refused to be cut; they were like liquid plastic – the poor hens must have been fed on plastic pellets. I persevered and after chewing for an extremely long time I won the day. The rice was good, the mysterious veg burned the roof of my mouth. I doused it with the soft drink. I hope I can digest this lot. I was feeling full.

I walked around the railway station; a herd of holy cows stood about everywhere, leaving their trademarks on the roads and pavements. The local fly squadrons were laughing as they landed on the dung piles; at least someone was eating. During my walk I fancied a mango and bought two, along with two cartons of orange juice. When I returned to the hotel, I asked the receptionist how to prepare the mango. He produced a knife and cut the skin into long sections. It peeled off no problem. I thanked him for the demonstration. I also asked him what the temperature was today. It was 45 degrees. I lay on my still-wet bed feeling slightly sorry for myself. The prickly heat was having a revival. My arm was not a problem, but I wanted to reduce the swelling. My night's sleep was intermittent; hot flushes woke me every hour on the hour.

Kanpur - overnight train to Calcutta

I was awake early. I showered and dried with my wonder towel. I did feel better although sweat poured from me almost immediately after my lukewarm shower. 'Action, Mac,' said the Inner Man. Decisions now. Calcutta? I'll go by train. I was not allowed to cycle in the state of Bihar; the only towns I'd miss out on would be Allahabad and Varanasi. It was 1000 hours when I returned to the hotel. I told the receptionist I had failed to book on the train, which wasn't quite true. I could have booked myself but they wouldn't give me a ticket for the Goose. I had queued for an hour. 'No problem,' said the receptionist; it was nice to hear those cure-all words. 'I'll get the tickets for you – see me in one hour's time.' I glanced at the temperature recorder; it was 44 degrees. Must be on the blink like my cat eye computer. I smiled on my way to my room. I returned after an hour to reception. 'Sorry, Sir, I was unable to get your bike on the train,' said the receptionist. With that, the manager appeared. 'Have we a problem?' The receptionist and I explained the difficulty with the Goose. 'I have a friend who is an agent,' he said. He phoned. 'No problem – the tickets will be here this afternoon. The train goes this evening. It will cost you more as there's an agent's fee.' 'But of course,' I said. My God, I thought, was I also becoming corrupt?

Later that afternoon the tickets arrived. Could I pay for them now please? The rupees were taking a hammering. I was getting short of the readies. 'The bank closes in an hour, sir,' said the receptionist. 'There is one up the road, about a mile.' For the first time in my life I sat in a bike rickshaw. 'Bank of India please.' He nodded. I looked at the guy. He must have been in his forties, but life had been hard; he looked all of sixty. He didn't have an ounce of fat or muscle, only the sinews in his legs protruded. I felt like putting him in the seat and telling him I'd pull the rig. As we reached the bank I asked if he would wait. He nodded. I went through the same bank procedures as before; it took all of three quarters of an hour to draw out my money. I was lucky; it was closing as I left. As I waited in the bank, a guy walked around serving cups of tea to the staff. Me, being a smart arse, asked for a cup. 'Thanks,' I said as the guy handed me a cup of tea. He held out his hand for money. Not so smart, were you, Mac? It was good tea.

The rickshaw guy was waiting for me, resting in the seat. I enjoyed my rickshaw ride back to the hotel. It's the best form of transport, with a relaxed view. I packed my bags and unlocked the Goose. I paid the receptionist; it was a cheap lodge. The manager allowed him to come to the station with me. I wheeled the Goose, he carried the bags. People moved like ants, beggars prostrated themselves in various horrendous poses on the ground – begging bowls in the raised position. I was glad the receptionist was there. The Goose was booked in the goods carriage. The number one boss man played out his dominance for all to see; it was he who ran the show. I stood in front of him; he was not a happy looking man. He barked orders to his scruffy, willing porters, who ran in all directions to fulfil his every wish. He looked at me. 'My bike to Calcutta, please.' 'Ticket,' he said, holding out his hand. He produced a piece of cardboard with the word 'Calcutta' painted on in black paint. The porter tied the cardboard sign to the handlebars of the Goose. He then held out his hand. 'Twenty rupees,' he said, 'and ten rupees for each of the porters. Forty rupees. The receptionist caught my eye and nodded. I paid reluctantly. As I said, bloody corrupt; to them it's a way of life. I hate it; it destroys democracy. It's not unlike a cancer. I bought some nuts and a bottle of water on the platform. When the train arrived I found my seat, thanked the receptionist and gave him a more than generous tip. He smiled, wide-eyed, held his hands in praying attitude and bowed his thanks. At least I'd made someone's day.

The seat was also my bed. I stashed the bags, one at either end of the seat; one for my head and the other for my feet. The babble of people was overwhelming. I sat and watched the sights of the world. No comment.

Yes, in my opinion I'd made the correct decision. The guard's whistle shrieked out its high note and we were under way. Opposite sat a well-dressed Indian man. We acknowledged each other with a smile. The carriage I was in held four beds; two at ground level and two higher. There was no one above him or myself. Good, I thought – peace and quiet. I was in need of rest. The rate the train passed through the countryside hypnotised me. My eyes closed and I cat-napped.

I woke as the train shunted out of a station. 'How far are you going?' asked the man. 'Calcutta,' I said. 'So am I,' said the man. We spoke. He was a railway employee; a track engineer. He knew every station and all the views and the names of the rivers; he was a mine of information. I was lucky to have him as a fellow passenger. I lay back eating my nuts; they were a little musty but I was hungry. When I'd finished I looked in the bag. There was a weevil. How many I'd eaten I don't know; I didn't taste the meat.

I sat back in the train seat daydreaming. I couldn't believe what I saw. A beautiful woman's ankle appeared over the side of the upper bunk. No shoes, and immaculately manicured toenails painted black. A gold chain hanging gracefully from her ankle completed the display. The rest of her appeared, dressed in the local sari. She was dark, young, pretty, wearing heavily applied mascara. She melted my surprise with a dazzling smile, opened the carriage door and was gone. The guy opposite accepted this show as if it were an everyday occurrence; he showed no surprise. I expect he saw her when he came in. On her return she gave the same mischievous smile, put one dainty foot on the handrail and disappeared into the top bunk above me. My God, I thought – what will Gill say when I tell her I slept with an Indian woman? Ha!

I lay full-length across the seats. I was aware of the constant jerking movement; it was like having sex with a carriage seat. I slept. Good night.

Calcutta

When I awoke the next day, I drank half a bottle of water for my breakfast. I also had indigestion. That's unusual for me. I was full of interest to see the dawn appear over India. I do like travelling by train. The ever-changing scene flickered past the window like a picture book. Even this early people were about their chores, men carrying little bottles of water stooping down in the field to carry out the call of nature. It must be hard to find an unused spot if they've been doing that all these years. When in Rome, Mac.

The young lass above appeared and smiled – that 'nice to have travelled with you' smile – and opened the carriage door and disappeared. The background colour changed continually with the strength of the sun. 'Calcutta next stop,' said the man opposite. The train came to a stop. 'Not yet.' My fellow passenger showed his disgust with a scowl. 'Do you know what's happening?' he said. I shook my head. 'You see these people carrying those sacks, and bundles of vegetables and rice?' Yes,' I said. 'They are unloading here to dodge paying tax. If they unload in Calcutta they must by law pay tax. Corruption is widespread,' he said. 'See the police? They are here to stop this kind of thing happening. They are paid, as are the train drivers. All corrupt.' We watched in silence. Tons of produce were unloaded from the train on to lorries and carts by porters.

The train gave a big shunt; within the hour we were pulling into Calcutta railway station. The Indian passenger and I shook hands and wished each other well. I bagged up – my, they were heavy – and set off to find the Goose. Calcutta was not unlike Paddington station in the rush hour. Find the Goose, Mac. I started to walk down the train towards the goods van; I was walking against the tide of folk. The Goose appeared from under a pile of luggage. The Goose was part of me; I was worried. I soon checked it over. A railway porter grabbed the Goose from me and started to walk away. I was shouting; he took not a blind bit of notice. My bags were heavy as I struggled to keep up with the guy. The next thing I knew we were at the station exit. The guy stopped and as he did I grabbed the Goose and said, 'you cheeky bastard,' and 'up you, Jack,' as I turned on my heel and walked away. He waved his arms angrily and shouted at me. I was in the mood for anything and anyone. When I looked again he had gone. The taxi bluebottles descended on me. You never learn, Mac. I pointed to my bike and made the international cycle sign. They disappeared, or should I say, left me alone. The adrenaline still flowed after the porter's antics.

I bagged up the Goose then studied the street map. Where do I go? From where I stood I surveyed a very busy city; what a seething mass of humanity. The roads were full of traffic and people. I was about to join that throbbing mass of ants. I had done my homework well. My format sheet detailed the city hotels and the district. I moved into the main stream of traffic.

I was nudged off the bike more times than I was on. Red alert; this called for all my cycling skills. I rode across the bridge. It was a beautiful piece of engineering. In the distance I could see another one. British engineering at its best. 'This is not the time for sightseeing,' said the Inner Man. With that, a taxi nudged my rear panniers as if to say 'move it.' If I stopped I'd be a dead man; concentration was the name of the game. The heat of the day helped to trap the hydrocarbon fumes in the city's built-up streets. This was air pollution at its worst and I was breathing it in. It took one-and-a-half hours to break free from the city's gravitational pull.

My head was thumping from the hydrocarbon fumes. 'Hotel, sir? Yes – that way,' said a young, smartly-dressed policeman. I thanked him and turned off the main road. The hotel looked like a well-used city hotel. 'Yes, we have a room.' It was music to my ears. 'You can leave the bike in the foyer. It will be safe, under supervision at all times.' I thanked the receptionist as I chained the Goose to the stair rail.

In my room I lay exhausted on the bed; I didn't feel well. The pain in my stomach increased, causing me to sweat. I was unable to lie on the bed. I twitched and moved with the pulsating pain stabs. I felt as if I had a ball in my stomach. I couldn't take much more of this. I crawled to the toilet and sat down. Oh my God – what have I passed? I don't know. I felt instant relief. I was now on the toilet floor, panting like an old dog. I just lay there, afraid to move in case the pain returned. I thought it must be like that when a woman gives birth. I shakily got to my feet and looked in the toilet pan. Whatever it was had gone. I was well-trained; I'd pulled the chain. I felt physically drained. I lay on the bed and slept.

I awoke feeling fine and looked at my watch – 1400 hours. 'Come on,' said the Inner Man, 'if you want to see Calcutta, move your butt.' Don't mention that word! After a quick shower and a change of clothes, I felt like a new man. I asked the receptionist directions to the Thai airline office. This involved walking the main streets of Calcutta. I did enjoy it. There's the office. I walked up to the desk to be greeted by a big smile. 'What can I do to help you today?' 'One single, plus my bike, to Bangkok,' I said. 'No problem, sir.' I paid with my credit card. The tickets had the time of departure printed on them; tomorrow afternoon. Great, that suited me fine. I thanked them. That was short and sweet; no problem.

I felt a bit scruffy so I bought a shirt. At least I'll look tidy travelling tomorrow. The cafes on the main street were of a high standard. I was tempted so I bought a giant ice cream. I was so hungry; the taste was out of this world. I refrained from eating too much after this morning's happenings. I enjoyed the rest of the day sightseeing.

On returning to the hotel, I asked a porter if someone could clean the Goose. 'No problem,' was the reply. That evening I ate at the hotel restaurant and enjoyed a substantial meal. I decided to have a relaxing evening. The lounge was open-air with small tables and easy chairs; on each table was an English newspaper. It was warm and balmy. What a great atmosphere, and what service. 'Yes please, a pint of beer.' Nectar of the gods. What a life. I retired to my room. Good night.

Calcutta

At breakfast I ate a morsel of everything. I was hungry and thoroughly enjoyed it all. The pain of yesterday had not returned, and although my arm was still swollen, it wasn't any worse. The porter whom I'd asked to clean the Goose stood by with a money smile on his face. I paid him. He still smiled so he was a happy man. I unlocked the Goose and bagged up. If you want a good job done, do it yourself. It's a true saying. If he had cleaned the Goose, I'll eat my hard hat.

I checked the time; I had time enough to reach the airport. I had a last look at the map before launching myself into the traffic, which was medium to heavy. I stopped at various points and watched the world go by. I think it's the most relaxing form of therapy. The international airport sign pointed in the same direction as I was cycling. I was on the right road.

I was cycling through the poor part of town, and in all my travels I had not seen the like. A shanty town followed the contour of the main road. I had seen shanty towns in other countries and been in them, but this was unbelievable. I would go so far as to describe them as a rabbit warren of people, or a rats' nest. The name I gave them was a warren of humanoid rats. The only time they washed was when it rained; their sole possessions were what they stood up in. They were highly trained at begging, acting and theft; it was a way of life. In my opinion I was looking at people whose survival was in-bred. Hereditary factors play a big part. You or I would die in under a week if we lived in the same conditions. The medical profession would do well to isolate the survival genes of these people. A study could be revealing. I looked on them with pity in this so-called modern world.

The sign said 'Calcutta airport'. The door opened automatically into the main building, but to reach it I had to run the gauntlet of the beggars who were lined up outside, trained not to enter the building. I surveyed the inside of the building to get my bearings. There it was; Bangkok Thai Airways check-in. 'Yes, sir – you have a box for the bike?' 'No.' I said I was not told when I booked in yesterday; concern was written all over my face. 'Could you please swivel the handlebars, lower the seat and let the air out of the tyres? Oh, and remove the pedals.' The final thing he said with a smile. I failed to remove the pedals with my spanner. Two keen young boys took over; they also failed. 'Never mind,' said the official. I checked in my pannier bags. In turn, they gave me my boarding pass. I kneeled down to put my passport back in my handlebar bag; my hand touched the glass dividing the inside from the outside. Outside, a young beggar woman with a baby in her arms followed my hand with hers along the plate glass. Both misery and anguish were written all over her face. She could have been a professional beggar, I don't know. I thought, a top actress would get an Oscar to look half as convincing as the beggar woman – with more money than she would ever see in her lifetime. I removed my hand; tears streamed from her eyes. The other side of that glass I was in a different world to hers. Makes you think, doesn't it?

I changed my rupees back to dollars; I had kept my receipt. I passed through security with no problems, but as I entered the departure lounge a security man said, 'is this bike yours?' 'Yes,' I said. He pointed to the pump. 'Could you tell me what this is?' I showed him how it worked. He smiled. I re-tied it to the crossbar of the Goose with a wide band of Velcro. The tannoy spoke: 'flight 123 for Bangkok now boarding.' I sat relaxing in the aircraft seat. Cheerio, India!

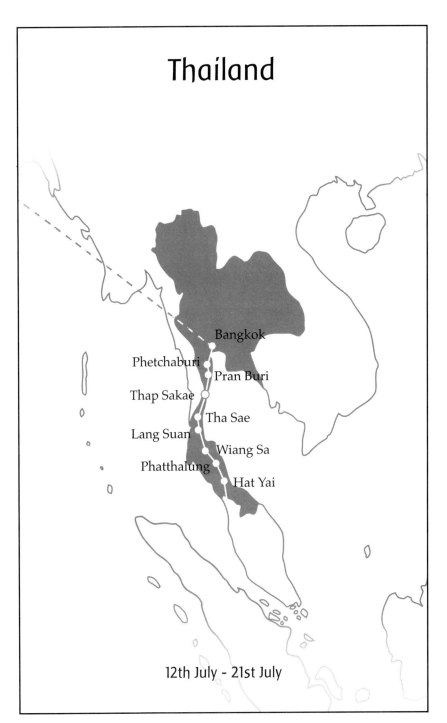

Thailand

Bangkok

Phetchaburi

Pran Buri

Thap Sakae

Tha Sae

Lang Suan

Wiang Sa

Phatthalung

Hat Yai

12th July - 21st July

Calcutta to Bangkok

You will never believe what happened in the airport after boarding the Bangkok flight. Take off time had come and gone. The tannoy spoke: 'This is your captain speaking. We have a slight problem. We are unable to account for an item of luggage a gentleman checked in. He is not on the plane himself.' The captain spoke again after a while. 'The plan is to lay out all the luggage on the tarmac. Passengers when called will leave the plane and identify their individual luggage.' My name was well down the list. When called, I duly left the flight and pointed to my luggage. An airport official marked it with white chalk and moved it to the plane. Two hours later the luggage was re-packed; the offending luggage had been found. It is better to be safe than sorry.

We were soon airborne. The flight food served was top class. Sitting in the seat next to me was an Australian lass. We had a good old chat, as they say. She had been visiting her husband in India and was returning to Australia. She was a teacher and a new term started next week. The air hostess handed out purple orchids. 'What do I do with this?' she exclaimed. My suggestion was to press it in the folds of a book, and when it was dry mount it in a picture frame.

The flight was soon over. The air hostess announced, 'fasten your seat belts please, we are landing at Bangkok, Thailand.' The airport was a bit glittery and very clean. The staff were efficient, friendly, helpful and happy, with smiles on their faces. I quickly passed through customs and immigration. 'Visa. British?' 'Yes.' He stamped my passport. I was in Thailand. I collected the Blue Goose and my bags from the luggage carousel. The fact that the pannier bags could be clipped together was proving its worth; one piece of luggage to find instead of two. I wheeled the Goose to a quiet corner and readjusted all the settings. I also pumped up both tyres. I was ready for the off – the question was, where? When you go on holiday there is usually a holiday rep on hand. You must look after yourself when travelling alone into a new country. You soon learn.

The airport was packed, but the directions and information signs were clear and helpful. There were courtesy phones by the dozen: 'hotel bookings here'. That was for me. I booked an airport hotel and paid with my credit card. 'The hotel adjoins the airport building, sir. That way.' She pointed to a lift. 'Third floor.' As she smiled she revealed a beautiful set of white teeth, just like piano keys. Money. I changed my money to the local currency. I returned to the lift; the Goose and I filled it. Third floor: the hotel was straight ahead. I came to the hotel coffee house and stopped and gazed like a schoolboy at the display of pastries. I'd forgotten that food like that existed. I made a mental note of the shop's position. I signed into the hotel, the Goose was housed in the left luggage. I was assured it would be safe.

The room was of a high standard; the bath looked inviting. I was soon immersed in the scented soapy hot water, scrubbing the dirt and sweat from my thin scrawny body. It was my first bath in a month. I was reluctant to get out. My clothes were clean, but scruffy. I felt a new man. I was booked in for two nights; I was in need of food and rest. I rested for an hour after my bath. You must eat; the signal flashed through my mind. What a choice – three restaurants. I sat down at a clean table and ordered. Onion soup, followed by chicken, followed by an enormous ice cream and a glass of white wine. I was fed and watered. I returned to my room and rang Gill. All was well. I had a ticking off for not phoning before. I lay on my king size bed. What a life. Good night.

Bangkok

I'm the first to admit I overslept; I must have needed the rest. Washing day, today. I washed all my spare clothes and hung them out to dry. I ate a hearty breakfast. A notice on the wall read, 'courtesy bus to the city'. The timetable suited my need. Why cycle? The coach stopped in the city centre.

Within the hour I was sitting in the front seat of the coach, enjoying the trip. The traffic was busy. One noticeable factor was that no horns were sounded. The roads were well-maintained and well signposted. From the hotel to the city centre took half an hour. I made a mental note of the time the bus returned.

Bangkok. After walking around this very busy city, I decided I liked it. The local folk were friendly and happy. It must be market day every day; the shopping stalls on the pavements stretched for miles. I even bought a replacement cycle top. My old one had worn well but was washed out. For a morning snack I bought cherries and apples; first class fruit. The sun shone relentlessly and it was humid; it soon saps your energy. I was fascinated by all the food I saw; it made me feel hungry. I sat down in the food market and ordered a Pepsi and two fancy cakes. To finish, I ate a vanilla ice cream.

While eating my ice cream I witnessed an act I'd never seen before or since. In the open food market one could buy anything from an ostrich steak to a bee's knee sandwich. In front of an open steaming kitchen stood a local chef dressed in his white clothes. He was very agile and talkative and the kitchen pots and pans stretched in a steam-laden atmosphere, laid out before him waist-high. Local Thai food could be ordered at the counter; the slip of paper was read by the chef. With great sleight of hand and agility, plus the verbal spiel, he acted out a dinner plate-filling ritual; both his actions and the verbal commentary were exaggerated. He moved with the dexterity of a ballet dancer. He balanced the plate and when it was full presented it to the recipient with an exaggerated gesture and a ring of his bell ready for the next customer. This resulted in great applause and laughter from the public. I sat riveted to my chair, rating his act with a ten-plus. This was far better than watching television. I was crying with laughter; I had not seen the like.

I returned to the hotel having thoroughly enjoyed my trip to Bangkok. I completed my chores by cleaning the Goose and oiling the chain ready for tomorrow. It was against my better judgement to have moved all the bike settings, both seat and handlebars. The seat is the problem; it must be reset in the same position as it was previously. I set it to where I judged to be the right place. My clothes had dried; I repacked ready for tomorrow. I studied the map to work out my route through Thailand, and spoke to a tourist rep in the hotel. He was against me taking the Burma-Thailand mountain border route, which, he said, wasn't safe because of bandits and drug smugglers. My mind was set; I intended to take the Burma border route. I double-checked everything; all systems were go for tomorrow.

I enjoyed my evening meal and even sat relaxing in the lounge, sipping a glass of port. The open road was calling. I was ready. My bath and the king size bed were also calling. I wrote my log, catching up with the happenings in Pakistan and India. If asked what I thought of India, my reply would be, sadly corrupt. I think there should be a twinning system between Pakistan and India; they are so alike. The social extremes cause discontent.

Bangkok to Phetchaburi

I ate a hearty breakfast and checked out of the hotel. I had enjoyed my stay. I picked up the Goose and fitted the panniers. I had that same feeling as when I started the trip; euphoria. 'On the road again; just can't wait to get on the road again.' What road? I was not allowed to cycle on the road directly outside the hotel. There was a road bridge over the motorway. I wheeled the Goose to the lower step. How do I get over that lot? I slung the Goose and the attached pannier bags over my shoulder and began the slow, deliberate haul, counting step after step until I reached the summit. I walked across the flat top of the bridge, wheeling the Goose, until I reached the steps going down. I walked slowly down again with the Goose on my shoulder, counting 50 steps up, 50 steps down. I was knackered. 'You stupid man, Mac,' said the Inner Man. 'You're not as young as you used to be.' My legs were sore.

I launched myself into the traffic. Navigation was not easy; the gravitational pull of Bangkok city held until the afternoon. I was slowly leaving the concrete jungle for a fresh, green jungle; the traffic was noticeably less. The standard of road I was not used to. There was one word for it: brilliant. On either side of the road there were approximately three metres from the edge to the white line. This was for motor bikes, scooters, cyclists, pedestrians and water buffalo. The remaining road was for everyday traffic. There were no irate, horn-crazed lorry drivers; the flow of traffic was very civilised and safe. People who passed waved and gave the appropriate greeting of the day.

I had not ridden on roads like these for months, or so it seemed. Long may it last. The day was hot and humid, but not excruciating heat like India, thank goodness. I was enjoying my cycle but had to reset my seat position a few times as my inner leg was rubbing on the inside of the seat. I could feel my legs were sore in the area of my thighs. I dismounted and could hardly walk. The alarm bells sounded. I remounted. I could cycle, which was a relief, but the pain was excruciating to walk. I glanced at the cat eye computer; it recorded 70 miles. I came to a hotel and booked in. Yes, they would also garage the Goose. My mind was working overtime. What was the mechanical problem with me? I swallowed two aspirin and slurped water. I know! It came in a flash. Those damn steps over the road. I'd carried the Goose and the bags up and down 100 steps in one go. 'You silly old fool.' I found it virtually impossible to walk. I went to bed early on Paladrine and aspirin. What a mix. My arm was still swollen with water retention.

Phetchaburi to Pran Buri

The night's rest had helped me, but my legs were still sore from the knee to the top of the thigh. I enjoyed my food last night and breakfast this morning. The Goose was bagged up ready to go; I'd left the bags fixed in position for the morning. I was on the road early. School children waited alongside the road dressed in their uniforms, carrying their back packs. To a child, they all smiled and wished me good morning. I was very impressed by their manners.

I could still cycle at my own speed. I was enjoying the cycling and the day's temperature and climate suited me well. The road standards continued to impress. As lorries passed by, my love/hate feelings were on the wane. I had the feeling I was back in a civilised country. I had that feel-good factor.

Between villages, there was jungle on each side of the open road. Some houses on stilts appeared. Black, pot-bellied pigs busied themselves along the road sides; chickens ran around as if demented. A sluggish dog gave me a look and went back to sleep, I'm glad to say. Scooters were everywhere; they had taken over from the bicycle. The Japanese must be making a fortune from the scooter market. The scooter was the family horse; it was common to see three people on one machine. We all know the saying – how many folk can you get in the family Mini? Well, today I witnessed six people on a scooter. Father was on the seat, three children on the front pan and two on the back; they carried a hoe handle stretching the length of the scooter. Each individual had his arm locked around the handle for support. Is it ingenuity or stupidity? You may well ask.

My legs were playing up; I was now in no doubt as to what had happened. It was Saturday and I was in need of some money. The banks are closed on Saturday. As I cycled through a village a Visa sign appeared on an international cash dispenser. I entered my pin number and requested the cash. In two minutes, the cash was in my hand. That brought a smile to my face. Rural service!

I checked the cat eye; 60 miles. My legs must be rested. I cycled to a hotel just off the road. The Goose was also housed. I could only walk with firm commitment and determination. The room was clean, except for an army of ants which stretched from a hole by the toilet door, across the wall at the head of the bed, and disappeared through a hole in the ceiling. I lay back on the bed and observed. What do I do about it? In my toiletries bag I had a small bottle of TCP antiseptic. With the aid of a paper hankie I dabbed the ants' road with TCP for a length of six inches. Within the hour there was not one ant to be seen; they would neither pass over nor go around the smear of TCP. What jungle message was used to transmit the road works ahead to the ants, I can only wonder.

Later that evening I struggled to the village shop and purchased food for an evening meal and breakfast for the morning. I spoilt myself with a tub of vanilla ice cream.

Pran Buri to Thap Sakae

I was well-rested and the pain in my legs was not as intense. I ate my breakfast which consisted of the goodies I bought in the village shop last night. I checked my Timex watch as I hit the road: 0630 hours. The weather was ideal for a cycle. No, the ants never returned to the ant motorway above my bed.

My legs definitely felt stronger as I rode along. It lifted my spirits;

I had that get up and go feeling. It was a hard ride today over the mountain roads running along the Burmese border. It was strange, somewhat different, scenery: jungle and scooters. From narrow jungle paths alongside the road, scooters would suddenly appear and just as quickly disappear. They sounded like bumble bees.

There was no roar from the jungle animals; the only roar came from audio systems. Some of them were in the bush. The roads were first class; it makes a cyclist's job much easier.

My appetite was returning. I was fast catching up on my eating habits. I had never seen so many petrol stations; every ten miles to my reckoning. I soon learned that one could buy most things at a petrol station, including Thai food. Hole-in-the-ground toilets completed the roadside services available.

I was now eating Thai food daily; rice with what? Your guess is as good as mine. If I wanted breakfast or dinner I used sign language; 'not too hot'. I drank iced water with my meal. Supermarkets also began to appear. I was spoilt for choice; they even sold ice cream.

As I entered a small village the sky blackened and the clouds opened. Rain! The old cats and dogs and frogs scenario. Lightning flashed across the sky and thunder rumbled in the jungle. Mostly it rains in the later afternoon; today was no exception. I was lucky. I sat in a roadside café and sheltered as I ate a bowl of rice. The road was soon flooded to a depth of two inches. School children were returning from school on different forms of transport. I saw a motorbike with a modified sidecar body. The sidecar had been removed and replaced by a purpose-built, four-metre square frame solid base with handrails. Seven school children were on the motorbike and sidecar, holding on to the rails. One was water skiing with one foot in the flooding water, hanging on the back clinging on to the handrail. No form of rain protection was worn by the children. They all smiled as the motorbike passed. I ordered a second bowl of rice and shook my head in disbelief at the wonders of the world.

It was still raining and was also getting dark. I asked the waiter in the café if there was a hotel, or rooms, in the vicinity. 'Five miles down the road,' he replied in good English. I thanked him and was soon on my wet way. Five miles passed in a flash. There it was. 'Yes,' said the receptionist, 'we have a room. You can also leave your bike in the room. Do you want TV and air conditioning, sir?' 'Yes.' 'That will be extra.' I have never been asked that before.

The sheets were clean and the bed hard; the springs must have died years ago. A pool of water stood under the Goose. When I was showered and dried I went to the supermarket across the road and purchased my dinner and breakfast. What a good choice. My legs were almost new; I was pleased that I could walk. I returned to my room and found the lock on the door was of no use. I slammed in the door wedge and placed the Goose across the door. I ate my evening meal while watching TV. I was getting spoilt in my old age. I glanced at the cat eye; 70 miles today. I was happy. Good night.

Thap Sakae to Tha Sae

My cycle clothes had dried overnight and my legs were as good as new. My arm was still swollen. I'll be glad when I stop the Paladrine. Having said that, I need to take my weekly dose today. Reluctantly I swallowed the tablets and ate my shop breakfast. The Goose was bagged up; it had drip dried overnight. I checked the tyres, oiled the chain and was ready for the off. The time was 0630 hours, the traffic was light to moderate; the weather was warm, with a slight head wind to keep me cool.

Still cycling the Burmese border, the roads were not as good as they had been, but rideable. I was enjoying my cycling. I learned that it rains every afternoon, so I must be aware. It's a case of being under shelter at the right time.

As I cycled through a small village in the hills, I stopped at a roadside stall and bought some small bananas. They were not more than three-and-a-half inches long, but they were sweet and nourishing. I hooked some on my bag and cycled on. Down the road I stopped for a drink of tea. I felt slightly embarrassed because everyone was looking at me. Some fit looking Thai youths were playing cards; bragging was the game. Gold hung from them like Christmas tree lights. They all wore jungle-type uniforms, camouflaged. A Merc car was parked outside on the roadside. A well-dressed elderly gentleman stood nearby surveying all that was going on. Twice I saw him give a wad of money to women in the group. One young guy was asleep on a wooden put-you-up bed by the card table. I have never seen so much gold on a man in all my life. I named him Fort Knox. He was young, good-looking and virile. A girl nearby was transfixed by him. I don't know if it was him or the sight of so much gold. Ding, ding, I got it in one. Drug-runners. The card game was heated at times; I was invited to play. With a smile I declined. Knowing my luck I'd win one of the women. I slowly beat the retreat, waving as I went under the all-seeing eye of the 'godfather' with the Merc.

It was a demanding cycle over hills in the heat of the day. My legs were feeling good and strong. In the late afternoon clouds gathered on the horizon; it would be raining within the hour. There was a B&B on the roadside. With sign language, I enquired if there was a room. The

Thai man nodded his head. He pinched my arm to see if I was real. I shook his hand; he smiled broadly in front of the group of men he was working with. You would think he had won the pools.

The room was wood-panelled on the floor, walls and ceiling. It was red wood. I wondered if it was Malayan red wood? It was as clean as a button. The old lady showing me around pointed to my shoes; no shoes on the polished floor. The house stood in an enclosed paddock. At the entrance gate a young man and his girlfriend were performing some serious love-making under cover of a sheet. The old lady shouted at them. The girl's head appeared. She pointed at the girl, then at me. I twigged the sign language. I shook my head and said 'no thanks'. My saviour; it rained as if to order.

As it rained the road works outside transformed into a mud bath. I was hungry. A petrol station stood on the crossroads. The rain had now thankfully stopped. I joined the owner and whom I took to be his wife having a very heated family squabble. I slowly chewed my food. What transpired before me was as good as any soap opera on TV. I watched and listened, enthralled. I decided there was no winner. More's the pity, there were no subtitles. I was fed and watered. My cat eye read 75 miles. Good night.

Tha Sae to Lang Suan

It was now second nature to complete my morning chores and be on the road by 0630 hours. I was aware that my legs were now pain-free and felt normal. My arm was useable but still swollen with water retention. The weather was warm and sunny as I cycled along the main road. The traffic was mainly scooters, although there were some cars and lorries.

Even at that time of the morning, young girls and boys stood at the roadside awaiting their school transport, the girls dressed in navy blue skirts and white blouses, the boys in navy blue trousers and white shirts. It became a morning ritual to be greeted with a smile and a 'good morning', with a flash of white teeth gleaming against their ebony faces; they radiated happiness.

As they passed the young girls and boys, people on scooters shouted and waved; they sounded like bees. For the first time in weeks I started to see cattle in paddocks; they looked in good condition. I came across an accident – a pick-up had left the road and the passengers looked to be badly hurt. Ambulances and medical staff were in attendance, thank goodness.

It rained earlier than normal. Damn – I was enjoying my ride. I pulled off the road at a petrol station with a café and shops, and sheltered with the Goose under a lean-to. The rain fell in sheets; I was lucky to shelter. A Thai family lived next door to the shelter. Two hours later I was still there. An elderly lady came out of the house and smiled at me; she was my age, I thought. She handed me some plums that she extracted from a bottle of alcohol. I thanked her and slowly ate the plums; they darted through my veins like wildfire. I felt suddenly lifted; my gloom from the two-hour wait in the rain vanished. The old lady smiled as she lit a charcoal fire. What an expert. I followed her every move – I had nothing else to do in the rain. When the fire was well-established, she produced some bananas, removed the skin, cut them into two-inch lengths, sprinkled them with sugar and wrapped them in fresh green banana leaves. She placed the bananas on the hot charcoal and left them there for about a quarter of an hour. She then removed them and unwrapped the hot leaves. There on a plate was a fully cooked sugar banana. I bet that tastes good, I thought. With that, she handed me two. What a fantastic taste. The rain had now stopped. Should I kiss her, or what? To show my thanks, I took the easy way out. I shook her hand and slightly bowed my head. She was happy and smiled and waved as I resumed my cycling. I was thankful, and pleased with my Thai cooking lesson.

The roads soon dried as I cycled along. I was well out in the wilds, rumbling through the jungle. There was not a village or petrol station in sight. I could see the rain clouds massing on the horizon. Within the hour the rain was back and man, it rained. There was no shelter in the immediate vicinity. I was wet, so I just rode on into the fast-falling dusk. The road was gradually becoming unrideable; pure mud covered it from half-an-inch to four inches deep; it was like cycling through slurry. What a bloody mess. The Goose and I were covered from head to toe in mud. In the murky darkness, a petrol station and some other buildings appeared. I asked with the aid of sign language if a room was available. 'Yes,' came the answer. I looked up and thanked someone. I saw a water hose wound round a tank, requested the use of it and was given a nod. I hosed down the Goose, spinning the wheels as I washed off the mud. I also washed it off the pannier bags. I then asked the guy to hose me down. This he did, with a smile on his face. I locked the Goose in a garage; the guy gave me a key. I carried the bags up to my room; it was clean. I showered and changed into dry clothes, then washed my dirty gear. My shoes were wet. I put plastic bags over my socks and went for a meal.

I awoke at my usual time; I must have an implanted alarm clock. All my washing had dried, my legs were fine and I thought the swelling had reduced in my arm. I checked the cat eye last night; I had cycled 100 miles. I was pleased, to say the least. I hope it doesn't rain as much today. My meal last night was rice and I don't know what. I enjoyed it.

I cleaned up the floor in my room and lugged the bags down to the Goose. Opening the garage, I bagged up, oiled the chain and examined the other mechanical parts after all the mud and rain. Breakfast was served. I'm not sure what it was but I ate it gratefully.

What a surprise: when I looked outside thick fog enveloped everything – just like the fog we get at home in Orkney. I looked at my map; I was making good time. I'd promised to fly Gill to Singapore if I reached West Malaysia (formerly Malaya). I must make contact tonight – at least she can pack her bags. 'Move your butt now, Mac – don't daydream. Get some more miles under your belt before planning further,' said the Inner Man.

I flicked on my rear light and pushed off into the fog. Two hours later, the fog lifted and the sun shone; what a beautiful day to cycle. As the fog was lifting I took some photos; the sun and the fog playing on the landscape made some fine views.

Cycling through a village a young Thai man joined me; he was also a cyclist. Up until now I'd only seen two cyclists in Thailand. Through sign language we stopped and I bought us both a Coke. As we chatted, it was surprising how much we had in common. Cycling holds no language barriers. His interest was in Blue Goose; he had not seen modern innovation. He showed me his bike. He had himself devised a type of derailleur system. I was impressed by his engineering ingenuity. I heaped praise on him for his skills. He beamed. I must have made his day. He cycled with me for 25 miles then, with a wave of the hand, he turned back. It was nice to have company.

My concern about the wheel bearings was unfounded; the Goose just flew along. I stopped later in the day and oiled the moving parts. I was feeling sorry that in a day or two I'd be leaving Thailand. What happy people. I decided that a return visit was a must. In all the miles I'd cycled, I saw only two other tourists. They stick to the anthill cities and towns, that's my opinion.

As I cycled into town I saw a hotel. 'No problem.' I checked in and the Goose was allowed in my room. The room and sheets were clean. As I rested on the bed I looked at the ceiling; it was panelled with mirrors. I wondered what they would say if they could talk?

I spotted an old steamroller on the road outside; again I took some photos. The old steam engine was burnt out; in its place a hotch-potch job of a diesel engine and cooling radiator adorned the somewhat forlorn looking machine. It was in working order. A heavy-duty scarifier was fitted to the rear.

Dinner tonight was two tins of mackerel in tomato sauce, one large tin of mixed fruit and a bottle of beer.

I checked the cat eye; 99 miles today. That's 200 miles in two days. I was feeling fit. I'll ring Gill tomorrow. Good night.

Wiang Sa to Phatthalung

Last night I slept like a log. It must have been those tins of mackerel; they were like sleeping tablets. For breakfast this morning I had tinned fruit; it refreshes the palate. I cleaned the Goose last night – there were still traces of that damn mud, it was everywhere. The Goose was bagged up ready to go, the weather was fine and sunny. I can only hope the rain stays away.

I was soon on the road heading for Malaysia. It was strange not to have that rush hour feeling. Traffic was intermittent. Scooters raced each other, with children precariously holding on at the back. They were shouting and waving, like jockeys at a race meeting. The mud from the past rains had dried out. Some had disappeared but not all; care had to be taken when cycling.

Cycling today was through real jungle. There were no houses or villages; the growth of trees and plants hung close to the road, as if ready to reclaim the intruder. Sun and rain are the natural ingredients for maintaining a full flush of plant growth.

Cycling was effortless; the Goose was flying. It was a case of head down, butt up and go. I saw a police car stop a lorry and make the driver sheet down a load of dusty chippings. I wondered if that would happen in our country. The inside of my leg was sore; there was a lump. I lashed on the Vaseline. I'll need to keep a close check in case it festers.

You cannot fail to admire the scenery as you cycle. It was like a picture post card. It struck me that when I stopped to take a photo I was never in it; there is only the background scene and the bike.

This morning it was made obvious to me that Thai people are aware of pollution and the environment. I saw a gang of workers planting trees and plants along the roadside. It's hard to comprehend that in an environment of natural jungle growth, bare patches are replanted. It made me feel good. Instead of destroying the jungle, they were encouraging growth.

126   In the afternoon I pulled into a petrol station and ate a meal of rice

and whatever-it-was. Are you complaining, Mac? No, I just ate it. A bottle of Coke or Pepsi plus an ice cream is enough to energise the body to cycle 40 miles. It's just like filling up with petrol.

I was now, in my opinion, back to my normal, fit self. My weight loss was on hold, but I was eating good food. Tinned mackerel was my favourite; it was safe to eat and nourishing. I must admit I did have a sweet tooth for tinned pineapple. I found that strips of dried pineapple were a good snack when cycling. The other night I ate some strips of pineapple while writing my log. I left them on the floor by the side of the bed. When I went to retrieve them in the morning, they were walking with ants. One never learns.

I thoroughly enjoyed my cycling today. I entered Phatthalung and spied a hotel. 'Yes, we have a room, and you can take your bike to your room, sir.' The room and bed sheets were clean, but the bed and pillow were hard. I filled in my log, showered and went to the supermarket to buy my evening meal and breakfast. In that short time I was showered, fed and watered. I was tired. Good night.

Phatthalung to Hat Yai

I was on the road at 0630 hours having completed all my chores, bagged up the Goose and oiled the chain. The weather was fine; ideal for a good day's cycle. I awoke this morning with an angry-looking lump on the inside of my leg. Don't let it be a boil or a saddle sore. It does annoy me as I ride. I wondered if it was the result of shifting my seat position en route from Calcutta.

There was no fog today, and the second day of no rain. I had now left the Burmese border and mountains and was heading on the main road to Malaysia. With luck I should be there today, or the following day. Early morning cycling is cool up until 1130 hours, then the heat of the day hits you. You, in turn, hit the water bottle.

I moved my bike seat ever so slightly away from the offending lump on the inside of my leg. I also applied Vaseline mixed with TCP. It had the intended effect. Feeling happy with my progress, I burst into song. This was going to be a choral morning. I sang everything I knew; the humidity was good for the vocal cords.

I would advise other countries to adopt the design and lay-out of the roads in Thailand. Of all the countries I cycled through, the Thai roads were the safest. The roads kept all categories of transport in their correct lanes. One felt safe cycling on the left-hand side of the road.

The Goose just flew along. The jungle, with all its trees and wildlife, held the attention. I saw no pollution and the road surface was well-maintained. Being an avid reader of Second World War books, I had read about the Japanese army fighting in Thailand, Burma, Malaya and Singapore. I now realised the harsh conditions both sides encountered while advancing or defending. The realities of those encounters filled my mind as I cycled along.

It was mid-afternoon when I cycled into Hat Yai. My leg was playing up. Rest, I thought, was the best form of therapy. A hotel was in the right place at the right time; so often it's not. I checked the Goose and myself into the same room. Good, the Goose was in need of a thorough clean. The room was fine; clean, the sheets sparkling white, the bed and pillow hard as nails. It crossed my mind that the Thais are keen on hard beds and pillows. The shower was hot; the water just what the doctor ordered. I was soon washing dirt, sweat and hydrocarbon oil film from my body. I turned up the heat and examined the inside of my leg, massaging both cream and TCP on to the angry swelling. The shower invigorated me. I took advantage of the hot water and washed all my dirty clothes and strategically placed them around the room to dry. I worked out it was eight days since I had showered with hot water. The skin on the sore leg was soft and supple; it would now come to a head or disappear.

I worked on my Malaysia map and came up with a date of entry into Singapore. I rang Gill – I do love to hear her voice. I gave her my proposed dates; all was well on the home front. I rested and ate my food from what I'd bought at a supermarket, saving some for breakfast. I find that if you cycle every day, you need plenty of rest. The only answer is early bed. Good night.

Western Malaysia

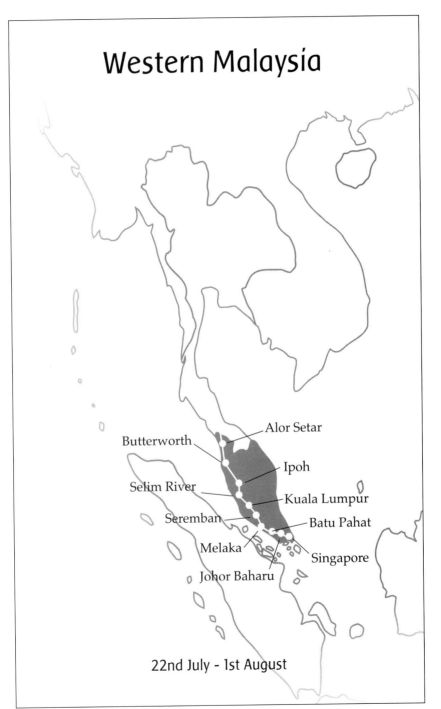

Alor Setar

Butterworth

Ipoh

Selim River

Kuala Lumpur

Seremban

Batu Pahat

Melaka

Singapore

Johor Baharu

22nd July - 1st August

Hat Yai (Thailand) to Alor Setar (Malaysia)

As I awoke I had Gill on my mind; I will see her in a few days. I was excited. I had something to gee me up. The lump on my leg was smaller. Whatever I had done had relieved the pain and swelling. I must have charmed it like a wart. I liberally dabbed it with more of the same.

I bagged up the Goose ready to go. I was on the road heading for the Malaysian border at San Dao. There was more traffic than usual, especially lorries. The weather was fine and warm. I was still in Thailand when I stopped for a cup of tea in a clean-looking café. I also succumbed to a plate of lychees. They always remind me of conkers or chestnuts; I did enjoy them. It's strange, but the last five or ten miles of a cycle always seems to be the longest; the roads go on forever.

I was at the border crossing, San Dao. I dismounted and searched out my papers. Where did I put them? There they are. Passport, money; I'll change it in Malaysia. Border crossings are similar the world over: them and us. I joined the queue, Goose in hand. It was very busy; the queue stretched out of sight. It must have been a mile long, or so it seemed. I filled out all the necessary forms; I would also need a visa.

A very high-ranking Malaysian passed. 'Excuse me,' I said, 'is this the queue for visas?' He nodded. 'Is this all the paperwork I'll require?' I asked. 'Come with me,' he said. He walked me to the front of the queue, checked and stamped my passport and handed me a visa. He smiled; I thanked him. I felt self-conscious – I don't like queue-jumping. I moved on to the final check with the police. It was the last hurdle. The Malaysian policeman was smartly dressed. 'Where are you going? Where have you been?' he asked. I repeated my well-rehearsed one-liner, 'cycling the world'. He smiled. 'You look very fit,' was his comment. 'Take care,' he said, with a smart salute. I was over the border. Malaysia.

It's not the first time I'd been to Malaysia; I was here in the 1950s as a young soldier. What did the policeman say? Change your money down the road: cycle one mile, turn left, the bank should be on your right. I was on my way. The road was unlike anything I'd cycled on before. I soon realised I was cycling on the hard shoulder of a motorway, or, as they call it, a freeway. I sailed along; I felt as if I were being spoilt. Half a mile down the road there was a police check under a bridge. They waved me in. They just looked at me, saying nothing, and waved me on. Funny, I thought. I turned left after a mile and there was the bank. 'Sorry, sir, we don't exchange Thai money, but if you cycle back to the main road and turn left, there is a restaurant 100 yards down the road. You will be able to exchange it there.'

I followed the instructions and exchanged my money, no problem.

Where was I heading? I stopped and checked the map. Alor Setar – I was on the correct road. Again, it was cycling on the left-hand side, but in all my travelling this was the first time I'd been allowed on a motorway, although only the hard shoulder. It was all systems go; the Goose just flew down the road. I became aware of a scooter tracking me at speed. It was a young guy with a very elderly woman precariously sitting on the rear set. 'Good afternoon,' he said. I returned the greeting. 'Hope you don't mind me riding along with you? I'm a student studying English; my final exams are next month. Would you mind if I practise my English on you as we ride along?' I couldn't think of a reason why not. I uttered the famous words, 'no problem'.

As I cycled we discussed politics and world problems; we also talked about my cycling trip and the people and places I had seen. All this time, the old lady balanced on the back of the scooter not uttering a word. Her face was expressionless as if this was an everyday occurrence. Half an hour had elapsed. My neck was sore from turning continually to the right. 'I live down here,' he said. 'Would you like to come to tea?' Declining, I said I had to reach Alor Setar before nightfall. 'That's my grandmother on the back,' he said. I smiled, turning my head round further to nod to her and nearly crashed the Goose. He took evasive action. Thanking me, he turned down a side road and was gone. I'm sure he spoke better English when he left me than when we first met.

There were alternative routes to Alor Setar. I stopped at a road junction, reluctant to leave the main highway. A car pulled up alongside. 'Problems?' said the driver. I explained where I wanted to go. He advised me on the best route and was gone. That was really helpful, I thought, with a smile. What did he say? Ride on, only a few miles to do. The sign said 'Alor Setar'. I booked in to the nearest hotel, the Goose was allowed in the same room. It was a tidy room with a clean bed and shower.

What a storm we had during the night. It raged on for two hours. As it abated I was grateful to be tucked up in my bed. I'd had a busy day, I felt sleep coming on. Good night.

Alor Setar to Butterworth

I was one hour later on the road this morning – I hadn't allowed for the time change. The storm last night did keep me awake. The lightning was like a grand firework display. There were tea-making facilities in my room of which I took full advantage; four cups and an apple pie is a good breakfast. I bagged up the Goose outside and oiled the chain. The weather was settled, the sun turning up the heat. Traffic was sparse; as in Thailand, the scooter was the 'in' form of transport.

After giving it some thought, I decided to rejoin the motorway. Why not? Cyclists should assert their rights. After a few miles I was back on the hard shoulder, still cycling on the left-hand side, as in Thailand. Cars and lorries dominated the motorway by driving faster than the norm; hydrocarbon fumes were more apparent on the freeway than on the standard roads.

Road miles quickly passed. The surrounding countryside was not unlike Thailand although there were more signs of cultivation, with cattle and fields. Hills on the freeway were few and far between. To my surprise, I came across a motorway café. I pulled off the road and had a grand meal; the facilities were very similar to those in the UK. Fed and watered I was soon back on the road, cycling for Butterworth. The food recharged my batteries; the Goose flew down the open road.

My mileage today so far was approximately 50 miles. I gave some thought to cycling on the freeway. Yes, it has its definite advantages, one being quick cycling from A to B. But in the bottom of my mind I felt that the freeway was faceless; I soon grew tired of open, fast roads. You become the same as the motorist; you go fast between two points without seeing the normal everyday folk and being able to converse when you wanted. I also missed the sights and smells of rural life. In my mind, the disadvantages outweigh the advantages.

The heat of the day was telling; sweat flowed freely and the water bottles were in demand. The sign said 'Butterworth'. What an English name. I wonder who named it? Within the hour I was approaching a small town with well-built houses and facilities. I glanced at my cat eye – 70 miles. That's enough today. It's strange how you make your mind up on the number of miles done in a day, irrespective of how hard a ride it has been.

The sign said 'Hotel Berlin'. Those Germans are everywhere, I thought. 'Yes, we can accommodate you and your bike.' The Goose accompanied me in the room. Great, I knew it was safe. The bed had clean sheets, a white pillow and it was soft – what a difference – and there was even hot water in the shower. When I'd showered and changed I was out on the street because I'd spotted a Kentucky Fried Chicken establishment on the way to the hotel. I have a soft spot for Kentucky Fried Chicken. Did I enjoy it? It reset my hunger pangs and relaxed my craving for food.

Back at the hotel I wrote my log, washed my sweat-filled clothes and hung them up to dry. Gill was on my mind; I would see her in days. What a life without a wife. Good night.

Butterworth to Ipoh

I was awake early, even allowing for the time change. The hotel was quiet so my sleep was not disturbed. Monday morning. I dislike taking my double dose of Paladrine tablets. It's my intention to stop taking the tablets next week. The weather was unsettled; rain was on the window and the sky was overcast. I bagged up the Goose, ate a tin of fruit and topped up the water levels in my bottles. As I greeted the day it engulfed me in a cloak of humidity. The roads were quiet except for scooters about their business.

The rain held off thankfully as I cycled on the freeway. The first 35 miles passed quickly. I decided to leave this faceless cycling, however, and turned off the freeway for secondary roads with more character. All too soon the hills started to appear. It was granny gear mile after relentless mile. I could feel the exertion requirement on my legs. Come to think of it, I'd not been cycling in the hills for weeks. The sweat glands were working overtime; it was running off my nose and chin like a tap. The water bottle levels were dropping too quickly.

On the side of the mountain road, a part of the overhanging rock had been cut away to allow for the road. This left a sheer cliff face and a waterfall cascaded down from the rock face. It looked all too inviting. I was, as they say, hot and bothered, and traffic on the road was virtually nil. I parked the Goose against the cliff face, stripped off and showered under the cooling water. Two cars passed while I was showering – they blew their horns. I turned discreetly to the side and gave them a wave. I dried off with Gill's wonder towel and dressed in my sweat-filled clothes. I felt fully refreshed and ready to face the demands of the rest of the day's cycling.

The day was hot and the sun shone relentlessly. I stopped in a village café and snacked on ice cream and Pepsi and topped up my water bottles. The Goose flew down the road effortlessly. I just held on, enjoying the experience. The road sign said 'Ipoh'. It was later afternoon and I'd cycled further than I'd intended. The first stop was a hotel. As I walked into reception I could see it was a cut above. 'Yes sir, we have a room. You can park your bike in left luggage – it will be safe.' I also booked an evening meal in the hotel. My room said it all; the beds and sheets were inviting. I'd not bathed in ten days. I ran the bath and emptied all the scented soaps and shampoos into the water and soaked myself for half-an-hour. I scrubbed off all the accumulated road dirt.

I must have looked a scruff in the restaurant; most of the guests were well-dressed young executives in their white ties and suits. So what? Been there, done that. Some guys walked around the hotel as if they had earache, holding their phones to their ears. What a load of posers. This was a good class of hotel, I must admit. On returning to my room, I washed the sweat-filled cycle clothes and hung them up to dry, completed my log and checked the cat eye; 95 miles. It's a good day's work. The TV was English-speaking. I lay back on the bed and listened to the latest news. I breathed a deep, relaxed sigh. What a life. Good night.

Ipoh to Selim River

As I awoke, two things crossed my mind: it was only days before I would see Gill, and what a good hotel this was. For the first time in days I went to breakfast and ate all the good, nourishing food. I drank tea and orange juice to the normal high level of my back teeth. I really enjoyed it. As I went to breakfast, I was surprised to see a newspaper lying at my door. I slipped it in my bag; I'll read it tonight. I bagged my clothes and then the Goose. The weather was overcast and humid. I oiled the chain. The traffic was heavier than of late; a mini rush hour.

Again I held to the secondary roads. Somehow, I felt jaded – it might have been the hills yesterday. The road sign said 'tunnel ahead'. There was also a sign which said to use your lights in the tunnel and to press the red button before entering which would alert cars and lorries that a cyclist was in the tunnel. I stopped and flicked on my lights and duly pressed the tunnel button. It activated a red flashing light to warn in-coming drivers. When I entered the tunnel the noise of the traffic was deafening; the roof lights and moving lights from cars and lorries became a wall. It's hard to describe, but I became disorientated. My immediate action was to remove my glasses. Everything settled down to normal. My glasses are progressive lenses; I mention this in case it happens to someone else. I have since travelled through many tunnels and have always removed my glasses. I have never had that disorientated feeling again.

The sun had burnt away the haze and there was a slight back breeze which helped me along and kept me cool. I was cycling through a built-up area and could see the sign in the distance, 'Southern Fried Chicken'. I stopped for a late lunch: two pieces of chicken, a bun and a drink, all for six dollars. I did enjoy it. It was a hot afternoon; I cycled within my limits, nothing too strenuous. The road sign said 'Selim River'. Within a short space of time I entered the village. I soon found a bed for the night in a Chinese hotel. I was allowed to park the Goose in my room. I sweated as I carried the Goose up two flights of stairs. The room was small with all mod cons. It was also reasonably priced.

The hotel restaurant was open-air, attached to the hotel front. I ate a grand meal and enjoyed it. I also ordered a pint of Tiger draught iced beer. Was that a tear in the corner of the eye? The dusk had fallen so no one could see. As I tasted the beer, memories came flooding back of my army days here in the fifties: the smells, the sounds, the humidity, and just relaxing over a pint of beer. I smiled when booking in the hotel when the proprietor said, 'welcome to my country.' I thought, well, my brother and I did our bit in the fifties – you could have shot at me or I could have kicked your butt. It's a funny old world.

As I drank my beer I was given a flying display second to none. Swifts or swallows caught flies in the glare of the lights outside the hotel. They also dived in amongst the fan blades disturbing the flies. Acrobatically they missed being hit by the rotating blades in the confined area. I was witnessing a magnificent aeronautic display, better than the Red Arrows. The electrical cable now became the roost for 250 birds. I'd not seen the like before. What a show – what a display. It was 250 birds; I counted. The electrical cable bowed under the weight strain.

I went to my room a happy, contented man and read the paper. As I finished my eyes were tired. I lay back on the bed. Good night.

Selim River to Kuala Lumpur

The noise from the traffic must have woken me. I glanced at my watch; it was time to get up. It was a bit noisy last night, but I was grateful for the rest. I had my usual tin of pineapple for breakfast and four cups of tea. I bagged up the Goose. The weather was fine and sunny. With luck, I should make Kuala Lumpur by late afternoon. I was on my way.

Miles just melted away like a dream. The roads were not as good as the roads in Thailand. Jungle was sparse, there were more open, cultivated fields. I wondered about planning permission. Could you just build where you wanted to? What I missed were the petrol station food stops. Cafes were usually in villages. Today was no exception. Pepsi and ice cream filled the Inner Man. No rain so far. The Goose was flying with the slight tail wind. It ate the hungry miles as if I were on a magic carpet.

Mid-afternoon the road sign read 'Kuala Lumpur'. I glanced at my cat eye; it read 65 miles. I kept my trained eagle eye open for a hotel as I cycled into the centre of town. I had a choice and settled for a good class of hotel. I checked in for two nights but caused a problem for the hotel security: what were they to do with the Goose? I suggested my room. The guy was relieved and immediately agreed. The Goose and I rode the lift to the second floor; the room was first class, with a bath.

Kuala Lumpur is a very modern city. The buildings and roads are well laid out. Traffic was nose to tail, with the scooter being the most popular form of transport. At the traffic lights the scooters are all lined up as if on a racing grid, awaiting the flag for off. There can be as many as twenty, all with their front wheels on the line. When the light changes to green the throttles are opened; the noise and hydrocarbon smoke and fumes engulf everything, including the pedestrians.

The Goose was in need of a clean. I soon had it looking good with the use of toilet roll and shampoo; it was sparkling clean. I took great care not to make a mess. I ran the bath and steeped in hot water and what was left of the bath additives. I decided to go into the shopping centre for a walk. On the way I saw, yes, you guessed it, a Kentucky Fried Chicken restaurant. It was a little early for an evening meal but the thought of that fried chicken dulled my willpower and I succumbed.

Speech and hearing-impaired boys and girls staffed the restaurant. To order a meal you pointed to a picture of what you wanted on a printed picture card. The system worked and the restaurant was well-patronised. In all my travels I had not seen the like. I was glad I had stopped because I really enjoyed the meal. I never reached the city centre. I'll see it tomorrow. I returned to the hotel and drank a pint of Tiger beer in the lounge bar (or was it two pints?). When I returned to my room I rang Gill to confirm her arrival time, and most importantly the day and date. She even gave me the flight number; KL 837. I'll meet that flight even if I have to go all the way by taxi. 'Determined talk, Mac,' said the Inner Man. As my father used to say, 'give me the man who can talk in the morning, not the man who can talk at night.'

Did I enjoy my rest day? You bet I did. I walked my legs off window-shopping. When I weakened and went to buy an item, I asked myself the question – who is going to carry it? Result – I never bought a thing. Kuala Lumpur, I did enjoy my short stay. Would I visit again? Yes.

Kuala Lumpur to Seremban

I set my inner clock last night as usual and was up early for breakfast. I was spoilt for choice but left space for my tea and orange juice. I bagged up the Goose and rode the lift to the ground floor. The weather was slightly cloudy and humid, and the traffic was surprisingly heavy for 0630 hours. With a final check of the map I joined the flow of rush hour traffic. My senses were soon on red alert. Here in Kuala Lumpur drivers were going faster than the norm. Where two lines of traffic converged, they would drive straight into the line irrespective of anyone else. There was no quarter given; every man for himself.

Navigation was demanding; four to six lanes of traffic was not unusual. Leaving Kuala Lumpur was an effort; a continual uphill climb. To change traffic lanes was to take your life in your hands. If I had stopped for any reason then, in my opinion, I'd be a dead man. The red alert lasted for five miles until I broke loose from the city.

It was one of those days when rain could start at any time. I thought of my arrival in Singapore. As I was entering by land, I only had a visa for fourteen days. If I overstayed I'd have to apply for another visa. That would be a pain in the butt. There was a need to time my entry, so there was no rush. I enjoyed the country and the cycling was the name of the game.

A shower of rain quickly brought me to my senses; the sky was dark and full of rain clouds. My cat eye read 50 miles. I'd had a good cycle once I left Kuala Lumpur. The road sign said 'Seremban'. I cycled for town and within the hour was requesting a room in a hotel. 'Sorry,' she said with a broad smile, 'we are fully booked.' I will always wonder if they are trained to say sorry with an 'I'm full, Jack – tough luck' smile.

I soon booked a hotel in the centre of town. The Goose would have to stay with security in their office. It was always manned. By this time the rain filled the sky; I was lucky to be off the road. It rained for three-and-a-half hours. I would have been soaked, to say the least. I washed all my clothes and hung them up to dry in my room, then showered and changed. I decided to walk around the shopping precinct in town. I went to a barber shop for a haircut and within a short time had lost all my straggly hair and my head looked like a well-cut lawn. The town was clean and it lacked for nothing; every conceivable item was on sale. I dodged the rain in and out of the shops as I made my way back to the hotel.

The receptionist was a smart young Eurasian girl. When I told her of my cycling exploits, she wanted to know more. 'How old are you?' she asked. 'I'm sixty.' 'You don't look a day over forty,' she said. I smiled. She made my day. I retired to bed early and watched TV. The phone rang. Hello, who wants me? 'This is reception. On the third floor we have a lounge bar with pretty girls; also, if you like to sing we have a karaoke room.' How does that work?' I asked 'It's a soundproof room – you can drink and sing your heart out to your own sweet self.' I smiled and thanked her. I was sixty, not sixteen. I hold on to the money in my pocket for other things. Good night.

Seremban to Melaka

As I awoke, last night's phone call made me smile. I checked my money, it was still in my pocket. 'You are a good boy,' said the Inner

Man. Breakfast was a tin of pineapple; it was fresh, like a good wash. I carried the bags down to the Goose, bagged up and oiled the chain. The weather was cloudy and humid. The traffic, I'm glad to say, was not like yesterday morning. The road followed the coast. There were no hills, just a morning sightseeing cycle; most enjoyable. My camera was working overtime; photo calls came often.

It is strange when cycling, you see so many sights that in your mind's eye need recording. Sometimes you can't be bothered – you can go for days without taking a photo. The next day, around every bend, is a good photo when you least expect it. Just like today. I turned a bend in the road crossing a bridge and glanced quickly at the river; it was flowing fast and was a dark chocolate colour. There, on a small sheet of polystyrene sat a native lad, fishing rod in hand, oblivious to the dangers. I stopped and took a photo, shook my head in disbelief at what I'd seen and cycled on.

Rain showers persisted all morning; one minute I was wet, the next I was drip-drying. At the start of one downpour I was lucky to shelter in a bus stop, only to be joined by two locals. I felt kind of uneasy. No one spoke for a while then one scowled. 'You English?' he said. 'No, Scottish.' 'I don't like English,' he said. I looked him straight in the eye and showed no fear. He dropped his gaze. I was on red alert. The rain stopped, intervening at the right time. I was glad to see the back of those very unsavoury characters. Those English must be a bad lot, I thought. I've heard that so many times.

The humidity increased after the rain and sweat ran off me, washing the Goose. I replaced my water level with drinks from the bottle. Talking about water, my arm was still swollen, but I was due to complete my malaria tablets in the next four days. Mid-afternoon I entered Melaka; 60 miles was enough for today. The choice of hotels made accommodation no problem. I checked into a good standard hotel and was allowed the Goose in my room. I showered the sweat off my body, slipped into clean clothes, washed my cycling clothes and hung them up to dry.

The river flowed through town and I decided to take a stroll. I followed the river and came to the shopping area. It was so humid, the heat was screwing me into the ground. Sitting at a shaded table at a roadside cafe I ordered my usual Pepsi and ice cream. Damn, I did enjoy it. I was harassed as I walked along by a bicycle rickshaw guy who gave me the hard sell. 'Special price for tourists,' he said. 'No,' I said in a very commanding voice. On the next breath he halved his original asking price. I gave him no trade.

The river through Melaka was fast-flowing and the water was a chocolate colour. I witnessed what I thought were sheep or goats in the river. I was wrong – they turned out to be monitor lizards. What a size. I stood with other people and watched them hunt for food. I had my camera and took a photo. What a fine sight.

Somehow, somewhere, I lost my film of Malaysia, but the lizards still loom life size in my mind's eye. My evening meal was again from the supermarket and I purchased breakfast for tomorrow morning. As I sat in my room my mind was active, planning the American cycle. There was a list of things I had for Gill to bring out to me, including maps and clothes; I must finalise the list soon. I was tired; the humidity has that effect on folk. No interrupting phone calls tonight, please. Good night.

Melaka to Batu Pahat

Sunday morning. 'No, you can't stay in bed; move your butt, Mac.' It was only a thought. I looked out of the window; blue sky. The sun was on time; it don't get a lie in. I bagged up the Goose. All my washed clothes were dry. 'Breakfast is served, sir.' The Inner Man spoils me. I enjoyed my breakfast and drank my liquid level of orange juice and tea. Yes, I do take my Paladrine tablet every morning; it sits on my daily log. I've now decided to stop them when I reach Singapore. A newspaper was at my door. I slipped it in my bag to read tonight.

I checked out the Goose's air pressure and the state of the tyre casings and oiled the chain. All systems go. The traffic was light; no rush hour on a Sunday. Soon I was out of town and enjoying my early morning cycle. I noticed that from mid-morning to after lunch, the village and country restaurants were full of local folk. I think the reason is that no one cooks on a Sunday; they all eat out. I cycled through the large, picturesque town of Muar. A tidal river runs through town and there were boats with young children fishing. They expertly hung on to the boats and rods making a very colourful spectacle.

The sun was at its zenith at 1130 hours; sweat ran off the end of my nose on to my cycling shirt. My liquid level was in need of replenishment. That was a good enough reason to stop for a drink, or, as they say, a 'livener'. I bought a litre bottle of ice cream soda and an orange iced lolly. I adjusted the cycle seat; the inside of my leg was rubbed raw. I coated it with Vaseline as a lubricant. It helped.

The roads ran through heavy jungle growth. The humidity enveloped you; you were never sweat-free, there was always a warm wet film on the body. I think that's one of the reasons I've rubbed the inside of my leg. I cycled on until late afternoon. Only scooters broke the silence, passing me like jet fighters. What did the road sign say? Batu Pahat. The cat eye recorded 70 miles. I found a good hotel, reasonably priced. It was above average and I checked in. 'The bike in your room? No problem, sir,' said the receptionist. 'Restaurant tonight, sir?' 'Yes, please,' I said. Why not?

As I showered I checked out my leg; it looked angry and red. Holding on to the back of a chair I gave it the neat, no-holds-barred, TCP treatment. It brought tears to my eyes. The hotel was a well-run establishment; it's bit hit or miss to find a good hotel every day. I sat down and read the Sunday paper in a relaxed mood. My evening meal was first class. Johor Baharu tomorrow. Both Gill and Singapore were on my mind. Good night.

Batu Pahat to Johor Baharu

I awoke with the first light of dawn. Sleep last night was undisturbed; I felt fully fit and rested, ready to meet the new day. My leg was a good deal better. I gave it a covering of Vaseline before slipping on my cycle shorts. For breakfast I drank three half-pint glasses of orange juice. It was the first time I'd seen chips for breakfast and there were plenty of boiled eggs. I was full; what a good meal.

Last night I wrote post cards to my grandsons John, Paul and Garry. I had stamps, so I would post them in reception on the way out. I bagged up the Goose, oiled the chain and was on the road. The traffic was light as I pushed off for Johor Baharu. I do enjoy cycling first thing in the morning; you can see everything in life – what makes a country tick. There was a slight face breeze; it kept me cool. The Blue Goose was flying effortlessly on the flat roads. I checked my tyres again this morning; other than slight wear, they were both perfect. Continental touring tyres, made in Germany – in my opinion they cannot be beaten.

In the distance I could see a dust cloud. I wonder what it is? Turning a corner I soon found out: road works. Oh no. For as far as the eye could see the road surface was being scarified. Lorries, JCB loaders, diggers, tractors, as well as the cars, lorries, scooters and bikes, mingled at will, threading a weary path through the uncontrolled road work mayhem. I checked my map – there was no alternative road. In my opinion, the enemy would be the dust; it would rip out the lungs. Action, Mac. I stopped before my attack. I decided to wear my windproof jacket and the towelling scarf my daughter Karen had made for me would go around my neck. I also wet my wonder towel and wrapped it around my face and over my head, with only slits to see where I was going. I must have looked like a bloody bandit. I was mad. What about my tyres? The road had been ripped apart; the dust cloud just hung around looking for mugs like me to hang on to. There must be better ways to repair the roads. The ripped up surface consisted of stone chippings, sized from half-an-inch to dust with holes and ridges – if you could see them through the dust cloud. I worked it out; the road works were all of two miles long.

When I was through I stopped. What a bloody mess we were in. I cleaned up myself and the Goose. My concern was the tyres, but on checking them I found them in good condition. I looked back at the unplanned chaos in wonder and disbelief.

That road took the biscuit, as they say. My navigational skills were called upon; road junctions were now coming fast and often, and the traffic was increasing by the mile. I saw a sign, it said 'Johor Baharu'. It made my day. I glanced at the cat eye – 80 miles. I felt good even though it was hot and humid. Traffic increased and my senses clicked into red alert. The sign said 'railway station'. I followed the roads; hotels were plentiful. I must be near the centre of the city. I planned to stop for two days so I chose a moderately priced hotel. There was no problem booking in and the Goose was allowed in my room on the eighth floor. I lifted the Goose and bags to the room. What a view. I could see the city and, in the distance, Singapore. Two days. That gave me time to plan my move into Singapore. I rang Gill, cleaned the Goose and washed all my clothes. I was spoilt for choice of food. I bought two cans of Bud beer. Sitting on the bed I pulled the ring pull on the Bud and Inner Man said, 'well bloody done, son. Cheers to you.'

Singapore

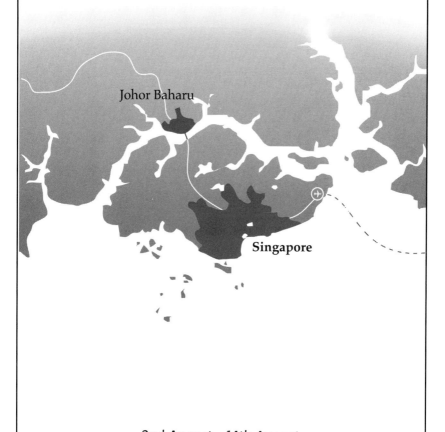

Johor Baharu

Singapore

2nd August - 14th August

Johor Baharu to Singapore

Singapore today. Bed was furthest from my active mind as I dressed. My leg was not so inflamed but I gave it a TCP dab. I'd bagged up the Goose last night and packed away my washed clothes. I really enjoyed my two nights in Johor Baharu. My breakfast was, you guessed it, tinned pineapple. I was on the busy road early, joining the lines of traffic across the straits. After some stops and starts I was at the border crossing. I showed my passport to the policeman. He looked me over. 'Been here before?' he asked with a dead pan face. 'Yes,' I said, 'in the fifties.' His expression did not change. He stamped my passport. 'Fourteen day visa,' he said, handing it back to me. What a happy man, I thought.

I asked a policeman the best way into Singapore city. 'Can I cycle on the freeway?' I asked. 'No,' was the reply and he pointed out an alternative route.

As I cycled along the various roads, the high standard of cleanliness quickly became apparent; everything from the houses, gardens and roadside verges to the roads themselves. I cycled past a road sign which read 'Nee Soon'. It was the road to the old army camp where I stayed in the fifties. It brought back memories good, bad and sad. It didn't twang my heartstrings.

Navigation was not easy. I followed the number 17 bus stops. It worked, bringing me into downtown Singapore. My plan was to stay at a cheap hotel for two days until Gill arrived. I would then join her at our holiday hotel that had been pre-booked. I found a hotel. The Goose was left with security. I checked it out; it was safe. As I walked through the hotel foyer, a very smart, shapely Chinese girl was walking towards me. She was one of those girls who warrants a second glance, with her short skirt, high heels and black sweater. My eyesight is not as good as it used to be – what was that written on her sweater? 'Don't fart and sneeze at the same time.' You can go off women quickly, can't you?

That's all folks. I could do with a gallon of Tennent's Lager from Alfie and Marion's, my local pub back home. I'd arrived, and to prove it, I'm here. Singapore.

Singapore

It was Saturday afternoon, 1400 hours. Singapore airport was one of the cleanest I'd been in. I had checked into our holiday hotel; the No 1 porter was concerned about the Goose's safety, but settled for left luggage. As I wheeled the Goose across the hotel foyer some leftover colonials from the past gave me some funny looks. I had made the airport in good time and was now sipping a cup of tea, waiting for Gill's flight to arrive.

My mind was active; it was just like a blind date waiting for her. What would she be like? I was dressed in my clean scruffy clothes. When I saw Gill last I was fifteen and a half stone; I now weighed under thirteen stone. Two and a half stone lighter. I was so sunburnt I could be taken for a local.

I wondered if she would recognise me. The tannoy spoke, announcing the arrival of the KLM flight. I was all nerves, like a small boy waiting for Father Christmas for the first time. There she was. Her silver hair shone angelic-like; the glass partition held us worlds apart, like that beggar girl in Calcutta airport. I just stood and drank in my dreams. Her worried face looked for someone. Who? Me. I waved; she saw me. Her worried look changed to that familiar smile and a slight frown. She cleared immigration, we locked together. No one could unlock us, I'd thrown away the combination. We stood back to catch our breath. 'You're too thin,' she said with a smile, 'I must feed you.'

What a holiday! No, I'm not going to tell you about it. See you in America.

Setting off from Orkney
May 1st 1995.

Boulogne harbour

Mac and the Blue Goose in the Swiss mountains.

Italy,
Brindisi harbour

Greece,
Igoumenitsa

Greece

Greek
landscape

Turkish
sunset

Buses, Pakistan

Pakistan

King Faisal Mosque,
Rawalpindi, Pakistan.

Taj Mahal, Agra, India.

Fishing boats,
Thailand.

Malaysian
countryside

Mac and Gill,
Singapore.

Gill, Singapore

Florence, USA

Big country

Fellow travellers, USA

Mackenzie
river, USA.

Yellowstone National Park

Old-timer

Bison, Yellowstone
National Park

The 45th parallel

Continental bed and breakfast, Missouri.

Yorktown

Blue goose, boxed
and ready for home.

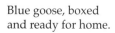

Around and back again.

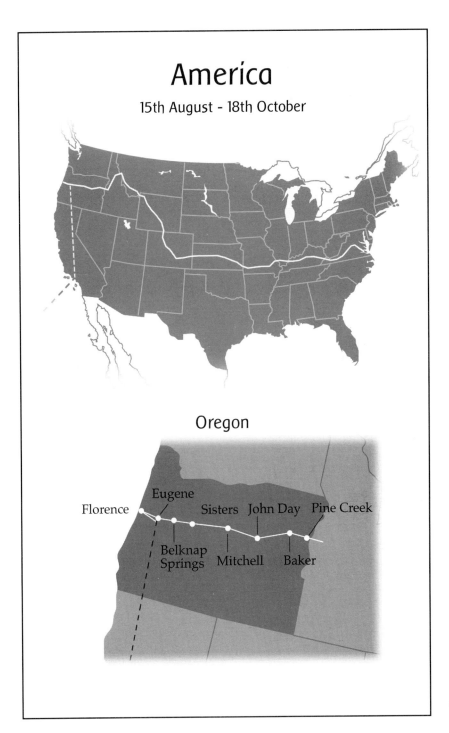

America

15th August - 18th October

Oregon

Florence · Eugene · Belknap Springs · Sisters · Mitchell · John Day · Baker · Pine Creek

155

Singapore to Oregon

As with all dream holidays it was fast coming to an end. Gill was due to fly home on Sunday 13th at 2300 hours. I had a flight booked to Los Angeles via Tokyo leaving 2245 hours on the same day. We travelled together to the airport. I had booked a London-type taxi, big enough to carry Gill, me, the Goose and the cases.

On arrival at the airport we both checked in. 'But, Sir,' said the Japanese baggage handler, 'we have not transported a bike before.' 'What's the problem?' I said in a matter-of-fact voice, as if I did this every day. 'No problem,' he replied. 'Could you remove the front wheel and deflate the tyre?' I was relieved; deep down I expected more trouble. 'Take care of the bike,' I said with a smile. The handler bowed his head and smiled back.

Gill's departure lounge was at the opposite end of the airport to mine. It was time to go; time to part. So many words have been written about time. It's a non-descriptive word; meaningful yet meaningless. I walked her to her departure lounge. She was well-versed on her flight connections. We said our farewells; this time it was final, we had been through our rehearsals. We were like two teenagers. Who cares? We stood in the lounge of a thousand eyes and kissed. It was strange – as we parted we both looked back at the same time, waved and smiled.

Within minutes of arrival at my departure lounge, the tannoy spoke: 'Japanese Airlines, flight 126 now boarding for Tokyo.' Soon I was on the jumbo upstairs, in the gods, as they say, next to a window. A young Japanese lass sat next to me. Within half an hour the announcement came to fasten our seat belts; we were on our way.

Food was served. I don't know what I ate. I was also handed a pillow and a blanket. The approximate flight time was six hours. Good night.

Tokyo to Oregon (via Los Angeles)

The in-flight tannoy woke me from a deep sleep; within half an hour we would be landing at Tokyo airport. I glanced out of the window. We were passing Mount Fuji – it looked just like an iced cake. We soon landed. I had eight hours' transit time. I asked the flight attendant if I had enough time to visit Tokyo. She advised against it, saying it would take two hours to get there and two hours back. I was tired and slept for a few hours in a lounge chair. On waking up I was hungry and had a cup of orange juice, a small cup of vanilla ice cream and a cup of tea; ten US dollars. If I had known the price beforehand, I would have slimmed. I enjoyed my captive time in transit at the airport. I had a full view of the main runway for both take off and landing. What a busy airport. Where is everyone going to and coming from? I could but sit and wonder.

The airport tannoy spoke: 'flight 127 Japanese Airlines to Los Angeles now boarding.' Time goes in whatever direction you want it to. I'd never flown over the Pacific before. I was directed to the sharp end of the jumbo. From the passengers I could see, I was the only westerner on board. Soon we were airborne. I was aware of the noise of the wind on the nose of the jumbo; it was quite significant. A pillow and blanket were handed out. My seat extended so I could stretch my legs. I left my shoes on; I had a problem getting my shoes on my feet after the last flight, as they had swollen. I was in a relaxed state of mind and body. Good night.

The tannoy system is far better than an alarm clock. It's guaranteed to wake the whole flight from slumber land in one small sentence: 'fasten seat belts, this is Los Angeles.' Soon we were landed. What a busy airport. Planes were taking off like rockets and dropping out of the sky, landing. I could only marvel at the demanding work involved to maintain flight safety in such a large airport. As I walked down the stairs to customs and immigration, I was aware of an over-sized picture of President Clinton smiling down at us. I looked at him twice – did he move his lips? 'Welcome, Mac.' 'Thanks, Bill.' I was soon brought down to earth; 'you haven't filled in your arrival form.' Damn, would I ever learn? No, they did not give me a form and that's the truth. I reluctantly filled in the form and rejoined the queue. I was asked the question, 'do you have any food: fruit or meat?' 'Yes,' I said, 'apples'. 'Dump them, please.' This I duly did. The very officious official checked my passport and announced that I could stay in the States until the end of November. I thanked him; I was in.

I looked anxiously for the baggage. The Goose and bags were waltzing round the carousel. I dived in among the Japanese and retrieved my worldly goods. I checked out the rig, blew up the tyres, fitted the front wheel and hooked up the rear bags; I was in business. Where's the exit?

'Where are you going?' said the Inner Man. I don't rightly know; I want to go to Oregon but… 'No buts, ask the guy.' 'Excuse me, can you help me, please?' The guy was huge in all aspects, both height and weight. 'I want to go to Oregon,' I said. 'Why, no problem.' Nice guy, I thought. He checked his computer, deftly touching the keys with his shovel-like hands. 'When would you like to go, man?' 'As soon as possible,' I replied. 'Right,' he said. 'Los Angeles to San Francisco, change for Eugene, Oregon. Your flight would go in one hour from now, landing in Oregon at 1850 hours; flight United Airlines.' I handed him my flexy friend. I always felt apprehensive when I paid with a credit card. Have you noticed that no one speaks when the cashier feeds the card into the mouth of the machine? Although the cashier sometimes says 'come on, come on,' as if to hurry it up. The machine rattled, out spewed a slip of paper like a lizard's tongue. Sign it, please, you have now spent your money. Painlessly he handed me my card and ticket. 'Go to Terminal 7, sir,' he said with a smile. 'Have a good day.' I smiled back and thanked him.

He did say they would transport the Goose. Terminal 7 was three quarters of a mile up the road. No, I won't ride; I'll walk. My legs think my butt has taken over my body transportation. It was warm; I was in need of a walk. There it was – Terminal 7. The Goose and I rode the escalator. At the United Airlines check-in desk I handed the attendant the ticket and pointed to the Goose. 'Sorry sir, all bikes must be boxed.' I looked up. Why me, Lord? 'No Sir, we don't box the bike – you must do that. I can sell you a box; the box plus transportation will cost you 60 US dollars. How much? For that I'd want it gold-leafed.

They had me, as the saying goes, by the short and curlies. I paid my 60 US dollars and boxed the Goose. I was still unable to remove the pedals; say nothing. I managed to fit the Goose in the box and handed it over to the guy. 'Thank you, Sir,' he said with a smirky smile. I was now sweating profusely and feeling pissed off. Don't say it, no, don't say it – but he did: 'have a nice day, and thank you for flying United Airlines.' In the time I had left I changed my money to dollars. I was ready to fly to Oregon.

Los Angeles to Eugene, Oregon

I must here and now sing the praises of air travel in the States. One can purchase a ticket just before the flight takes off. All other countries have a lesson to learn from the Americans in the department of air travel. Well done.

The flight to San Francisco was so revealing; it was like a video on travel. I was lucky to have a window seat. From San Francisco to Eugene, my nose was glued to the window, drinking in the view. What wonderful scenery; what a big country.

All too quickly we had landed in Eugene airport. It was a good internal flight – no immigration checks. My bags and the Goose made their stage debut, pushing through the curtain on the carousel. I retrieved them quickly and set about reassembling the Goose: pumping up the tyres, straightening the handlebars, resetting the seat. I was bagged up, ready for the off. I looked about me; the airport was empty of passengers. It reminded me of Kirkwall airport at home; as soon as the flight is gone, it's so quiet. I checked the map and pushed the Goose out on to the road.

I gave a shiver as I felt the autumn air in my bones. Light was fading fast as I mounted the Goose and cycled for town. 'Remember to ride on the right-hand side,' said the Inner Man. The road sign said 'Eugene'; my butt landed gently on the leather seat and I was on my way. I began to sing. 'On the road again – just can't wait to get on the road again.' I'd been out of the seat for what seemed to me to be an age; it fitted me like a glove.

The outskirts of the town soon appeared. Darkness was falling. The sign read 'Mum's Motel'. I must admit it looked a bit grotty and seedy. Give it a try. I entered reception to be greeted by an over-large lady and a brood of kids; a solemn-looking man followed in the rear. I requested a room; I don't think I was the norm. She handed me a key. 'Room 17,' she said, with a big smile. The questions came thick and fast once I said I was cycling the world.

I walked to the room. On the way I met two teenage girls. 'You won't like it here,' said one, with the biggest black eye I think I've ever seen. The colours were as you'd see in a film, black, blue, yellow and red; the eye rested as if on the cheek. The parked cars were all suffering from abuse – broken windows or windscreens, doors and boots smashed in and wheels missing. I checked out the room; it was clean and the doors and windows shut. I could also make a cup of tea. I returned to reception and paid Mum's $28.

I was so, so tired; I was suffering from a case of double jet lag. I ate the Walker's shortcake Gill had given me for a flight snack; it made a good dinner/supper. I slipped the wedge in the door and put the Goose across it. The window was closed. I fell on to the bed like a wet rag. Good night.

Eugene to Florence

As I awoke I felt both refreshed and relaxed. Yes, I'd had a good sleep. The Goose was packed ready to go. The weather was fine, if a little cold – the time was 0830 hours. When I left Mum's Motel not a solitary thing stirred; it was like a ghost town.

I checked my map; I needed to cycle from Eugene to Florence and back again. My plan was to start my cycle across America from the Pacific to the Atlantic coast. Florence was my start point on the Pacific.

My navigation skills soon picked up the road to Florence. I stopped at a roadside café for breakfast; fresh cakes and tea. I was now ready to meet the world. The roads were fairly quiet. Yes, I did remember to cycle on the right-hand side.

I was soon cycling in the country. It could have been anywhere in Scotland; there were dense pine forests. I was feeling cold but the cycle up the first hill of the day soon warmed me. Cars and pickup trucks passed at a fair speed. It must be the Eugene rush hour. I was feeling happy with myself. I sang all my known hit parade songs. The roads were well-surfaced and signposted. In the centre of the road stood a teenage girl, hand indicating for me to stop. She held a mobile phone to her ear. No, I said to myself, there can't be a poser out here. I smiled; she smiled back. I stopped. 'Traffic coming through,' she said. 'Wait here for five minutes.' On my trip I was to see many more girls and women directing traffic at road works. I suppose it's employment. Some were glad to chat; it must have been very lonely out there on the roads.

Photo calls were many; what beautiful scenery. Soon I picked up the Mackenzie River that flows through Florence to the Pacific. What a majestic river. Fishermen in small boats became numerous. Some stood fly-fishing, others dangled the rod over the side of the boat, all waiting for a fish to bite. This was the kind of cycle I liked, through wonderful wooded country. This was, as they say, a new ball game; the sights, sounds and smells of the scenery were something new for me to get used to.

The road sign said 'Florence, two miles'. I rode slowly into town following the main shopping street. Shops and supermarkets dotted the route, and a choice of motels. I booked in a money-saver motel of a very high standard. I dumped the bags and rode between the sand dunes for the sea. The Pacific soon came into view as I followed the flow of the Mackenzie River.

I stood and daydreamed: this was the start of my journey across America. As I rested on the handlebars I could only wonder what lay ahead. The shop said 'locally made ice cream'. It must be good, local folk were filling the shop. I ordered my usual vanilla flavour, sat at an outside table and watched the world go by as I slowly ate my ice cream.

This area had been Indian country; what a beautiful place to live. I met two fellow cyclists. They were both American and dressed, like myself, in cycling clothes. We sat and had a good yarn. When I said I planned to cycle over the Rockies they expressed their doubts. Had I left it too late in the year? Their concern was the snow. We wished each other a safe journey; they were cycling to Canada. The conversation had placed thoughts in my mind. The tyre size on their bikes was 700+20; my tyre size was 700+35 – softer on the butt. They also travelled light.

I noticed as I set off this morning I had good control and the Goose felt lighter. I had given Gill maps, format sheets, coat, shirts and films; in other words, I had unloaded my bags.

I had now stopped the Paladrine tablets for a week. My arm felt better already and the swelling had gone down. I bought my dinner in the supermarket and retired to bed early. I had covered 65 miles today – what a good start. Good night.

Florence to Eugene

I slept so well last night; I must still be suffering from the jet lag hangover. I ate my supermarket breakfast and bagged up the Goose. Last night I balanced the panniers; it will make cycling easier. The inside of my leg again looked inflamed, and was sore to the touch. I must clear it up. The weather was cold, with a slight face wind. The clouds on the horizon looked like rain on the way. Hope not. As I cycled off there were no cars or angry lorries; the time was 0700 hours.

I enjoyed my return cycle to Eugene following the great Mackenzie River. Yes, even that early in the morning, fishermen were casting their rods for the elusive fish. The heavily-wooded pine forests swept right down to the river's edge. I stopped for photos, trying to capture the still pictures to help my future memory recall. I see they have problems with nesting bald eagles; they nest on the electric pylons, like the hooded crow in Orkney nests on electric poles.

I smiled to myself as I cycled past an old roadside store, still in use. It nestled in the heart of the quiet countryside. Above the door the sign said 'Walton's'. In the background was a table mountain. I wondered if this location was where the series *The Waltons* got its name? Stranger things have happened. I can't answer that question. I thought I heard someone shout 'goodnight, John Boy,' as I cycled by.

On the roadsides folk were picking blackberries. I stopped and tasted the delightful berries. Leaves were now falling to earth in the slight breeze; this was the first sign of autumn I had seen. The taste of blackberries was still in my mouth. What I'd give for a blackberry tart and custard. I was enjoying my return cycle. The young girl I'd seen directing traffic was still there. She waved and shouted in recognition. I waved back. It's nice to be known, even in America.

My return trip now took me through town. I thought it a good idea to stop on the other side of town so I could make a quick getaway in the morning. The Eugene county fair was in full swing. Should I go? The question was answered for me in a flash; the threatening rain followed. The rain hampered navigation through the town, but I found tomorrow's road, and a Holiday Inn. At reception they said, 'Yes Sir, we have a room for you and your bike.' I settled the bill there and then with my flexible friend. What can you say about the Holiday Inn? It's of the highest standard.

My cat eye recorded 65 miles. I enjoyed my stay. The swimming pool looked inviting and I now had a swimming costume thanks to Gill. I'll swim tonight. That also reminds me to ring Gill tonight. I spent late afternoon studying the maps of my proposed route. My leg still looked and felt angry and inflamed. I gave it the neat TCP treatment. I did a form of Highland fling, with tears streaming from my eyes as it soaked in. I smelt like a doctor's armpit. I looked at the Goose; it's not easy to find the original seat setting. I know what you're going to say – I should have marked the setting. I did for height, but not lateral movement.

I ate pasta in the dining room; it had a TCP aroma. Even the waitress looked at me funny-like. I thought TCP was good for you; what an advert.

Yes, I did swim after my meal; it washed the smell away. I rang Gill; all was well at home. It was great to hear her voice. As I looked out of the window it was now dark and the rain was spattering against the glass. I finished my log. I was ready for bed; my computer mind was ready to be switched off. Good night.

Eugene to Belknap Springs

I was awake early next morning, raring to get going. I slapped some Vaseline on the angry-looking swelling on my leg before slipping into my cycle shorts. Breakfast I ate in the hotel and thoroughly enjoyed it. The Goose was bagged up ready. I checked the map and oiled the chain outside the door. The weather was cold, with rain clouds, but the sun was generating heat in readiness to sustain life. Most of the traffic was entering town; the start of the rush hour. I slowly sat on the seat; it wasn't too bad. I pumped the pedals at my normal pace. I was under way.

Today as I cycled I witnessed the most scenic route of the whole trip. Every turn was a picture, each bend in the road unfolded a new world. There was a need to re-programme my senses; this was exciting, mile after scenic mile. The route followed the Mackenzie River. The cycle route I'd chosen across America was the Bi-Centennial Trans-American Bicycle Trail. The route promised to cover all the old Indian trails and interesting sights; no freeways and hills on hills – a real cyclist's dream.

After all that build-up I was held up for an hour. The road was blocked with logs which had fallen off a lorry that had overturned on a bend. Wait for it, the rain started. I sheltered under a pine tree with the Goose. Within the hour the logs had been moved to allow a single line of traffic.

I saw more cyclists today than at any time on the road. In all, I saw approximately 300 cyclists, all going in the opposite direction to me. I spoke to one or two; apparently they were cycling from Idaho to Oregon. It wasn't a race, just a jolly ride. I was fully enjoying my cycling. Mile followed mile; the Goose was flying and the rain had stopped. In the late afternoon I stopped for a Pepsi and a cake; the small roadside café was full of cyclists. It made me think there could be a problem tonight finding a bed. I cycled another 20 miles and enquired about accommodation. As I had expected, they were all booked up. You know, I didn't mind because they were cyclists. If they had been footballers, say, I would have been the first to moan.

I stopped outside a motel. This looks a tidy place, I said to myself. 'Sorry,' said the lady, 'all booked up.' As I turned to leave she shouted out, 'wait a minute – I'll phone round.' There she was, as busy as could be, and she was trying to help. 'There's a very nice place ten miles down the road, named Belknap Lodge,' she said. 'The sign is on the roadside, so look out for it. It's expensive; do you want me to book it?' Beggars can't be choosers, as the saying goes. 'Yes,' I replied. 'What's your name?' 'Petrie.' I thanked her and asked her name. 'Diana Rae,' was her reply. I made a mental note to send a thank you card; must log that tonight.

There is a saying, 'there's nothing stranger than folk.' This became very apparent as the day wore on. I found Belknap Springs and folk were queuing out the door just to book in. The cost of a bed was displayed on the wall in reception; 65 dollars. When you're tired and it's raining and you have just cycled 70 miles, a bed is a bed, irrespective of cost. As I waited my turn, an elderly man and woman stood in line with me. The man was all of seventy years old; tall, slim and straight-backed. Life had not bent him. They began speaking to me, asking all sorts of questions. When I related my cycling experiences in the countries I had been in, they became more and more engrossed. The queue had now vanished; it was my turn. As I was about to speak, the elderly man said to the receptionist, 'give him a room for tonight free.' Was I hearing right? The receptionist gave me a room key and I mumbled thanks like a kid who is unexpectedly given a sweet. In his fine American drawl, the elderly guy said, 'I am the owner of this lodge; my grandson is running it for me.' By now I had found my voice and I thanked him again. There is, as I repeat, nothing stranger than folk.

'In return for my gesture, son,' said the man, 'I want you to advertise the Belknap Springs Lodge as you journey across America. Goddamn it, man, the young 'uns of today are not a patch on us old 'uns. They don't know what it is to work or want.' He followed this up with a spit, as if to make the point. He carried on by saying, 'if you're down here in, say, half an hour, we'll take you for some grub.' It sounded good to me. I followed it up with a nod of the head. 'I'll be there,' I said.

The Goose was lodged in the manager's office. I found my room, showered and changed into clean clothes. The interior of the lodge was all pine panelling; what a beautiful place. The room, from the bed to the ceiling, was also pine. There were tea-making facilities, but no food. I sat in the lounge as a pickup truck pulled in, driven by the lady. In the passenger seat sat the lodge owner. 'Just shove in here,' he said. I sat in the front seat. We briefly introduced ourselves: 'Rick McDougal and my friend, Clare.' I shook hands and said, 'Mac Petrie, pleased to meet you.' Rick went on to say that he did not live here but was only visiting. Clare drove with confidence. We stopped at the lodge where I'd met Diana Rae; we both gave a recognition wave on seeing each other. We sat ourselves in the dining room, which was busy. The room was finished in pine; I would say it had character. We ordered food and had a long wait; I was starving. I could've eaten a horse, as they say. We passed the waiting time talking. I found it of great interest; life on the road can be lonely at times.

The food duly arrived. That's when I made my big mistake. I started to eat; they started to pray before eating. I felt embarrassed; it put me off my food. I apologised and they both nodded understandingly. It was a good meal. I offered to pay. You'd think I'd bitten Rick's leg off; he wouldn't hear of it. I thanked them both for a first class meal. When Clare had driven back to Belknap Springs Lodge, I so very nearly fluffed it again. I said my farewells and thanks. Clare and Rick looked at each other; all three of us were sitting in the front seat. 'We will say a little prayer for Mac's safety, Rick,' said Clare. 'OK, Clare – you say it.' 'Please God, keep Mac safe on his journey and see him safely home, Amen.' We shook hands. I was touched. We said our goodbyes; they were returning home that night. As I sat in the quietness of my room, I felt good. Human nature was not all bad.

A unique lodge feature was the natural thermal spring. Hot water rose to the earth's surface; a two-inch pipe carried the water to a swimming pool and it supposedly contained all the natural minerals of life in the water. I thought of my leg. Yes, I did go for a swim and enjoyed it. The outside air temperature was cold, yet the water was warm. I had a really good soak. I was fascinated to think that natural hot water could come out of the ground. Pine trees grew all around the pool. From my room it was strange to see wisps of white steam floating above the trees, condensing in the cool of the evening and returning as water to the river that flowed past the lodge.

I'll say it again, there is nothing stranger than folk. It had been a most enjoyable day. I slept well; I think I was still suffering from jet lag. Goodnight. Safe journey, Rick and Clare.

Belknap Springs to Sisters

As usual, I was up early, drank my working level of tea and ate an apple for breakfast. I carried the bags down to the Goose, oiled the chain outside, thanked the receptionist and I was on my way. It was cold but fine, the sun shining through the trees and constantly changing the morning scenery. Photo calls came all too often; I was continually spoilt. For my route today I had two choices: cycle over the Mackenzie Mountain or go the long way round, skirting the mountain and adding 25 miles to my journey. A fellow traveller who last night drove over the mountain told me there was at least two inches of snow on the mountain road. Decision time; I would take the longer route.

The Mackenzie Mountain looked so picturesque and majestic in its blanket of snow in the early morning sunshine. The blue and green background gave it a real post card, or, dare I say, Christmas card look.

The route I'd decided to cycle was by no means easy; it was a continuous hill climb for thirty miles. I'd forgotten the fact I'd been off the Goose for the duration of my holiday. I felt it in my legs; the physical exertion required for such a ride. I was in need of sustenance and for the first 40 miles there was none; I'd been in granny gear for four hours. The sign said 'country park'. It also named the facilities, one being a shop. It was an outdoor park with a horse riding/mountain bike route, and walks. I bought my breakfast and some sticks of liquorice. I ate the sticks with gusto, as if I had a mineral deficiency; just what the doctor ordered. I ate my breakfast outside at a table. I relaxed, giving the fast food time to top up my energy levels. I glanced at my watch. Did I say breakfast? It was also lunchtime. I sat and contentedly watched the world go by. The day passed too quickly. Soon I was cycling into the outskirts of Sisters. The Three Sisters mountains glistened in the first fall of snow; what a great sight.

The motel looked inviting. 'Yes, we have a room with all facilities, and a fast food breakfast is served in reception in the morning. The outside pool is hot water.' The lady also informed me she was the owner. She had a dignified look; she was Dutch, I had it in one. She was not young but her silver hair was tied back and she had that Nordic look about her. She could play Maria von Trapp in *The Sound of Music* with her Dutch/American accent.

I found my room had all facilities and was as clean as a pin. I slipped the Goose in through the door when no one was looking. I washed all my sweat-laden clothes, rigged up a line outside and hung them out to dry. The pool looked inviting. I went for a swim and felt refreshed. The large supermarket was across the road. I bought my evening meal and a snack for the morning. Three separate paddocks in the motel's grounds held sheep, llamas and deer; I'd not seen that before. My arm and leg were feeling fine. My arm was near to normal size and something had worked on my leg; the inflammation was all but gone. I wrote my log, laughing at some of the back pages; even I couldn't read them. I studied tomorrow's route from the map. After last night an early night will do me good. Good night.

Sisters to Mitchell

Nature called; time to get up and cycle. My leg was looking and feeling better. Soon I was on my way for the fast food breakfast in reception: tea, coffee, fresh cakes and buns; well worth the effort. My washing was dry. I stashed it away, bagged up the Goose and oiled the chain. The weather was fine, but cold. In the supermarket yesterday I bought a pair of thermal gloves for one dollar. This morning I was in need of them. I checked out my route for today and was under way. Traffic consisted of only the odd car or lorry.

The countryside was white with frost. Within the first two hours, the gloves had paid for themselves. By 1130 hours, the sun dominated the landscape; it was a new day. My gloves and windproof coat were returned to the pannier bags.

The countryside had changed so quickly; I was now cycling through dry and parched country; the kind of country where cowboys or Indians could appear over the hill at any time. The day was so warm I was now cycling in my shorts; I could even feel the morning sun burning my leg. I cycled past the first dead coyote I'd ever seen and stopped and watched a beaver at work; sadness followed by gladness.

The fields were big; twenty acres or more. Water was supplied by a portable sprinkler system. What a length, and what a cost it must be.

Cycling was demanding; hour after hour up a mountain; it was a long, slow climb. A passing cyclist stopped and talked. He looked like a weather-beaten cowboy. He was cycling the other way across America. I asked him what his biggest problem was. 'Water,' was his reply. He looked really knackered. I poured one of my water bottles into his bottle; he couldn't thank me enough. We wished each other all the best. That's my good deed for the day.

What did he say? The head of the pass is five miles up the road; nothing changes. I had reached the summit. 'Ochoco Pass, 4,720 feet' – that's what the sign said. No wonder the going was tough. It's a true saying that what goes up must come down: hold your horses, we were on a downhill run. The Goose was flying. As I hung on I applied the brakes intermittently so as not to overheat them. My speed was too fast at times. Traffic was virtually non-existent.

Late afternoon I arrived in Mitchell; my cat eye recorded 95 miles. It was a small town straddling the main route. Originally it was a gold mining town; records say it burnt down in its short history. I had a Pepsi and a cake in the café; most enjoyable. Talking of food, if I keep eating I'll end up like some of those Americans. Fat on fat – I've never seen the like. If they get any bigger, they'll forget what their legs are for. Male and female drivers would pass me, one hand on the wheel, the other holding a plastic cup of Pepsi or Coke. It was a recognised way of life.

There were two motels in town. I chose the smaller of the two, farther away from the noisy road. The window of my room faced a garden and in the distance were the hills. I ate my evening meal in the local restaurant; it was home-made food and enjoyable.

An American guy sat at the next table. We talked and he informed me he had also cycled from Sisters that day, and was in part following the same route as myself. Man, could he talk. He was staying in the other motel. If he could ride as he could talk, he must be good, I thought. He promised to meet me on the road outside his motel so that we could ride together. I retreated to my motel and sat in the quietness of the porch on an old rocking chair; the resident dog was sure friendly. I was so relaxed I started to nod off to sleep, only to be woken by midges biting my face, arms and legs. I retreated to my room and left the dog to fight the army of midges. Good night.

Mitchell to John Day

What a sleepy, quiet town. I slept, as they say, like a log. I had promised to meet the American cyclist at 0700 hours this morning. As I dressed I glanced out of the window. What a sight. A fully-grown deer was stretching upright on its hind legs with the dexterity and grace of a ballerina, picking and eating apples from a tree in the garden. One could see from its movements that its senses were on full red alert. I decided against a photo, knowing that the flash from the camera would frighten it away. I stood transfixed as it ate its fill of apples, then it majestically

167

jumped the hurdle gate and disappeared into the mountains. In my entire life I had never seen nature demonstrating such natural wonders. That scene is etched on my mind forever.

I ate my breakfast. My leg was now virtually healed. Belknap Springs swimming pool – I wonder if it was the minerals in the pool? I will never know. The Goose was bagged up waiting to go. Weather-wise it was cold; I wore my dollar gloves. I wished the old dog good morning as I pushed the Goose out on the road. He wagged his tail as I oiled the chain. I waited for the American rider for all of ten minutes. No sign; I never saw him again. I thought of his bike; it had two water bottles fixed on the rear seat and an American number plate fixed to the cross-bar. It all looked effective. He said he had found the number plate on the side of the road.

The mountain was tough cycling; granny gear in autopilot. The cycling effort required that I held on to the edge of the pain barrier. I was well rested; it does make a difference when effort is demanded first thing in the morning. It was cold but bright. The sun would soon warm me up with the help of the mountain cycle. When I reached the summit it read 4,700 feet. I was warm. I passed through a small town and purchased my usual Pepsi and ice cream; my fix for another thirty miles. I saw what I can only describe as the biggest, fattest man I have ever seen. To my reckoning he was all of 30 stone-plus; I was a mere thirteen stone. Same heart and lungs. I could see that it was only with a great effort he could walk. These people must eat for eating's sake. I felt sorry for him; he rolled as if in a trance as he walked.

The roads were good and vehicles as this morning, few and far between. Pickup trucks are the common form of transport. I marvelled at the size of the country – prairie as far as the eye could see. I saw some old tractors and farm machinery parked outside some farms and houses and recognised some of the makes. Their condition was good; it must be the constant temperature and lack of salinity that protects them from rusting.

I could see the town in the distance, the sign said 'John Day'. I rode the main street and checked into a motel. The room had all facilities and the Goose was with me, safe. The local supermarket was down the road. I purchased my meal for the evening and my breakfast. I found it was far cheaper to stop in a motel and eat from the supermarket.

The Goose was cleaned and I washed my day's clothes and completed my log. I rang Gill and studied the route for tomorrow. As they say, never a dull moment.

I lay back on the bed and relaxed. Good night.

John Day to Baker

I jumped out of bed ready to meet a new day. There was frost on the window; I dressed accordingly. Breakfast was fruit and yoghurt, and tea until the back teeth level was high. The inside of my leg was healed and my arm back to normal; I felt a fit man. The Goose was bagged up; I oiled the chain outside the motel door.

It was cold and frosty on the deserted road; there was no sign of traffic as I cycled out of town. The roads were in good condition. I checked my map. Yes, I was on the correct route. The countryside was mixed, from fields to forests to prairie. There were hills, or mountain passes, I should call them. Granny gear was the name of the game. Cycling today was slow and deliberate; energy was in demand. The first pass summit road sign read 4,000 feet. This morning again I saw a dead deer on the side of the road. Yes, it upset me to think of all the animals worldwide getting killed every day. It makes me wonder if my grandchildren's children will see wild animals, other than in a zoo, in their lifetime. One can but ask how long before the animals become extinct? We all shut our eyes to the inevitable when we should be taking action. In my opinion the first line of defence is the schools, to bring it to the attention of children. Am I opinionated? No, I now feel I have brought it to the attention of folk.

I just completed my second mountain pass. What did the sign say? 4,000 feet. It's already mid-afternoon. Today's miles are hard fought for; the water bottle is in demand. As yesterday, the sun cleared the frost by 1030 hours this morning; it then turned into a grand cycling day. It's just a little hot this afternoon – I can feel the sun burning my legs.

I cycled for the top of my third mountain pass of the day; my body and legs let it be known it had been a demanding cycle. I was in need of a rest. The roads were still quiet and the vast countryside sparsely populated. The sign said 'Baker'. I free-wheeled into town and glanced at my watch; it was 1530 hours. I was on the road at 0630 hours this morning – 9 hours in the saddle. I was in need of sustenance and a room, in that order. The Friendship Motel looked good. I checked in no problem with the Goose in the same room. The room was clean and tidy. I washed my clothes, showered and went for a walk. I soon found a café and ordered Pepsi and ice cream; I sat and watched the world of Baker City go by. Across the road was a cycle shop. I spent an hour looking at the latest American mountain bikes and all the accessories. I also bought a water bottle to replace the bottle I lost in Pakistan.

I had a few photo calls. I saw various country and western-type metal-made objects; they really caught my eye. The theme and the standard of finish was, in my opinion, first class. I always regret not having found out who made them while I was there.

My evening meal and breakfast I purchased in the supermarket. I went to bed early only to be woken during the night with an itch on my arms. I switched on the light to see four or five lumps. I saw the reason; bed bugs. I caught three and squashed them; the blood squirted on to the sheets. My arms were now itching badly and it annoyed me. Only one thing for it – the neat TCP treatment. I also rubbed some on the bed mattress. I went back to sleep with no further bites. It took all of four days for those bites to completely clear. I must remember TCP also helps one sleep. Good night.

Baker to Pine Creek

I was awake at my usual time even though my sleep was interrupted last night. I ate my breakfast, bagged up the Goose and applied TCP to my arm lumps. I oiled the chain. White frost painted the town. Only one or two pickup trucks passed by; one with a dog in the back, window-shopping.

I moved out on to the road, itching as I cycled out of town. The weather pattern was the same as yesterday; cold enough for my gloves. For the first 40 miles, the Goose flew across the flat prairie. I stopped and admired some old tractors and took some photos. I rode to the top of a hill; the frost was long gone and the gloves and cycle coat stashed away. The heat of the sun shimmered the road, dulling the clarity. A strange form emerged through the shimmering heat. It was not a mirage, but an elderly lady cyclist. She was my age-group, with long silver hair tied back. She sat tall and stately. If anything, she looked like a character out of Don Quixote. The sun had tinted her features light brown, not over-done. She was dressed in shorts and a loose blue top. Her bike was bagged up; she was as clean as a new pin. We greeted each other with a smile. 'Nice day,' she said in a cultured voice, not American. Canadian? Ah! 'Yes,' she said, 'I have cycled from Canada. I do like cycling in America at this time of year.' She looked like a dream. 'How far are you cycling?' she asked. I gave her my well-rehearsed answer. 'I'm sure you will enjoy it,' she said. 'My father was also a cyclist; we cycled these roads often. She gave a smile that wouldn't melt the ice off the mountain-top. 'Oh well,' she said, 'have a safe ride.' She mounted her bike with deft grace and was gone. As I rode down the road I wondered if that had been a dream or a mirage.

For the next 30 miles I cycled over mountains, hills and passes; it was hot work. I passed two cyclists but only one stopped. He sat down with his head in his hands; I could see he was psychologically done in.

He was having one of those days when you have had enough. I knew he was beaten as he sat on a stone; his head was down. We talked. He was from Virginia and had been on the road for a few months. His father ran a business back home. He had problems with his wife so he thought it was time to prove he could do something on his own in life. He asked what I was doing. I answered in my usual way. For the first time, he looked me in the eye. 'How old are you, man?' he asked. 'Sixty,' I replied. It brightened him up no end. 'These bags of mine are so heavy,' he said. How many times have I said that? 'How far is it to Florence, Oregon?' he asked. I quoted the rough mileage. I didn't lay it on too much. I didn't overdo the number of hills either. I made a suggestion: 'Why not drop your bags off in Baker and re-direct them home?' 'What a good idea,' he said. 'That's the answer to my problem.' I told him not to give in, but to cycle all the way. It was all downhill from here, and it would be character-building. He'd be a better man after completing the trip. He stood up, straightened his back, smiled and shoved out his hand. 'Sure great to meet you, sir,' he said. 'If you are in Virginia, here's my card; give me a call and I'll come and pick you up.' We said goodbye and I watched him ride off with a spring in his legs. 'I didn't know you were an agony aunt, Mac,' said the Inner Man.

The sign said 'Hell's Canyon 20 miles, Pine Creek 10 miles'. That'll do me. When I arrived the only accommodation was a caravan site with shop. I booked in. The caravan was suitable with all mod cons; shower, cooking utensils. I purchased my evening meal and breakfast from the shop. I had made someone's day. I was happy. Hell's Canyon. Tomorrow's another day. Good night.

America
Idaho

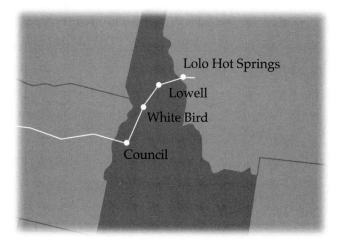

Pine creek to Council

I enjoyed my first night in a caravan. In the morning I was pleased to see I had no more bites. I ate my supermarket breakfast. The ground outside had been painted white with frost. I bagged up the Goose and oiled the chain outside, then slipped the caravan key through the letter box at reception and rejoined the road, heading for Hell's Canyon. As I cycled down the road I started to wonder if I would cycle the Rockies. I decided to give it a good go.

Soon I was cycling through Hell's canyon. It didn't catch my imagination; I had cycled through more spectacular canyons. I was now following the waters of Brown Lee Dam. What a sight. Some fishermen were already out in their small boats. The scenery was outstanding; sometimes so impressive it couldn't be caught on film. The area was too vast and the colours continually changing with the morning light.

On the hill or incline out of the canyon, it took me four hours to complete 20 miles. The slight wind was blowing in my face. I didn't mind; it kept me cool. I stopped in a local shop and bought some post cards. I wrote them out there and then. I sent one to my son, Stuart, of a horse carrying a great fish the length of its back, strapped to the saddle. The hills were now flattening out. I was on my second wind and what did I see? A dead moose lying on the side of the road. Even in death it was beautiful. It spoilt my day.

I climbed some big hills no problem, and also walked a few. The traffic was from light to non-existent. I rode through a small town and changed money to dollars in a local bank. Yes, I couldn't pass up the chance of a Pepsi and an ice cream. I cycled for another hour. Nine hours in the saddle; I'd had enough. The sign said 'Starlit Motel'. I booked in; the Goose was in the same room.

I have never seen so many additives for the bath. The rooms, from the beds to the curtains to the shower and toilet, were more for stolen weekends and honeymoons. Yes, this would do me. I found the supermarket and purchased my evening meal and tomorrow's breakfast. I was now getting hooked on supermarket shopping at the end of the day. It had fast become part of the ritual, like having the Goose in the room and doing the day's washing. I've never slept in such opulent surroundings. Good night.

Council to White Bird

I awoke with a jolt. Half asleep, I looked around the room. Without my glasses all I could see was this fancy décor. Where the hell am I? I thought. I came down to earth with realisation as my mind clicked into gear. What I like about cycling clothes is that within minutes you are dressed, ready for the road. I ate my breakfast and bagged up the Goose. From the window the weather was fine; no frost but a strong wind was blowing the pine trees opposite. I oiled the chain. The traffic consisted of one passing pickup.

I joined the main road. My destination today, if I could make it, was White Bird. Yes, you guessed correctly; the wind was very strong and in my face. The undulating, winding road followed a wide, fast-flowing river. Open prairies can sometimes become faceless, but following a river has ever-changing, built-in scenery. I first heard the screams above the noise of the wind. Was I hearing right? The next bend revealed all; a rubber raft was shooting the rapids, the screams of pure fear came from the captive occupants as the raft tossed and bucked like a wild horse. They were holding on to the restraining ropes for grim death. I smiled as my camera clicked. That was one way to have fun and pay for it. Very exhilarating, I should think. I would like one day to shoot the rapids.

The head wind was so strong in places I had to pedal downhill. It was obvious the river was a great tourist attraction; many people were to be seen in the area enjoying their holiday pursuits. A burger bar caught my eye. I ate as a snack the best chicken and tomato burger I've ever tasted. The waitress fussed over me like an old broody hen; I couldn't shake her off. They say that the best way to a man's heart is through his belly. She got the second part of it right; well done.

In the shelter out of the wind the sun was hot. I find that cycling is easier with the flow of the river rather than against it; it must be because the river flows downhill. 'Shut up, Mac,' said the Inner Man, 'you make me feel stupid.' I was cycling with the flow, but against the wind. Determination was etched on my face. I could feel the physical effort necessary to make headway against the gale; I was feeling the strain. The road sign said 'White Bird, 5 miles'. I passed one motel, but I was determined to reach White Bird; I could see it in the distance, nestled in under a great mountain. I won't be beaten. The road turned to the right off the main road, and there it was in the valley. I pulled into the motel. 'Yes sir, we have a room..' I could see as I wheeled the Goose through the door it was suitable. I soon found the local supermarket and bought my food. I also bought a bottle of iced tea. What did it say on the label? Natural, real-brewed tea. I was hot and thirsty after cycling 90 miles. I popped the cork and took a good, deep swig. My facial expression turned from one of expectancy to 'what a load of…'.

I caught up on all my washing and my arms were now back to normal. TCP had got rid of the lumps. I filled out my daily log; I was pleased with today's mileage. Early to bed, early to rise, in my opinion, makes a man. Good night.

White Bird to Lowell

When I awoke this morning I was not sure of the time; the time changes are coming fast and often. I felt well-rested and ate my breakfast. The Goose was bagged and ready. I checked my map. I had two options: follow the main road directly over the mountain, or cycle the mountain through the old Indian burial grounds. I decided on the latter. I oiled the chain and checked the tyres; a few pumps of air were needed in the rear tyre and we were off. Within a mile I was in granny gear; progress was slow. Personally, I think the best time to climb hills is first thing in the morning. What magnificent views; the photo calls came fast and regular. Only one car passed me.

This mountain was demanding. I could well understand why the Indians fought so hard for their country, and why the scalping of white settlers was the deterrent of the day. I stopped a few times and daydreamed. It was the Indians who named the mountain as we would name a town today. I was also seeing what they would have seen first thing in the morning. There was a feeling of solidarity and sadness; even reverence. From where I stood I could see the top; a concerted last energy-sapping effort and I was on the summit. I stood and caught my breath. There was a chill in the air at this height. The vast, panoramic view was indescribable. The White Bird mountain to me is more than a memory; I did feel the reverence.

What a way to start the morning; 11 miles in two-and-a-half hours. I was now back on the main road and lorries, cars and pickup trucks soon brought me back to reality. I stopped in the small town of Granville and celebrated my mountain climb with a bacon and cheese roll, followed by an ice cream. I know what you're saying: 'that man is eating too much.' I fully agree.

The cold chill of morning was now gone and the day was warming up. The Goose flew the flat surfaced roads; I was a mere passenger enjoying my cycling life. National parks became a common part of my cycling day, eaten up in the vastness of the ever-changing country. The parks were well cared for and cherished by one and all. Please keep up the standard. I can only congratulate you on a job well done.

The only way I can describe this vast country is an ever-changing picture; an all-seeing eye dictates our inward and outward view. Place names stimulate memory recall. 'Lowell 10 miles.' I glanced at the cat eye; 70 miles. That's far enough today. I stopped at the first motel. 'Yes, sir, we have a room.' I wheeled in the Goose, washed my clothes and showered. What a difference to be wearing clean clothes. I was now finding the different foods to eat, but tinned fish was my staple diet. Was there a change in time again today? My inner clock was confused; I'd better check with reception. No peace for those who worry. Good night.

Lowell to Lolo Hot Springs

As I awoke, at least I knew what day it was – Saturday. I was following no plan; just a quiet country cycle. I ate my breakfast, bagged up the Goose, oiled the chain and joined the very quiet road. I was on my way. The time was 0630 hours. The weather was cold but fine; it should warm up by, say, 1030 hours.

I was following the river. The trees on my left-hand side grew close to the road. I caught a shadow in the corner of my eye. I turned my head. There, running behind me, was a young coyote, or, as they say, wild dog. He looked no more than six months old and jogged beside me as if he's been there for miles. He seemed to be in good condition, his grey coat blowing in the morning breeze. My camera was in my handlebar bag, but I thought if I moved for my camera it would frighten him away. The unannounced appearance of a pickup truck eventually did just that. I enjoyed the company. I saw more coyotes on my trip, but they flew across the roads like bullets, very shy of humans.

Following the river was an excellent way to see all the sights and unfamiliar animals and birds; it kept your attention. I was aware that the road was ever so slowly rising on an incline. I was, as they say, in the heart of no man's land. There were no farms or houses or signs of human habitation. It was mid-afternoon; the hunger pangs were kicking in. I came upon some log cabins built on the incline of the hill. The planning was well thought out; they blended in with the surrounding countryside. There was also a shop and a café/restaurant. I decided to eat and kill those hunger pangs. The food was good; I really enjoyed it. The dining room had character, except for the heads of dead wild animals which adorned the room. They looked down on me as I ate; it made me feel self-conscious.

I had a chat with the storekeeper. He talked of hard winters, but the spring, summer and autumn made up for it; no, he wouldn't change it for the city. Nor would I. 'Any rooms?' I enquired. 'Sorry, we are always full,' he said. I could well believe it. I enquired if there were any motels in the vicinity. 'Over the mountain pass, another 30 miles,' he said. My options were few. My cat eye recorded 70 miles today already. I said my goodbyes and left.

I mounted the Goose and slowly paced myself up the mountain, vowing never to leave such a climb until last thing again. It was one of those days; the top never came. The scenery was fantastic; only the odd car passed me. I reached the top, stopped and took a long swig of water from my depleted bottle.

I was over the hill, as they say. What goes up, must come down. I was on a flyer. I held on to the Goose. I was eating the miles and enjoying it when I felt a sharp sting behind my ear. Yes, I had been stung by a bee. It was painful. I stopped and doused it with anti-sting cream from my medical pack.

Dusk was falling fast. There it was: Lolo Springs Motel. 'Yes sir, a room – no problem.' It was Saturday night, a very interesting day. My cat eye recorded 90 miles. I pushed the Goose the last few yards into the room. There were all the modern facilities. The room was a log cabin set out like an army fort; even full-sized Indian tepees could be hired. I showered and ate in the restaurant. I decided I'd rather eat my supermarket food.

It had been a long, hot day and I fancied a pint in the bar. I opened the door; I must have looked like something the wind blew in with my scruffy clothes. The place looked like a scene from *Star Wars*. There were big, ugly, hairy guys, some slim in their cowboy gear, with high heels and cowboy hats. The dart board was being hammered; the noise was deafening with the country and western music and the loud American accents. I did not like it. I downed my Bud and hit the road. I cleaned the Goose and washed my cycle clothes. I was tired; it had been a hard day. Good night.

America
Montana

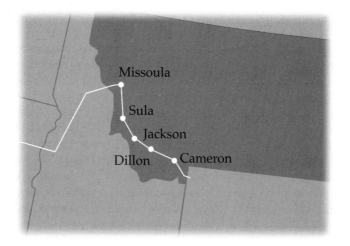

Lolo Hot Springs to Missoula

I was a little late getting up; I could feel the cold. I ate my breakfast and bagged up the Goose. I looked out of the window; it said it all. Everything was white with frost. The sun was still asleep. I dressed for the cold; it hit me as I wheeled the Goose out into the fresh air. Today my plan was to cycle to Missoula. I had more time to view the motel in the morning light. Painted with frost, what a picture it was; the log cabins and Indian tepees. From one, smoke rose from the centre, whisking into the cold morning air. The lake was frozen over and ducks fought to keep their balance and footing on the slippery ice. Steam rose from the thermal springs. The hot water joined a river flowing alongside the road; it left a tell-tale white cloud of steam as it condensed in the cold river. Looking at the Indian tepees, all sorts of thoughts were conjured up. For authenticity a paddock of piebald ponies stood in the foreground, their hot breath condensing in the frosty air. It was well-known that this was an Indian wintering spot.

There were no other tracks on the road except mine. I must be the first on the road. Care had to be taken; it was slippery. The road continued downhill. Nothing moved. It was strange following the steaming river. The weak sun's rays shone on the frost making the picture ever-changing by the minute. What a sight. I was so pleased to be part of it.

What a way to start a day's ride – all downhill. Care was the name of the game. I was fully aware of the cold; my hands and feet were so cold I thought I'd get frostbite. I can honestly say that I have never been so cold in all my life. Cycling through a ravine, there were high rocks on either side. At one low point in the hills, the sun's rays were lighting the area and I felt the temperature difference. I stopped for quarter of an hour to thaw out; even my teeth were chattering.

Cycling through a small village I spied a café. I soon stopped and chained up the Goose. I was so cold when I stopped, I could hardly lift my leg over the seat. I walked stiffly to the door of the café. As I opened it I was met with the smell of fried bacon and was hit by warm air. Four guys were eating breakfast, obviously friends; they were laughing and joking, their plates piled high. It's strange, but when Americans eat they don't remove their hats. I suppose it's the way you are brought up. 'Yes, sir?' said the homely-looking waitress, standing with her pen and notebook at the ready. I pointed to the guys' breakfasts. 'I'll have one of those, please.' She smiled. 'Toast and coffee?' 'No, tea, please.' I had begun to thaw out; my circulation was slowly torturing me to submission. I could move my legs, but my feet did not belong to me. I was, as they say in Orkney, 'coming at' slowly. The breakfast arrived.

My, can I eat all that and still cycle? I was game. The result was a complete refuelling of the body as blood rushed to every part of me, chasing away the cold. I was fed and on my second mug of tea and felt very content with life. The sun warmed the morning air, chasing away the early frost. I was warm again as I unchained the Goose. I thought of the Rockies. Would I be able to cycle if it was that cold?

I cycled for Missoula feeling a new man. It was a very big, modern town with all facilities. I decided to book into a motel and come off the road early today. The sun was now warm. I parked the Goose in my room and took a stroll around town. K-mart. I decided to shop and bought thermal gloves, a thermal long-sleeved vest and thermal extra-length socks. My basket was full. I could now face the cold mornings. I found the thermals useful. I would wear them for the first three hours of cycling, then change back to my normal clothes when the sun warmed the air. I returned to the motel pleased with my thermals. I washed all my clothes and cleaned the Goose. Good night.

Missoula to Sula

I awoke at my usual time and looked out of the window; frost. The sky was clear. I dressed in my thermals for the first time and was protected from the cold. Not like yesterday in Lolo Hot Springs. No wonder I was cold yesterday; the height was above 4,500 feet. I bagged up the Goose and was on my way. Traffic that early in the morning was sparse, all heading into Missoula. I was cycling in the opposite direction. Within the hour I stopped for my breakfast in one of those quick-serve burger places. They promise to fill you up for virtually nothing. I again learned that in this life you don't get nothing for nothing. I was still hungry when I left. I put it down to the power of advertising.

With my new thermals I was ready to face the world. The slight wind was cold. What a difference; I felt a new man protected from the elements. I changed back to my normal cycling clothes at 1100 hours. It was now a beautiful sunny day. The roads were wide; two lane traffic in and out of Missoula. No rain. Don't mention it. I'd come to accept the days would all be the same; they had been up till now, anyway. I was enjoying my cycling out of the hills; farms and fields started to appear more frequently. I couldn't believe what I was seeing – there was a farmer bailing hay. Admittedly it wasn't a heavy crop – but bailing at this time of year? Photo call. I stopped and took a photo with the hills in the background. They were white with a fresh covering of snow.

This is a vast country. I felt at times like a micro-dot in the vastness of Windows 96. I cycled through a pretty town by the name of Hamilton. What a homely-sounding name. Along the roads are strategically placed car parks, with notice boards relaying all the local information. These are readable from an open car window. I found them very informative; they also relate to the historical past of the district. Today was a day of continual change: farms with fields, prairie, woodland, towns and solitary country roads. I enjoyed it.

It was that time – late afternoon – when a night's shelter is foremost in the mind. I found a country motel. The receptionist booked me in. The room, again the log cabin-type, was clean, tidy and homely on the eye. It had all facilities. I wheeled in the Goose, washed all my clothes, filled out my log and rang Gill. She gave me a row for not ringing sooner. I chose to eat in the restaurant.

I was later informed, while drinking a pint in the bar, that the establishment had been built and run by a local madam. She built the motel on the cheap, as they say, from help and gifts from her many admirers. It was still as she had designed it. It was obvious she had an eye for architecture and other things. The story goes that she was so well-established with the local gentry, she used her source of information to her advantage. The local wives resented her alluring charms and collectively managed to shut down her establishment. I was now on my second pint. I met an American farmer and we talked about Aberdeen Angus stock. It was interesting. The bar maid kept asking how long I was staying in the district; she made it plain she had no man and lived alone. I was on my third pint – more than I had drunk at any one time during my trip. I was feeling tired and wished everyone goodnight. As I opened the door to my room, the Inner Man said, 'Are you drunk, Mac?' No, but I was happy. As I lay on my bed, a giant moth walked on the ceiling. What a beautiful colour. It was walking upside down. Was it drunk? Sweet dreams. Good night.

Sula to Jackson

I woke early, feeling good, and ate my breakfast. No tea; I drank water instead. I had dressed in my thermals – mountain pass cycling today. I bagged up the Goose and oiled the chain. As I left the room I looked for the moth but couldn't see it; it must have been drunk and fallen off the ceiling. The weather was cold, but there was no wind. The sun should warm the mountain route soon. Today's cycle was over the Chief Joseph's Pass: 7, 241 feet. Soon the inclined increased and we were on track for the pass. As the hills increased I became warm. I stopped and changed into my everyday cycle clothes. I was given a fright as a fully-grown moose ran crashing through the woods beside me, snorting and kicking as it went. A farm nestled in the lee of the mountain and the lone figure of a man was repairing the roadside fence. I greeted him with the customary 'good morning'. He returned the greeting. I asked what had caused the damage to the fence. 'Darn moose,' he said. 'I'll shoot the devil if I see it.' I never let on I'd seen it a mile down the road.

What a ride: granny gear for eleven miles over three hours - 7,241 feet. I rested at intervals; it was a case of stop and go. I did rest at the head of the pass. What scenery, for as far as the eye could see. Photo call. I did some panoramic photography. Soon I was cycling downhill; it brought a smile to my face. Oh no; turn left. I was still climbing for another five miles. My water bottle was well-used; the sweat on my brow had now disappeared as if by magic. I'd finally reached the top. The grass at this height was sparse. I now understand the saying 'one cow to the acre'.

My plan now was to head to Wisdom; on the map it was a small prairie town. I cycled through a small village and saw a café. Yes, why not? I had lunch; it was well cooked and presented and I was in need of sustenance. When I entered the café, three other cyclists came in and we acknowledged each other with a nod and a smile. One of the cyclists came and talked to me. I invited him to sit down. He said the three of them were cycling to Yellowstone Park; they had cycled from Oregon and were tenting every night. They asked where I was heading – when I told them it raised their eyebrows. 'Would you mind if we joined you?' they asked. 'By all means. We will cycle together.'

The wind had risen significantly since I had been in the café. Yes, you guessed it, I would now be cycling into a head wind. We introduced ourselves: Mack, Dale and Lyndale. Mack was fifteen years old, Dale was a scoutmaster and Lyndale a PE teacher. We decided to cycle the now-windswept prairie; each in turn would ride point (at the front). I had not cycled like this before and was surprised at the difference it made. Each would in turn take point position, changing every five minutes. It did work. We staggered the line slightly diagonally across the road. The head wind was so strong, passing vehicles occasionally made us break up, but the traffic was virtually non-existent.

We cycled this method all afternoon until we reached Jackson. It consisted of only a few farms and houses clustered together. I asked myself why anyone would want to build here? When I booked into the one and only motel, my question was answered: we were virtually sitting on thermal springs. The motel bedrooms were free-standing outside. The three friends set up their tents. I did not fancy a tent; I like my home comforts. There was plenty of piping hot water; the heater in the toilet was on the blink, it was continually in the on position. I took advantage of this heat and washed and dried all my clothes. We all ate together in the large restaurant, swapping cycling stories. We decided there and then that we would again cycle together tomorrow. I enjoyed the company but I was ready for bed; I said my goodnights.

Jackson to Dillon

I awakened just as dawn was breaking, then I heard it: the coyote's howl on the prairie. I lay and listened, enthralled by the new sound. I'd heard it so many times on western films. I found it acceptable, like a new record. I don't suppose the locals even hear it. I could see through the window that all was painted frost-white. I dressed in my thermals to greet the new day. I bagged up the Goose and was ready to go.

I opened the door and whistled; heads popped out of the tents but as soon disappeared. Mack was the first to rise. I called him in. His teeth were chattering so much he could not talk. I sat him in the toilet and shut the door. The heat in the toilet was like a steam room. Quarter of an hour later Mack emerged with a smile on his face. 'That soon thawed me out,' he said. Each one who emerged thawed out in the toilet. We had all bought breakfast the night before and we sat on my bed and ate in the warmth of the room. I made a mental note there and then; this camping lark is not for me.

We were all ready to go. Jackson is roughly at 6,000 feet and winter comes early at this height. We were soon cycling through cattle country. Cattle on the move with dogs and mounted cowboys blocked the road. I didn't mind; I took the chance to take some photos. It was just as you'd imagine; we were in a western film. The dogs worked hard. They were fearless, jumping immediately to every command; they were well-trained.

We had some time to make up; the mountains came our way fast. The first two were at 7,000 feet. What a pull. We worked well as a team on the flat, but on the hills it was every man for himself. Dale surprised me. For a man of forty, I thought he'd be the fittest, but he lacked stamina. Lyndale was what I would call average, while young Mack left us all standing on the first mountain. I could hold my own. On the second hill Mack was drained of stamina. I rode point, setting the pace; even I found it hard-going. I rode point all the way into Dillon. Dale had blown it, he was physically beaten. Mack was hanging on. Lyndale said, 'enough is enough.'

Late afternoon, when we arrived in Dillon, we stopped in a café and had a bite to eat. I had a cup of tea; they drank coffee. Before we split up, we agreed to meet at this same spot in the morning at 0700 hours. They went to their camping ground and I went looking for a motel. I was spoilt for choice and found a first class motel, which was very reasonable considering it was in the middle of town. I booked in, the receptionist gave me the key, I wheeled the Goose through the door and parked it ready for the morning. I washed all my cycle clothes and hung them up to dry. I showered, changed my clothes and walked into town looking for a supermarket. Again, I was spoilt for choice. I bought a bag full of food. I returned to my room and enjoyed my meal, then laid out breakfast for the morning. The ride was not great in mileage but it was stamina-sapping; those mountains do take it out of you. I completed my log and was ready for an early bed. Good night.

Dillon to Cameron

I awoke at the crack of dawn and looked out of the window; frost. I dressed in my thermals, bagged up the Goose and ate my supermarket breakfast. I enjoyed it. I had hot water facilities and drank my fill of tea. I checked my map; it was a tough ride today through the mountains. What time did we say we would meet? 0700 hours. I was there quarter of an hour before time. Dillon was coming to life real slow; pickup trucks were on the move and the odd person walked by. I waited until 0745 hours; no one showed. I was now cold. Had they gone before me? Did I get the time mixed up? I decided to cycle on my own. If they were late, perhaps they would catch me.

Even with my thermal socks my feet were so cold; I was cycling through a dead air at a very low temperature. But the weather was fine; I couldn't wait for the sun to kick in and warm me. Last night in Dillon I bought post cards and posted them to Gill, Alison, Karen and Stuart. I wondered how long it would be before the cards arrived home. A flock of wild geese flew over with their usual 'V' formation. What a wonderful sight. They were having a good chat. I wondered if they would see home before me.

I stopped and read one of the information panels on the roadside. It said 'gold country'. Soon the sign of torn and ripped land bore the trademark of the people's lust for gold. Man and machines had left it devastated. At some lonely houses gold ore was laid out on makeshift tables to lure the tourists into buying the 'yellow devil'.

I came to Virginia City. As I rode into town I could see it was a ghost city, living in the past from its former golden days. It was well preserved; the houses and shops were now for the tourist such as me. Abandoned trains and carriages, and other unrecognisable machines, were left to rust where they stood, littering the surrounding land. 'Do you want to pan for gold?' said the sign. No thanks. A very old fire engine drove through town, the fire crew dressed in their old fire-fighting clothes. It was a great sight; very authentic. I chained the Goose to the wooden sidewalk, entered the old-style café and bought myself a large vanilla ice cream and a Pepsi. I sat facing the road, watching the world go by, and watching for my three friends, but with no luck. The lady who owned the shop said the opening hours were seasonal; at the end of September it closed until next year. She said with a smile that she was looking forward to the shop closing so that she could go on holiday. We all yearn for a break, irrespective of what job we do.

I bade Virginia City farewell as I rode to meet the approaching mountain pass. What a ride, but the stop in Virginia City rested my cycling legs. I was now acclimatised to mountain climbing. The pass was 7,000 feet. The nearest resemblance to a mountain goat was the fact I was born in December. That makes me a Capricorn.

The views from some of these mountains are fantastic. Now, by experience, I realised why people go mountain climbing; the best view is always from the top. Just as night follows day, on reaching the top there are hills to go down. Downhill, here we go. The speed you could reach if you let yourself go could be classed as dangerous. I steadied myself with the brake levers; don't overdo it – you could soon burn out the brake blocks.

Cameron. It was a small collection of houses with one shop; the motel was log cabins. 'I only hire out the cabins, sir.' He said the price; I coughed. I only wanted to hire one, not buy it. I contemplated the alternative; another 30 miles today. No, thank you; I'd cycled far enough. I'll take it. The lodge was self-contained and slept eight folk. I thought of putting up a B&B sign to try to make some of my money back. The shop was run-down and poorly stocked, but I managed to purchase some food. Good night.

America
Wyoming

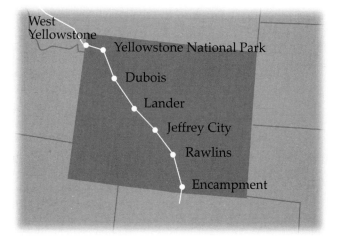

Goodbye Idaho. The dawn greeted me as I ate my breakfast and drank my tea. My mind was active; would I reach Yellowstone today? I bagged up the Goose, checked my map and oiled the chain. The weather was overcast to fair. The wind was, you guessed it, in my face.

Traffic was sparse as I cycled towards the foothills of the Rocky Mountains. Hills were plentiful; the granny gear was called upon on numerous occasions. Photo calls were tempting; the views from the higher ground were dramatic. Between the head wind and the mountains, reserves of stamina were called for; you had the feeling it was one step forward and two back.

I stopped at a crossroads. One road stretched to what looked like infinity. Beside the road was a collection of mail boxes, approximately 100, of all shapes and sizes, but there wasn't a house in sight. I wondered where these people lived? I took a photo; the boxes looked very lonely to me.

The continual climb seemed never-ending but the dramatic scenery helped one forget the physical demands. Dramatic is not the word to fully describe the aftermath of an earthquake; one can but wonder at the unleashed forces at work that day. To physically move mountains and flood rivers – the forces required to achieve such a feat are, to my mind, incalculable.

This was rough, tough, lonely country. I was still climbing uphill and the wind increased in strength the higher I climbed. I was under the whip and struggling. 'Don't overdo it,' said the Inner Man. It was late afternoon when I reached a plateau; the exertion eased and the Blue Goose took over and seemed to run itself.

Traffic started to increase; the odd lorry and pickup truck. I stopped and checked the map; there were two important turns to make along the way. Yes, I had got it right, the signpost said 'Yellowstone Park'. What a hard day. As I cycled into Yellowstone West, I felt a sense of personal achievement.

There was a good choice of accommodation; I chose a reasonably priced one which was clean and tidy and provided breakfast. The Goose was allowed in my room. Soon I was showered, changed and walking the town. It was a very impressive small town; pristine and built for the tourists. Soon I was watching the world go by from a roadside café with a vanilla ice cream and a Pepsi. It gee-ed me up; I felt regenerated and ready for anything. My mind was one jump ahead. It was Saturday tomorrow; should I stay for an extra day? I decided against, owing to the risk of winter weather crossing the Rocky Mountains.

I spent the last few hours walking the town and taking photos. It had been a hard day's cycle. I soon felt tired after the day's stamina demands. The evening meal was most enjoyable. I returned to my room, filled out my log and rang Gill. She assured me all was OK. It was grand to hear her voice. I cleaned the Blue Goose and made it ready for the unknown demands of tomorrow. Good night.

Yellowstone National Park

'Good morning, Mac,' I said, looking at my reflection in the mirror as I shaved. I smiled; my face was sunburnt, lean and showing my age. Breakfast was served in reception; tea and coffee, with a choice of fresh cakes delivered that morning. I chose the cakes with the most jam, to build up my energy reserves.

My plan today was to cycle Yellowstone National Park. The weather was fine with a sharp frost. I was on the road at 0630 hours; the sun was just peeping through to make a new day. Traffic was non-existent as I cycled to the pay lodge at the entrance to Yellowstone Park. The entrance fee was four dollars.

The staff were trained rangers; the guy taking the money could have stepped out of a make-up tent on a film set. He looked the part dressed in his smart uniform and hat, sporting a rugged beard. The information board thoroughly documented the 'dos and don'ts' if a wild animal tangled with you.

The Blue Goose was running well; I'd oiled the chain and topped up the tyres with a few strokes of the pump. I was feeling exhilarated. I must admit, it's not every day one cycles through Yellowstone Park. All the animals live in the wild; nothing is penned. Within five hundred yards of the start, wild deer were running alongside me, crashing through the undergrowth. What grace; their movements almost looked computerised.

The roads were generally good, although slightly narrow. Pickups and cars became more numerous as the day wore on. The soft edges to the road were not for cycling on, or only with care. During the day I must have cycled on about twenty miles of road under repair; it was rough on the butt and the tyres. Some cars ignored the speed limit resulting in stones coming off their tyres like bullets.

The rivers, trees, mountains, lakes, animals and thermal springs make the park the legend it is today, together with first class husbandry. The hot thermal springs fascinated me; steam was propelled into the air as far as the eye could see, condensing and returning to the ground in water form, leaving a slight atmospheric smell of sulphur. Each spurt of steam would rise as though orchestrated. Yes, I did see the grand-daddy of them all, Old Faithful. It was like the circus – when it rocketed up in the sky people would shout, 'Whoopee! Aww!' I think it played the crowd. All modern facilities were available; the car parks were full and tourist shops and supermarkets dominated the complex, together with cafes and restaurants.

Most of the time I was cycling along the roads were deserted. I saw a herd of buffalo, walking and grazing beside a river. It was a wonderful sight. They had the freedom of the park to roam as they liked. I just stood there and watched; I was enthralled. My mind wandered. The history books tell of thousands and thousands of buffalo moving at will throughout America. The Indian tribes appreciated them as part of their seasonal food chain. What a loss. The white man must be held accountable for our generation's loss. I cycled quite close to two old bison bulls; one was on the road approximately six feet away, the other crossed the road in front of me. I'm glad to say he was more interested in a parked pickup than me. I thought to take a photo but decided he was too close for comfort.

Nature heals and nature destroys: the sight of hundreds of tree trunks still standing was a stark testimony to the natural forces of the past. Water had made lakes that flooded the forests, drowning the trees. Fire in 1988 destroyed acres of trees; the blackened trunks stood in silent reminder. This is still earthquake country. One ray of happiness stood out in the midst of all this devastation; young trees were growing. Nature heals – true.

The rivers and lakes were favourites of the fishermen; they stood in all their fishing gear splendour, trying to fool the weary trout into swallowing their hooks. As I went along, I saw another cyclist, and, to my surprise, he was sitting in a car park, heating a can of something over, of all things, a fire. Fire was the last thing I thought I'd see in the park. It takes all kinds.

As I cycled I enjoyed the freedom. On seeing a point of interest, one could immediately stop and view. The cars and pickups were kidding themselves that their way was 'back to nature'; they were passing it by too quickly. The occasional park ranger's car passed, the driver keeping a close eye on the park. It had been a very enjoyable, different day. My cat computer read 80 miles; I had cycled from the west to the south of the great Yellowstone Park. As I cycled past the south entrance, cars, pickups and caravan trucks were queuing to enter. I smiled. One of my dreams had come true.

I soon found a motel on the outside periphery of the park. On enquiring about a night's lodge, the receptionist informed me that they had two motels. 'This lodge is fully booked,' she said with a smile, 'but we do have rooms available in the motel approximately one mile further down the road.' I booked in and she handed me a key. I found the motel in record time. The rooms were double-stacked and I was on the ground floor. I stabled the Goose. The room had a commanding view over a valley. It gave you a relaxed feeling. Soon I had showered and washed my gear. I was feeling hungry. The restaurant was back at the main motel complex. Without cycle panniers, I was soon there. I wheeled the Goose into the main reception, explaining to the receptionist that I wanted to eat in the restaurant. Where could I leave the Goose? 'Leave it here in reception,' she said. 'It will be safe.' As I sat down in the restaurant I had peace of mind to think that the Goose was in safe hands. Well, if you don't ask, you don't receive, do you?

The restaurant was well-staffed with young girls and boys. A boy approached with the menu. By his accent, he wasn't American, but I couldn't quite place it. 'I'm Spanish,' he said. 'I've been here training all season.' With that home-sick look he explained that he was due to go home at Christmas. He also explained that all the girls and boys were here on job training. As I ordered, I said, 'well, if they can cook as well as the Spanish, it will be good food.' He was delighted with my remark. I must have made his day, because what service he gave. He served me great amounts of food – enough for two. If I'd made his day, he made mine – just for one understanding remark. I left him an over-generous tip.

By the time I returned to my room it was getting dark. What a difference to cycle pannier-free; the Goose just flew on its own. It was looking forlorn and dirty after cycling the road works in the park. I gave it a good clean, until it sparkled. Relaxing on the bed, I switched on the TV to bring me up to date with the news. I also read a few pages of the Gideons Bible. It had been an interesting day, to say the least. No, I didn't see any wolves or bears. Next time, maybe. Good night.

Yellowstone Park south to Dubois.

I overslept by half an hour, but why not? – it was Sunday. I ate my apple pie breakfast, made my tea and drank three cups. Glancing out of the motel window, I saw that the weather was fine; slightly overcast. I had already dressed in my thermals. I bagged up the Goose, oiling the chain outside the door. For the first two hours, the roads were quiet and there was not much traffic. I was lucky to be cycling away from Yellowstone Park, because as the morning wore on, traffic was building up on its way to the park.

I was enjoying the Sunday morning cycle; hills were few and the farmland was well cultivated. There was also good grassland. It was fine to see Aberdeen Angus cross Hereford cattle, as one would see at home. I saw the odd moose, one with a calf at heel. When I stopped to look, other cars also stopped to see what I was looking at. It ended up like a crowd outside a football match.

Reading my map last night, it showed a big mountain. It would be late in the afternoon before I would cycle it. I suppose it was something to look forward to. During the morning I cycled through part of the Teton Grand National Park. Parks in these parts are very numerous, but essential in order to maintain the abundance of wildlife. I stopped for my usual tipple, Pepsi and ice cream. I'll need to watch; I think I'm getting hooked on it. In the afternoon the overhead cloud persisted, although it was quite warm. I cycled one or two small hills - they were a warm up for the big mountain. I could see it waiting in the distance. The road quickly rose. I changed down the gears to granny gear; I was soon on autopilot.

As I fought my way to the top I dismounted, and during my rest looked back at the mountains surrounding Yellowstone Park. What a wonderful sight: the highest Rockies in the range stood out as if painted in the sky. The grandeur took your breath away. The snow had been the final stroke of the artist's brush. I took a photo, realising that I was cycling the wrong way; sometimes the best views are behind you and you don't realise it. It's strange, but I had noticed this a few times; the old sayings don't always work: 'what the eye don't see the heart don't grieve.' I wanted to see everything. I thought I was on the mountain top, but the road went further up, and, to top it all, on reaching the summit the clouds opened up and it rained, turning to hail. As I sheltered under some pine trees, there was an information board. It read: 'Togwotee Pass, 9,658 ft. Continental divide. Named in 1873 by Captain W. A. Jones, honouring his Shoshone Indian guide, Togwotee.' What an uplifting thought. Indian guides were indispensable; they had the know-how.

I was now saying goodbye to the Rockies and cycling downhill. I'm not a great lover of going downhill; you have to concentrate. Late afternoon still saw me cycling downhill, but there was also greener grass; farms now appeared and houses were also part of the landscape. America can be a lonely place. One can cycle all day and not see a soul; even cars and pickups had faceless, dark windscreens. By my cat eye, I had cycled 85 miles. Motels appeared; Dubois must be close. The motel said 'welcome'. It was late Sunday afternoon. I checked in and the Goose was allowed in my room. An elderly lady was in reception. She looked as if to say, 'if I didn't have all this to do, I could be sleeping.' Nothing moved, not even the birds. I completed all my chores and had a great shower. I ate my meal in the local restaurant and enjoyed it. I relaxed on my bed, wrote my daily log and watched TV. I was tired. Good night.

Dubois to Lander

As usual I was out of bed early. One glance out of the window said it all. It was raining, and I mean cats and dogs. It rained as if it was giving Dubois a wash. The dust that had hung everywhere disappeared. I sat by the window and daydreamed as I ate my apple pie, followed by two cups of tea. I kicked my heels, raring to get going. Should I go and get wet, or wait an hour? As I pondered, the rain stopped and the sun began to push through the clouds. I was on the road in double quick time.

To my surprise, it was a downhill cycle; the miles passed as fast as dreams. Photo opportunities appeared but by the time I had decided to stop, the scene had changed and I was past it. I only stopped to photograph exceptional views; I was spoilt for choice.

The air after the rain was like a room temperature glass of white port; more-ish. I glanced at my watch; noon was fast approaching and I was still cycling downhill. As we know, all good things come to an end. It said on the signpost, 'Riverton straight on, Lander turn right'. Within four hundred yards of turning right, I was in low gear, going uphill on a road that had been freshly stone chipped. I don't like stone chips; they are as dangerous to cycle on as ice. The chips sung off my tyres like annoying bees.

The scene in front of me reminded me of cowboy country. The prairie stretched for mindless miles; not a thing moved, not a cow was to be seen. Hang on, what was that in the far distance? A herd of antelope, bounding recklessly through the bush. 'You cycling far?' I jumped in fright. I'd been so enthralled by the antelope I had not heard or seen two cyclists approaching. I recovered, smiled and said 'Lander'. 'We are cycling there. Mind if we join you?' 'No problem,' I said. 'Nice to have you aboard.' They were either German or Dutch, I thought Dutch. Yes, I got it right in one.

They were both in their late twenties and long-distance cyclists like myself, though not as weather-beaten as me, perhaps. They both rode mountain bikes. They carried what seemed to me to be a lot of gear: tents and backpacks. We talked as we cycled; both spoke excellent English while my Dutch was zero. When it comes to languages, the British are lazy – not a truer word said. I introduced myself, 'Mac': they also introduced themselves: Marica and Martin. Martin had a rear view mirror attached to his glasses. I had a handlebar mirror when I started my trip, but I found that the Velcro band on the brake lever obstructed my brake hood grip, resulting in the handlebars being out of balance. I'm an old fuss pot. We cycled on until we reached Lander.

McDonald's: I saw the sign at a thousand yards without my glasses. I was getting receptive to their good service and products. My standing order: 'ice cream and a Coke, please.' I always stand opposite the elderly ladies who are serving; they heap the ice cream cone full to overflowing. I always think the staff have an unwritten urge to pile on as much ice cream as they possibly can without spilling any, and make a perfect ice cream whirl. I'm hooked; to me it's a fix, then my hunger pangs are contented. The Dutch couple sat with me and we talked as we ate; they were also cycling across America. As we talked, I drooled over my ice cream. They laughed and immediately christened me 'Big Mac'. I'd been christened for the second time on this trip.

Martin asked if I'd mind cycling as a group tomorrow. I agreed. We intended to meet at McDonald's at 0730 hours the following morning. They were spending the night in their tent. I rode back to town to a motel I had seen and booked in just as it started to rain. What a storm. There was thunder and lightning; it was a good fireworks display. I ate in the motel and retired to bed. Good night.

Lander to Jeffrey City

Last night I slept well and was up early, feeling fresh. I bagged up the Goose, oiled the chain and checked my tyres. I arrived early at McDonald's to meet Martin and Marica and the sight of food twanged my taste buds. I ate breakfast and as I sat outside it was a fine morning. My mind went back to the thunderstorm last night. What a display of lightning; it crazily veered at every conceivable angle: white, blue and yellow, I was transfixed by the display. I had not seen the like for many a day. The storm lasted for over an hour; it played its game, then with the rain it disappeared, as you would turn off a TV.

A fire engine passed the motel last night in full voice; the motel owner told me this morning that a house had been struck by lightning during the storm. There had been a fire, but fortunately nobody was hurt. He smiled when he saw the Goose and said that ten years ago the main street had been dug up for over a year; if the rain had come then, the street would have been a mud bath. It reminded me of cycling through Italy; a road crew were digging up the road and re-laying the tarmac. Cars, lorries, we were all held up, hot and bothered and short-tempered. Down the road came a driverless tarmac-laying machine; the driver was actually walking alongside to see the quality of the machine's work. I hate to think what could have happened if the machine had run out of control. I had to smile because I thought of the saying, 'we are all Europeans'; that's what the politicians of the day say, trying to brainwash the gullible public by saying that all EU countries are the same. Knickers.

Martin and Marica arrived and had a cup of coffee; I had tea. We discussed the day's proposed cycle, and they told me that they had sheltered during the storm last night. Jeffrey City was approximately 45 miles away, and Rawlins another 65 miles. No thanks – 110 miles.

When we set off, Martin rode point and Marica and I were 'tail end Charlie'. Martin and Marica were accomplished cyclists; as I pointed out, their legs were younger than mine. On the hills Martin flew up; Marica at times found the pace Martin set too hard. I was always in the van of the group.

We soon found our pecking order and our limitations. On the hills I dropped back to Marica's pace and offered some fatherly psychological help. Martin was young and strong; he had the field. I found it strange to cycle with folk. As I said before, I had my own pace and did my own thing; I was not a group rider. We did enjoy each other's company, however, and cycled together for a week or more.

The weather was fine. The open prairie at times is faceless; mile followed mile. All too soon we had completed the day's proposed mileage. There were motels alongside the road, together with restaurants and cafes. I checked in for the night – yes, Blue Goose was allowed in my room. Martin and Marica set up their tent nearby; they also invited me to join them for an evening meal. I accepted their invitation. The area in which we were staying had, I'm sure, seen better times. The area across the road was bathed in a dust cloud. When I enquired, I was told that the whole place had once been, in the not too distant past, an open cast radium ore mine. The huge, earth-moving machines reinstating the site back to the original prairie caused the dust cloud. I watched and thought of the health hazard.

The café was of a good standard. I ate cake and drank a Pepsi. Whilst in the café we were joined by a group of car enthusiasts, and approximately six, drop head coupe Morgan cars were parked outside. These were cars from Britain, crossing America. I enjoyed the evening meal and thanked mine hosts. Retired early to bed. Good night.

Jeffrey City to Rawlins

I was up with the dawn, bagged up the Goose and was ready to meet
the new day. I ate an apple breakfast and drank my fill of tea. Speaking

about tea, when we left the café after talking to the Morgan enthusiasts, they paid our café bill. Many thanks. The evening meal last night was excellent. One problem: I couldn't do that every night after cycling all day; fit up the tent and make the evening meal, then wash up all the cooking utensils.

The weather was fine, although the strong head wind was against us. All three of us were on the road at 0700 hours. The day's plan was to cycle to Rawlins. After the first 40 miles, I felt unwell. We stopped. I had the urge to go to the toilet; one must obey the call of nature. The area where we stopped was flat prairie; there was only one lonely sage bush approximately two feet six inches high, 300 yards from the road. The problem of travelling in a group was now very obvious to me, but, as the old saying goes: 'when you gotta go, you gotta go.' This I did. During my restaurant calls, I'd collected a few serviettes for such an emergency. After the call of nature I felt better.

I drank some water and we resumed our cycling. I must say my cycling companions were very sympathetic and understanding. I had that morning, within the first hour of our cycle, stopped and eaten a meat roll. This was completely out of character, knowing only too well the hidden consequences. But do we ever learn? Was this the cause of feeling unwell? I'll never know.

Again we rode up the hills, which were plentiful, and the landscape had sparse vegetation. One could see for miles and farms were few and far between; it was very rough country. Rawlins appeared in the distance. My cat eye read 75 miles. That's enough for me today, thank you.

We were now cycling with more understanding as a group. If Martin was riding too fast, I would shout and verbally pull him back; there was no animosity. I found them a fine couple to cycle with. I soon found a motel and checked in. There was no problem about the Goose being stabled in my room. My cycling companions had found a campsite on the way into town. We agreed to meet and cycle together the next day.

The motel room was the one and only room I'd found with a microwave oven. I took full advantage of this when visiting the supermarket to buy my evening meal. I bought soup, a main frozen meal, frozen chips and a sweet, plus my breakfast for the morning. My window in the motel room let in the rays of the setting sun, so it was warm. The meal was good; more motels should fit microwave ovens. I completed my daily log and rang Gill. All was OK on the home front. It was good to hear her voice; she is my rock. Good night.

I was up early. The weather was overcast with the chance of rain. I put my rain clothes on top of the panniers so they were easy to get at just in case. The clothes I washed last night were dry; I placed them in plastic bags as a precaution. My breakfast was from the supermarket last night; I really enjoyed it. I also had hot water to make my tea, all four cups. I was ready to meet the world. I glanced out of the window; it was raining slightly, and the wind was increasing with the rain. I met my Dutch friends at the pre-arranged place. Encampment was the plan for the day. We were soon on our way. The traffic was light, it was too early for the rush hour. I stopped at a post box and posted a card to Gill; she'll be delighted to receive it.

The wind was still increasing and the wind direction was head on. Have you noticed that when it's raining, everything and everywhere looks the same? People don't smile; their heads are down and they look unhappy. That's how everything looked today, as if it had been painted with a wet brush. We did stop a few times to watch the antelope, but even the prairie looked bland.

My feet were now wet, but it was my own fault; I was too lazy to stop and fit my waterproof cycle spats. I'm glad to report that after my night's rest I was feeling completely better. There was no reccurrence of yesterday's problem. The morning passed all too quickly. Owing to the rain we were cycling and not talking, so the miles added up quickly. The route we were taking brought us on to the interstate road and we cycled on the hard shoulder for approximately ten miles. It's the equivalent of our motorways; the cars on the road were just flying by, cocooned in a water spray blanket. I must admit, it was different; it gave another insight into travelling you wouldn't usually see when cycling.

We were all wet and miserable – the rain never stopped. In the late afternoon, we arrived in Encampment. We soon found the local campsite. My Dutch friends were looking like myself, a bit like drowned rats. We pre-arranged where to meet in the morning. I felt sorry for them having to erect their tent in this rain and get into wet sleeping bags. Not for me, under any circumstances. I like my bed and a hot shower. I cycled back up the road and found a motel I remembered passing. 'Yes, we do have a room.' My visa card paid the man. It was clean and tidy and the Goose was stabled for the night. I showered and changed into dry clothes; what a great feeling. I washed my wet clothes and put them on the heater to dry for the morning.

I slipped on my dry, waterproof cycle jacket and walked to the supermarket. I was by now an expert supermarket food shopper, tinned fish being my staple diet. Today I also bought some vitamin tablets.

I take a few every week. Back in my room I enjoyed my meal while I watched the news of the day on TV. I was warm, dry, fed and watered; I felt a new man as I relaxed back on the bed. I wrote my daily log. The cat eye read 65 miles. Good night.

America
Colorado

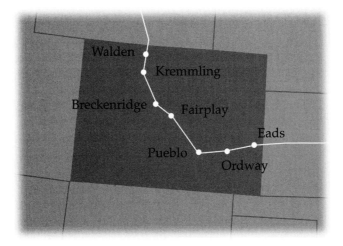

'Move your butt, Mac – it's time to get up.' I was out of bed in a flash. The Inner Man had spoken. I ate my supermarket breakfast, bagged up the Goose and oiled the sprockets on the chain. I looked out of the window; the weather was overcast and windy; it looked cold. I cycled down a quiet, traffic-free road to meet my cycling friends. They soon joined me and we were on our way. Walden, here we come. Today we were saying goodbye to Wyoming and hello to Colorado. Time is flying; that's three states I've cycled through already.

It now seems that my Dutch friends and I are cycling mates. Every day they say they enjoy my company and ask if they can cycle with me. I enjoy their company too. Their problems become mine, and vice versa. Cycling at the continuous high altitude was, to say the least, tough. It's taken me a few days to settle down as the 'tail end Charlie'. I must not cycle too close to Marica's wheel; slow down, Martin, you're going too fast. I watched Martin ride a hill like a young buck antelope, leaving Marica and myself to slowly but surely reach the top.

I had never cycled at altitude for so long, but I'm glad to say I had no problems with my breathing. At the time of meeting my Dutch friends I referred to them as carrying everything but the kitchen sink. Well, now I know what is in the cycle bags; Martin is a book worm, says it all.

I found Marica to be a very considerate, unselfish young woman. She was both physically and mentally strong, although on a steep hill sometimes she would get frustrated with herself for being too slow, but being the old granddad I am, I helped her over these personal lows. She did carry her share of the camping gear.

The ride today developed into a damn hard cycle; the weather was cold and sometimes wet. Two mountain rides tested our endurance to the limit. The day's mileage did not indicate the hard physical effort needed to complete the cycle, but then, it never does. The daily log sometimes misses the fact that a small mileage recorded on a day is the result of mountain weather, wind, health or mechanical problems. It knocks a hole in one's average miles. I remember a guy saying to me, 'only fifty miles today?' Have you noticed they always say it in a crowd with a loud voice, as if to discredit you? I answered as quick as a flash in an equally loud voice, 'I cycled it backwards.' It brought laughter.

Walden was another small prairie town and the land in the vicinity was well-cultivated. I had a shock today. I went to the bank to be told my Visa was over-drawn. My American Express travellers' cheques saved the day. I rang Gill, my administrator; it was good to hear her voice. She had forgotten to pay the monthly Visa bill. This was quickly rectified and no more of those surprises were had during the rest of the trip.

I saw Angus cattle today, which reminded me of home. On reaching Walden I checked in to the nearest motel to town. The room was clean and tidy with all mod cons. My Dutch friends and I agreed to meet the next morning. The room was blessed with a water heater and I made a welcome cup of tea. I managed five cups out of one tea bag. I gave the Goose a special clean. As I cycled today, it became very apparent that a problem was developing in the rear wheel. The pre-sealed bearing cracked a few times, especially if I exerted high torque pressure on the pedals. I concluded it must be the bearing, as everything mechanically checked out all right. I made a mental note of it, to keep my eyes open for a cycle repair shop. It had been a demanding day. Good night.

Walden to Kremmling

I could hear it on the motel window before I opened my eyes: rain. It was also cold. I dressed in my thermals and wet gear. My apple breakfast tasted real good, washed down with three cups of warm tea. I bagged up the Goose and checked all my gear was in plastic bags. I also did a quick visual mechanical check. I oiled the chain and cycled to meet my Dutch friends. The rain had eased. My mind's eye was imagining getting out of a sleeping bag, dressing, and folding the tent in this weather. Tenting is not for me. They were in the pre-arranged spot looking a bit dishevelled and wet. We agreed to cycle to Kremmling. The rain had stopped although the roads were still wet. The traffic was light this early in the morning; only a few farm pick-ups.

The terrain was mainly prairie; I expect it enjoyed the rain. The roads were in good condition, the hills we encountered not particularly steep. I was enjoying my cycle, but I did so want to ride point, and said so. It was agreed that we would take turns at riding point and change positions every ten miles. I decided there and then I was a point rider. Besides setting the pace, I was giving something to the group. The rain had now disappeared. We stopped and removed our wet gear. That was better; more freedom of movement. Cycling at altitude is so demanding; at times I felt drained of energy.

My rear wheel bearing was behaving itself; there was no undue torque on the pedals today. Despite the undulating road, we had made very good time. I wondered if changing the point rider had an effect on our cycle time? It was late afternoon and we were quickly closing down on Kremmling; we could see it in the distance. Soon we were
there. My Dutch friends were stopping in a campsite in the town centre.

They invited me to dinner that evening and I accepted. It was Saturday night. I soon found a motel which was clean and tidy and had a heater. I washed my wet clothes and left them near the heater to dry. The Goose was allowed in my room, no questions asked.

I was soon showered and changed and made my way to the main street to find a supermarket. I wanted to buy my breakfast for the morning. This I did and also bought a bottle of wine and a few cans of Bud for tonight's dinner.

Dinner was at eight o'clock. I left the panniers in the motel and cycled to the campsite. The wine and the cans were in my handlebar bag. When I arrived both Marica and Martin were busy preparing dinner. They worked well together, each knowing what the other had to do. In no time the meal was ready. I presented the wine and the Bud to mine hosts, who gratefully accepted this addition to the evening meal.

The meal was a chicken salad. It was very well-prepared, with a good nourishing selection of salad, followed by strawberry cheesecake. The wine and the beer made the end of the meal. The topic was cycling; what was to come and what had gone. I did my duty and washed up all the pots and pans, plates and cups. I thanked mine hosts for a most enjoyable evening and was soon on the Goose cycling back to the motel. As I opened the door I felt the heat; I had left the heater on to dry my clothes. I had been cold, so the heat was most acceptable. When I cycled home, my rear tyre did not feel true for some reason. I checked it in the light of the room and saw it was a slow puncture. I repaired it at once. As I checked the inside of the tyre wall, my finger came into contact with a sharp thorn. I removed the thorn, repaired the puncture and inflated the tyre. Job done for the morning. I felt the warmth of my room and it made me feel tired. Good night.

Kremmling to Breckenridge

As I got out of bed, I glanced out of the window. It looked cold so I dressed in my thermals, boiled the water heater for my tea and ate my apple pie breakfast. The rear tyre was still inflated from the puncture repair last night. I made my way to the agreed meeting point; my Dutch friends were still cycling with me. I oiled the chain on the Goose as I waited. Within minutes, they arrived. I don't know who thought up the sometimes inappropriate names of the small towns I cycled through. The weather was fine and cold; good for cycling. We all three bade each good morning, as had become customary; it was a good way to start the day. The road was traffic-free as we got under way, forgetting it was Sunday.

For the first time in America, we were on cycle paths. The paths passed through a tourist area which was very picturesque. The blue water in the lakes contrasted with the mountains; the multi-coloured yacht sails completed the picture. We were entering a built-up area, the class of the buildings showing its affluence. For the first time, tourist hotels replaced motels. Big, expensive 4x4 pickups passed, towing the latest gleaming new speed boats. Cars and camper vans passed, some towing secondary 4x4 runabouts. On the tail end of some, hung two or three mountain bikes. In the autumn Sunday sunshine it seemed everyone in the area was enjoying a fine sunny weekend. At regular intervals, mountain bikers passed us, some shouting encouragement or waving. This was certainly the in place to be: Breckenridge and Silver Thorn. We were well ahead of our predicted time; it was late afternoon and the strong sun shone, picking out the white strips of snow still clinging to the surrounding mountain ridges.

Mountain walkers became apparent, dressed in their gear, like cyclists; they do look the part. We stopped as if by intent. We were in a very busy town square, full of tourists. The shops and cafes were full of people. We sat on a bench and became part of the noisy mob. I bought ice cream and my favourite Pepsi. We looked at each other and smiled; we all had the same thing on our minds. Hoosier Pass. It's all we talked about for the last few days. Should we ride it today or tomorrow? Marica was complaining of feeling sick; she had also been sick in the mornings. Morning sickness? No, say nothing, Mac; perhaps they wouldn't appreciate my joke. I was game to ride the pass, as was Martin. Marica decided to use her feminine charms and thumb a lift in a pickup over the mountain.

Martin and I reluctantly left her on the roadside thumbing it; within five miles she waved as she passed, the bike in the back of a pickup. It was all too apparent from the start that we were on a steady climb. Up and up we went; again, the young legs of Martin were proving too much for me. 'You go on, Martin,' I said. 'I'll see you at the top.' Slowly he increased the distance between us and the road twisted and turned until he was out of sight. The road continued to snake; some cars and pickups blew their horns in understanding of our task ahead. I was in granny gear, sweating profusely. I was also in autopilot with the demanding effort. I stopped regularly to top up my water level. The sweat now ran off my head as if I had a leak. The more I sweated, the more I drank. This was some mountain pass. I had not seen Martin for some distance, but I felt I could do it; I was now in the overdrive determination gear. As I climbed higher I was seeing the first signs of snow stuck in the gullies from last year. Cars and pickups were few and far between. This must be the last rise, I told myself. No, another one.

I'd risen my hopes three times only to find up and up it went.

I rested twice to catch my breath and became aware of my short bursts of breath while inhaling and exhaling. I was not distressed. My, this was some pull. This must be the last one; I could see the mountain top taking shape. Yes! I'd made it to the top. There were Marica and Martin standing beside the road, jumping up and down, clapping and shouting their encouragement. With the last concerted effort I had done it – reached the top of Hoosier Pass; elevation 11,542 feet.

The sign on the mountain top read:

Continental Divide

Atlantic Ocean	Pacific Ocean
Water Shed	Water Shed
South Plate River	Blue River
Pike National Forest	Arapaho National Forest
Park County	Summit County

Department of Agriculture Forest Services

The sign said it all; I confirmed it with a photograph. I felt on top of the world. The snow was dazzling white; the forests were dwarfed among the high mountains. All the green colours melted into each other. I stood open-mouthed and drank in the breathtaking view on that late warm sunny afternoon. I wouldn't like to cycle the pass with inclement weather. Sometimes it's better to push on and complete a task rather than leave it until the morning. The big push had paid off. I checked the Goose; the bags were safe. I did hear a few rear wheel cracks whilst applying maximum torque on the way up. But we were about to apply the reverse – downhill at great rate of knots. Why is it I'm always last? Is it that the Goose doesn't run as freely as their bikes, or am I a little reluctant to give the Goose its head? I don't know. Anyway, I always catch up at the bottom of the hill. This was the first sign of the descent out of the mountains. The miles were flying by, the cycling was all downhill until we reached the small gold mining town of Fairplay. It still carried the scars of its mining days; it also still carried the old façade. There were shops and, I'm glad to say, a motel. Martin and Marica also fancied stopping the night in the same motel. It worked out cheaper to book two rooms with facilities than two separate rooms. We booked in. I glanced at my cat eye computer: the recorded mileage for the day was 77 miles; a nice Sunday run.

We decided to eat out. Marica was feeling better. We found a small local restaurant; the meal was good and reasonably priced. We celebrated our day with a nice cup of tea. We were all tired and returned to the motel. I was soon in my bed and slept like a log. Good night.

I was out of bed at my normal time. To say the least, it was strange to be in a motel with other people; at least I knew them. Marica had made breakfast; I had the feeling of being spoilt. I consumed three cups of tea; the tea bags were given to me last night by the restaurant owner because I thought we would need them this morning.

I bagged up the Goose and oiled the chain. I was glad I had dressed in my thermals this morning, because outside in the motel car park, the cars were covered in frost. The weather was fine; I hope it will stay that way. We were all ready to go. Although still in the mountains, downhill was the name of the game; it was so cold the frost was biting to the bone. During breakfast we decided to cycle to Pueblo, rightly or wrongly. The owner mentioned this morning that his motel was busy; the reason was that it was the first motel in the hills.

For the first 60 miles hills were plentiful. In the afternoon again, there were more hills than flat roads. We helped each other along, not pushing too hard. If one felt tired, we cut the pace. The roads were on open prairie and the breeze was in our faces. The sun shone in the afternoon, so the breeze kept us cool. I thought I'd be stiff after yesterday's exertion, but no, I felt good. We had not wasted any time on the road; we all rode with determination. I checked my cat eye at one short stop we made; the computer recorded 100 miles. The roadside shop where we stopped was shut, but there was a Coke machine. We checked our loose money and managed a can apiece.

Marica and Martin were discussing whether or not they should cycle the next 28 miles to Pueblo. There was very little enthusiasm shown. It was all right for them, as they had a tent, but I had no alternative but to cycle to the town. I needed a motel for the night. I pointed this out and made my feelings known. It was finally agreed we would ride for town. I decided I would ride point.

Before setting off, I needed some nourishment. I had some biscuits and apples that I shared with Marica and Martin; I also balanced out my water with them. We were soon on our way. I bit the bullet, as they say, and pushed hard for the next 28 miles. Soon I was on my own, but I couldn't stop because night was falling fast. When cycling I felt strong; like the first miles of the day there were no power-sapping hills, only gently undulating roads. I reached town, What should I do? I waited at a set of lights on the road leading into town. Half an hour later my Dutch friends appeared. Darkness was falling fast. We congratulated each other on completing the task we had set today; we had covered 128 miles in 12 hours of dedicated cycling; we were all happy. There was a motel in the distance. 'That's for me,' I said. My Dutch friends also decided to stay in the motel. I checked in and there was no problem with the Goose; I stabled it in my room. I told Marica and Martin that I was having a rest day tomorrow. They agreed that they would also stop the extra day. I'd now cycled for 26 consecutive days; I think I've earned a rest day.

We agreed to eat in the restaurant tonight; dinner at 2030 hours. We booked the time. A quick wash was called for and a change of clothes. This was a first class motel and the bath looked extra inviting. Decision made, I ran the bath, pouring in all the smelly soap, and slid in up to my neck. The hot water released all my aches and pains. I thought I was walking on air and was soon into my clean clothes and on my way to the evening meal. I must have smelled like a scented old man. The food was above average; we finished off with a glass of white wine and a can of Bud. I was as contented as a baby, and bade my friends goodnight.

Pueblo (rest day)

You know, it's funny, but when I'm awake I must get out of bed. I can't lie in bed resting and daydreaming. The time was 0630 hours. I made myself a cup of tea. I was feeling rested; there was no stiffness from the last two demanding days. The weather was fine. There was a slight touch of frost; that would soon clear with the morning sun. I looked in the mirror; my reflection met with my approval. I was trim, sun-bronzed and weather-beaten. My legs were slightly piebald where I'd been wearing my cycle shorts. My arm, I'm glad to say, had returned to normal. My hair was long and straggly; the barber for you today, my son. As I dressed I listened to the world news. O.J. Simpson? Who is he?

I found a phone book in one of the drawers in my room, equivalent to our Yellow Pages. I was concerned about the bearings in my rear wheel; the cracking noise was annoying me. Yes! Roberts Cycle Shop, Pueblo: times of opening, 0930 hours until 1900 hours. My intention was to be at the shop when it opened. The motel receptionist gave me directions; the shop was approximately one mile into town. I had removed my panniers and cleaned the Goose until it shone. Ah well – another toilet roll gone. I had also now purchased a small, double-sided sponge that I found very handy, and did a good job.

I rode to McDonald's for my breakfast and as I made for the cycle shop I felt like a racing cyclist; the Goose just flew. I was at the shop at 0900 hours and waited for it to open. It did, on time. I was invited into a very clean and well-laid out workshop. I spoke directly to the cycle fitter, explaining my wheel bearing problem. He nodded and said he would check it out for me. I also pointed out the problem with the front brake cable and brake blocks. He checked his watch. 'Come back at 1500 hours.' I left the workshop wondering if I would still be here tomorrow. One always thinks the worst.

I was now on shanks's pony. I spent the next hour walking round the shop show room looking at all the latest bike models and gizmos. I was tempted a few times but was stern with myself; the Inner Man kept saying 'no'. As I walked down the street I saw a sign for a barber/hairdresser. I was soon inside, sitting in the barber's chair. The barber was an elderly gentleman in a suit; he had enough gold on his fingers to open a jewellery shop. Good job he had ten fingers, or he'd be bankrupt. I smiled at my thoughts. 'What style, sir?' he asked, bringing me back to reality. 'Cut it all off, please.' 'How close, sir?' 'To the boards,' I replied. He laughed and uttered the famous words: 'no problem'. Within five minutes I was walking down the road 'scalped', as they might say in an Indian reserve.

When I returned to my room, I looked at the stranger in the mirror and laughed. At least now the wind wouldn't blow my hair in my eyes. I was the nearest thing I've seen to a Buddhist monk. The Inner Man said nothing; I knew he agreed.

I met my Dutch friends sitting on the grass near the swimming pool. When they saw me they congratulated me on my hair cut. How can it be a good cut, I thought, if I have no hair left? For personal hygiene, however, it's the best way to keep one's head clean.

I walked back to town and shopped in K-mart. McDonald's had my vote for afternoon tea. I returned to the cycle workshop; the Blue Goose was ready. I paid the man 21 dollars, plus tip. I cycled back to the motel a happy man.

Pueblo to Ordway

I was up early as usual and glanced out of the window; frost with a fine sky. I dressed in my thermals; I don't like to get cold first thing in the morning. I ate my apple pie breakfast and heated the water for my tea. I was ready to face the world. Last night, I bagged up the Goose, checked the air pressure in the tyres, and oiled the chain outside the motel. I was ready and waiting for my Dutch friends. They soon joined me and we wished each other the compliments of the day. We decided we would cycle for Ordway.

There was some movement of traffic on the roads, but as we left Pueblo it was quiet. We all agreed we had enjoyed our rest day and cycled with renewed energy and purpose. I was listening for any noise from my rear wheel, and I'm glad to say there was none; that was after the first 20 miles of the day. The brakes were working at a touch; what a difference. The repair was well worth the money; it also gave me peace of mind.

Thinking back, I had enjoyed my lone cycle into Pueblo. On that 28 miles alone, I had that feeling of being independent. But, all due respects, I do enjoy the cycling with my Dutch friends, and like their company. The roads had now changed, not unlike roller coasters. On checking the map today, we had two choices: 55 miles or 110 miles. We settled for the 55 miles. The weather had changed; the frost had gone and the sun was shining. One could feel the heat.

The railway line made an appearance, stretching for mile after endless mile. We even crossed the line, resulting in Martin having a puncture. When he repaired the tube, there was a sliver of metal in the tyre casing from the railway line. A goods train passed and, as it did, the driver sounded a mournful horn, as if glad of our company. We waved, and the horn sounded again.

We made good time. In the late afternoon, we were cycling into Ordway. It was a small railway town where the tracks crossed the road and passed beside the town. The town itself was so quiet, we hardly saw another living soul. There were no motels, but the equivalent to British B&B. I settled for a clean looking house. Everything was near the railway line; I could imagine the train noise at night or in the early morning. I was made welcome by what I would call two old maids, one trying to outdo the other; they fussed about nothing. The room was spotlessly clean, with all facilities.

I was invited to dine with my Dutch friends, and when I found the town campsite, dinner was being prepared. I delivered three, ready-made fruit pies and a bottle of white wine. I don't like red wine. As the meal was being laid out, all the flies in the district descended on us. I was like a tic tac man trying to fight them off, but to no avail. I wonder if they work as a team?

The meal was as usual tasty, filling and plentiful; the pies were good and the wine better than I'd imagined. Two flies committed suicide in my wine. Not being a wine connoisseur, I wondered if one would call it meaty? A train passed; the driver blew the horn ten times. The line of trucks was endless; one could feel the vibration in the ground as the train slowly passed. A pickup truck stopped and out got a very swarthy character with long black hair. 'Do you mind if I join you?' he asked. 'I just want a chat.' He plonked his butt on a nearby stone. 'I'm a painter,' he said, 'and a Mexican. We don't have a good name in America – they call us lazy. I've had a hard day.' The conversation continued, covering all aspects of life. It made his day; it made ours. He left us as quickly as he'd come, disappearing down the road in a cloud of dust. I thanked mine hosts for the meal and cycled back to my lodge. Good night.

Ordway to Eads

Usually I'm awake early, but this morning was an exception to the norm; my watch read 0530 hours. The slow passing train hooted 16 times; what a time to wake up the town. What an alarm. It must be like this most days. The locals must be used to it. I ate my apple pie breakfast and drank three cups of tea. My mind went back to last night at the campsite; that Mexican character must have been looking for the sympathy vote, that's my conclusion anyway. I did offer to wash up the pots and pans, but the flies must have heard me because they descended on them in droves. Marica declined my offer, saying there was a need to boil the water before washing the pans; rightly so. It was a good meal and I thanked Martin and Marica again when I cycled over to see them this morning. They too had been woken early by the train and were packing the tent after their breakfast. As I waited, I oiled the chain on the Goose. The weather was cold but fine; it would be warm today when the sun got up. I still wore my thermal gloves.

We were on the road earlier than usual; the agreed plan was to cycle to a town named Eads. The roads today stretched for mile upon mile across open plains and the roads were wide. I estimated the cars and trucks numbered around five an hour.

The trains were busy. I saw three trains pulling 100 rail wagons in one long, seemingly never-ending line; I may have missed one as I counted them. The railway lines followed the road. As the train passed, we all waved; the train driver let off a number of mournful hoots in recognition; it was a priceless sound.

Today I felt good whilst cycling; my rest day was but a dream. Grassland with the odd group of cattle started to appear. Marica punctured. With the deftness of a weightlifter she upended the bike, bags and all, and within half an hour she had repaired the puncture. Martin stood by, not offering any assistance, just taking all her actions for granted. I was speechless watching her. I congratulated her on her performance; she smiled. It pays sometimes to keep one's mouth closed. I'm glad to say I did.

It was late afternoon and in the distance we could see Eads. As we cycled into town, we were aware of the quietness and cleanliness. I saw a motel and booked in; the Goose was stabled in my room. My Dutch friends cycled on to the town campsite. In the late afternoon sun rays it was warm as I walked down the deserted street. The shop front doors were open, but no one was to be seen. The sidewalks, as Americans call them, were empty; there wasn't a single person. A pickup did pull up in front of a shop. The driver got out, disappeared into the shop, came out, jumped into the truck and was gone. What a way to shop. In my mind there was something missing; that human touch. It was not the first or last time I witnessed this in America. There was a supermarket. I bought my evening meal and tomorrow's breakfast, then retuned to the motel, washed all my clothes and cleaned the Goose. I'm glad to say the rear wheel was now mechanically sound; I heard no more cracking noises. I completed my daily log and rang Gill. I do miss her. 'Don't get homesick on me now, Mac,' said the Inner Man. I bagged up the Goose ready for an early start tomorrow morning. I thoroughly enjoyed my supermarket meal. I opened the Bible to an optimistic page and read. Good night.

America
Kansas

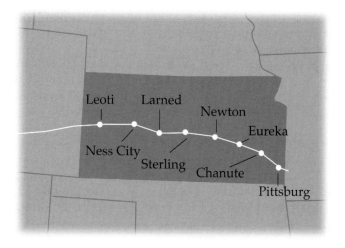

Leoti Larned Newton Eureka

Ness City Sterling Chanute

Pittsburg

As I glanced out of the window, the weather looked fine. There was a slight frost; this now seemed to be the norm. On a fine morning, one is guaranteed frost, or so it seems. I dressed in my thermals, just in case. I packed my washing into the panniers and the Goose was ready for the road. I ate my breakfast, washed down with tea, oiled the chain – the Goose looked spick and span – and was on the road. One or two pickups passed as I cycled to the campsite to meet my Dutch friends. They were on the ball, ready to go. We discussed the day's cycle and agreed we would try to reach Leoti. That meant we would be leaving Colorado and would cycle into the state of Kansas. When I looked out of the window this morning, I was not aware of the wind. It was strong and coming side-on.

The prairie stretched as far as the eye could see. I saw winter wheat growing. I stopped to watch a tractor and direct seeder working. I had never seen that before; it was very interesting. I don't know what was being planted, grass seed or corn. The tractor and seeder were both huge.

I saw it in the distance and my heart quickened pace. Well, I am a silly old oil man. It was an oil pump, or, as they call them in America, a 'donkey head'. The sight of it fascinated me. My Dutch friends must have thought I'd flipped my lid. I stopped and watched the non-stop action in wonder. This simple pump was the forebear of all the modern oil equipment. It was trouble-free and practicable, and unobtrusive even by today's standards. I'd never heard anyone complain about the unsightly oil pump. I thought the oil industry had something to learn from the old school. A lesson for those in today's industry; both living in harmony.

A passing train brought me back to my senses with two hoots of the whistle; priceless. I don't hear anyone complain about that noise pollution either. The trains were, and still are, the lorries of the prairie; it is the best form of transport. People ask me what I think about when I'm cycling every day. This chapter says it all; the mind and one's senses are priceless.

The weather had turned out grand. The sun was shining but it wasn't too hot; the wind had now subsided to a slight breeze. The weather could not be better if one planned it. In the far distance we could see Leoti. What was the difference between Colorado and Kansas? Nothing, as far as I could see. As we cycled into Leoti, we saw that it was a clean, above average town. I made up my mind to stay here tonight. I glanced at my cat eye computer; it read 81 miles.

For the first time I felt I was being held back by my Dutch friends;

I wanted to cycle alone again. I can't explain it. I enjoy cycling with them and they are good company, but I somehow felt restricted. I would speak to them in the next few days.

I checked into the nearest motel. No problem, the Goose was allowed in my room. The facilities were first class; the room was clean and the white bed sheets glistened. I showered and cleaned the Goose with the sponge and strong soap I bought in the supermarket. I also washed my day clothes. It's surprising the dirt one picks up on the road every day.

I shopped in the supermarket. I now knew the general lay out of the shelves; I was becoming an expert. I found shopping most nights in the supermarket made a break from the cycling; it was something different to do. Yes, I liked Leoti. What the name means I still don't know. Good night.

Leoti to Ness City

I spent a very quiet night after the noise of the train whistles the night before, and was up at my usual time – although the time zone had changed in Kansas and it was one hour ahead. I remembered to change my watch last night. The weather again looked fine; there was a wind, but from which direction? I'd know once I was outside. I ate my breakfast; yoghurt and fresh fruit. It was a change and I enjoyed it. I bagged up the Goose. My overnight washing was dry. I gave the Goose a visual mechanical check; all looked fine. I cycled to the campsite and there were my Dutch friends finishing packing the sleeping bags. We held a planning meeting and decided that we would try to reach Ness City. Within a quarter of an hour we were on the road. Despite the fine weather it was cold and the wind was fresh and veered from side to side. What were my first impressions of Kansas? VAST.

I thought I'd seen herds of cattle, but no, what I did see were cattle indeed, all penned up, and, at a guestimate, there must have been three to four thousand of them. They were fed from mobile feeder lorries, blowing the chopped food into troughs through adjustable auger heads. When we cycled by we could smell the feed and the cattle. I didn't find the smell obnoxious.

We stopped in a lay-by and ate our snacks; a mobile home was parked nearby. The driver came over and talked to us, wishing us a good day. He enquired where we had come from and where we were going. He spoke with authority on the different grasses on the roadside. The grasses are natural to Kansas and he explained the differences, picking a head of grass to demonstrate. The buffalo grass, apparently, has ten times more nutritional value in a bale than other grasses. There ended our science class. We thanked him and were on our way. One meets all kinds on the road.

Martin requested to ride point all day. So be it; I would tag along. What was now becoming apparent was that I was the dominant one on the hills; I had the legs of them both. I reasoned, rightly or wrongly, that at altitude Martin, being young, could outride me. I know that athletes train at altitude before big races and it helps them to win. The opposite was now apparent; I could ride the legs off Martin. I must admit, since coming out of the mountains, the hills seemed an easy ride. I felt fit and energetic and my stamina was high. I mention this as a matter of interest to others who have witnessed this phenomenon.

As we cycled, the oil donkey heads became more and more common. I was still enthralled to see them; they intrigued me. Marica punctured again. This time I offered to help, but she declined. Martin stood deadpan, his face showing no concern about her efforts to repair the puncture. She showed off her skills and never once complained or asked for help until she had masterfully finished the job. As she set the bike upright I applauded her; she did manage to smile.

It was late afternoon as we cycled into Ness City. It had seen better days. When the oil bubble burst, the city declined; it was one of the first places to feel the depression. Facilities were above the norm. The motel I booked into, for instance, had a swimming pool. The Goose was allowed in my room. My Dutch friends and I agreed to share in the cost of a combined meal. We ate it in the park. It was a beautiful evening and there was no rush; we could just sit and enjoy life and the good company. When I returned to the motel, I cleaned the Goose and checked out the tyres. I couldn't believe it - they were in such good condition. There were one or two small cuts, but nothing to warrant a tyre change. My cat eye had recorded 82 miles. I was one happy man. Good night.

Ness City to Larned

Early to bed, early to rise. I wasn't wealthy or monetary wise, but my head was a wealth of knowledge. You could call me, tongue in cheek, a wise old bugger. You live to learn; some say you never learn. That's only partly true.

As I got out of bed I checked on the weather through the window. I could see the trees bending; the wind was blowing strongly. The sky was clear and it looked cold. I ate my apple pie breakfast and drank my usual three cups of tea. I dressed warmly; it did look cold in that wind.

I bagged up the Goose, not forgetting my dry clothes, and checked the map. The nearest town was Larned.

When I cycled to the campsite my Dutch friends were packed and ready to go. We agreed that, with luck, today's cycle would be Larned. I oiled the chain as we were talking. It was soon very apparent that the wind was in our faces, but the traffic was again non-existent. Did anyone go to work? I never saw anyone.

Martin again volunteered to ride point; he was a glutton for punishment. I now answered to the name of Big Mac, and found it second nature to respond to it. The roads were slightly undulating, but mostly flat prairie plains. It was turning out to be a hard ride; no one laughed or joked today. All energy was required to cycle into the wind; it was a case of heads down, butts up.

This was a change – cultivated land started to appear. The fields were even fenced, though cattle were few and far between. My interest in old farm machinery was topped up for most of the day. It was apparently the 'in' thing to display old farm tractors, mainly outside farmhouses. I also saw the biggest combine harvester graveyard I had ever seen. Over one hundred in a group in a field. I took a photograph, but it was a bit too far away and didn't do it justice.

Young Martin was riding his butt off, but at one point he was noticeably slowing. This wind wasn't making our lives easy. I took over at point. We will earn every hard mile today. The only way to fight the wind is to lessen your exposed surface area; the other two tucked in behind for shelter. I kept up a good pace. It was a help when the wind wasn't gusting. Cattle, horses and people were as hard to see as hens' teeth. There was just no one there. It was as if one was riding back in time; it was strange.

It was late afternoon when we first saw Larned. Even from a distance it looked a fair size of a town. I could also see the McDonald's sign; it made my day. When we stopped we were wind-blown and thankful to have a rest. We enjoyed a snack to eat and a chat before splitting up for the night. I glanced at my cat eye computer; 65 miles. We earned every one today.

I had a choice of motels. I was ready for the home-spoilt feeling and chose a good class of motel. I checked in. Yes, they had a room and I could park the bike there. I showered, changed, and felt a new man. I asked the receptionist for directions to the supermarket. It was just up the road. I spoilt myself for an evening meal – ready-cooked chicken was on the menu tonight. I also bought my apple pie breakfast; I always find that these pies are fresh.

I needed to rub some cream on my face as the wind had burnt my skin. I thought I was weathered enough. I wrote my daily log.

As I rested on the bed I realised the room was, to say the least, above average. It's nice to spoil yourself now and again. I thumbed through the Bible I found in the drawer, thanks to the good old Gideons, and read a few pages of the good book at random. Good night.

Larned to Sterling

Last night I could hear the wind blowing outside, but as I lay in bed in the morning it was quiet. That's a good start anyway. I was soon on my feet and dressed. I glanced out the window; yes, it was dry. I bagged up the Goose and checked the tyres. All systems go. I ate my breakfast, washed down with tea, and checked my map. Sterling looked a fine day's cycle. I oiled the chain outside and set off to see my Dutch friends. They had overslept; the wind last night had kept them awake. They had not eaten breakfast. We all said it together: 'let's have breakfast at McDonald's.' It was agreed and within five minutes we were sitting down to egg and bacon, followed by tea. It set the mood for today. Everyone was smiling. We were an hour late getting under way. So what? We checked the map and agreed that Sterling was a good cycle today.

The weather was fine and cold; that strong wind had blown itself out. Traffic this morning was very light. If this was the rush hour, it was acceptable. As I exerted full pressure on the pedals, the rear wheel never cracked once. I'd given some thought to the rear wheel bearing problem, and concluded that one of the causes could have been the day I cycled through the mud in Thailand.

We were soon cycling through farm country. Corn was the main crop. In some fields it still needed to be harvested – I thought it was rather late. The area today proved to be of great interest to Martin and Marica. When I asked the reason, they said that this was where the first Dutch immigrants settled. It soon became apparent from the clean houses and well-kept gardens. My Dutch friends were also interested in the family names on local gravestones. They took some photos. As I waited, I smiled inwardly. I remember seeing a beautiful church with the graveyard situated on a high bank. With the hills and trees, it was very picturesque. A modest sign said, 'Sunnyside Church welcomes you all.' The road wound around the church and graveyard and came back out on to the main road. A big, blatant sign said, 'no entry'.

I was still enjoying my cycling. People might ask, 'aren't you fed up?' To be honest, no. I set myself a goal and I was enjoying seeing the new places and faces, as I've said before. Psychologically and physically it was top line.

In the afternoon dark clouds ominously rolled in. The sky was black and blue; it was just a question of when. The rain started slowly at first. I stopped and dressed in my wet gear, but my Dutch friends did not bother. Man, did it rain, and rain, and rain. At least it was warm; that was a help. As we rode into Sterling, the rain was running off my butt. I wished to be in Stirling, Scotland, but then I thought I'd also cycled through there in the rain. No real difference; it's all in the mind.

I'd had enough. We pulled off the road, and a motel appeared on the main road. I checked in and my Dutch friends also elected to stay there. The receptionist, or landlady, kept me in conversation for over half an hour. She was a widow in her late fifties. The motel complex was hers. Why do people always want to confide in me? It's not my angelic looks! As I say to my wife, who wants an old sixty year-old, with a grey thinning thatch like me? By the time we parted, I had partially drip-dried, resulting in the floor in front of reception being flooded. I paddled off to my room with the Goose in tow. My panniers were, to say the least, damn wet through. At least the plastic bags had saved the contents. I washed all my wet clothes and showered. The supermarket was across the road and I bought dinner and breakfast. I was fed, watered and warm; one contented, happy man. Good night.

Sterling to Newton

When I got up this morning the room was still warm, as I'd left the heater on to dry my clothes. I checked them out; they were dry. My pannier bags were also dry. I bought them on the understanding they were waterproof; I even waterproofed the seams. I ate my apple pie breakfast and drank four cups of tea. The tea bag was leached clean. The weather was cloudy but it wasn't raining. I bagged up the Goose and my Dutch friends and I walked out together. I oiled the chain and checked the map. Newton was agreed upon to be the cycle of the day.

The big faceless prairie changed to small well-cultivated fields. The grass fields were green and cows, pigs and horses became more plentiful. Here I was, halfway across America, but I'd seen more prime cattle in Orkney in one day than I'd seen here up till now. My favourite farm machines littered the farms. Oliver tractors must have been well-established in this area. While riding along on a slight incline, three lorries passed, nose to tail. One can forget the size of these great prairie hulks. I estimated their speed to be between 50 and 60 miles per hour. All three were high-sided and as they sped past, the forward wind pressure slowed me down to a virtual crawl. The third one stopped me; the air pressure held me as if in limbo. Air pressure entombed my very being, and then in seconds let go. A very strange feeling, to say the least. I remember the look of satisfaction on the driver's face – as if to say, 'you think that was bad? Wait until I've passed.' I have a name for those lorry drivers; I don't think it's printable. We cycled on, discussing the incident at a roadside café. It must have been the result of speed and the fact that there were three lorries in quick succession.

I bought a card and sent it to my dear wife. Martin planned to collect all his books tonight and post them off home; he was afraid they might get wet and spoiled. He also offered to post the maps I'd used up till now. I agreed to hand them over tonight. He said he would post them on to me at a later date. I'm still waiting, Martin.

Time was passing quickly, the miles were being covered at a fair pace. No rain or wind – just what makes a good cycling day. The sign said, 'Newton, pop. 16,332, All Services'. It also gave the police and sheriff's emergency phone numbers; very handy. I checked into the first motel along with the Goose; I've taken it for granted now that the Goose will be allowed in my room. No one ever complained and at least it's safe. I was sure I had a slow puncture. I pumped it up and made a mental note to check it later. I showered and completed my chores, and did my usual shopping. As I rested on the bed, I'd forgotten the slow puncture; I only remembered when I got up for a Jimmy Riddle about 0530 hours. I changed the tube there and then. The bed looked inviting. No, I decided against going back to bed. I ate breakfast and lost count of the number of cups of tea I drank. With my liquid intake, I must be related to a camel.

I was, as they say, fighting fit and raring to go; all my morning jobs were done. I had time, so I studied the map. In the past week, we had found instances of no road signs. The map might say to go for seven miles down a road then turn right, but if you don't check the miles from point to point, without signs one can very easily take a wrong turn. We also found roads closed with signs. It made me realise how easy it was to go wrong.

Newton to Eureka

I was outside the motel kicking my heels, showing my impatience to get going. The weather plays a big part in my cycling life. It is the first topic of the day for discussion, and it also controls forward planning. My Dutch friends arrived late. Never mind. The time was 0800 hours. We were on the road well before rush hour. There was a show of cars, but not too many. Today's plan was to cycle to Eureka. The name conjured up a few thoughts. We wished each other the compliments of the day as we headed off.

Today I enjoyed my cycle. The roads were well-maintained, sometimes flat, then undulating, and there were three steep hills which were very demanding. Some of the small towns we passed through showed no signs of human habitation, as we had seen previously. We now called them ghost towns. For the first time, we stopped to talk to two cyclists going in the opposite direction. They were Americans, cycling, like us, across country; they were hoping to make a church in Newton to spend the night. One produced an American flag. My mind did a boggle. He'd carried the flag this far west, he said, and asked if we would we put our signatures on the flag and pass it on to the next cyclists that we met. The flag was covered in signatures. We assured him we would pass it on. In his deep Texan drawl he wished us a safe journey; we did likewise. Martin stuffed the flag in his pannier. That's the last I saw of it. On the road you meet all kinds.

I was riding point today. Martin and Marica were both feeling the drag on the hills and I had to slow the pace. I had now been on the road for five months; they had only been going for six or seven weeks. I was more cycle fit than they were. Perhaps the enormity of the task was becoming more apparent to them - who knows? The day was a very demanding cycle.

As we rode into town I made a very lame joke. At the top of my voice I shouted 'Eureka!'. Marica smiled. Martin asked me the mileage of the day. I glanced at my ever-ready cat eye; it read 81 miles. I was a happy man. My Dutch friends elected to tent out for the night and cycled on for the campsite. I booked in the nearest motel to the town centre. I showered and washed my clothes. The heated drier was handy; it dried my clothes and kept me warm at the same time.

That evening I went with Martin and Marica for a pint of beer in the nearby pub. This was the first pub I'd been to in America. It was also the first time I'd drunk in a morgue. It was dark and dreary, as if no one wanted to be seen drinking. One pint and we were out; I never went into an American pub again. The evening meal was again from the supermarket; a chicken and pasta ready-cooked meal. It was good. I'd now concluded that supermarket meals were cheaper and superior to a restaurant. The weather had noticeably turned cold; there was wind and sleet, and snow was evident. What would tomorrow bring? I wrapped myself in blankets and hibernated for the night. I thought I might hear a knock on the door from Martin and Marica, and decided they could sleep on the floor in their sleeping bags if they came for shelter. Good night.

Eureka – rest day

I was awake early and cleaned the window with a sweep of my hand, peering out. It was still dark but the street lights gave a good indication of the weather. 'No cycling today,' I said to myself. Everywhere was coated in snow; it was blowing and sleet was evident. My first thoughts of the day went to Martin and Marica, tenting out in this weather – what a way to spend the night.

I ate my breakfast, drank my tea and watched some TV. At least I was in the warm. Martin and Marica arrived on their bikes; they came into my room visibly shivering. Marica's teeth were chattering. 'We left the tent where it is – we're not riding today. Are you?' he asked. 'No,' I said, 'not in this weather. I'll call it a rest day.' They agreed, smiling, and I offered the room's facilities. 'The shower will warm you up,' I said, handing Marica a clean towel. They both accepted the offer of the warm shower. I made some tea and we all sat down and watched TV, paying particular attention to the weather forecast. As the daylight came in, it unveiled a winter scene.

The shower brought colour to their cheeks and a warm smile. I made the motel room available to them for the rest of the day. We all went to a nearby café for breakfast, my second, and thoroughly enjoyed the food. I bought some post cards and dutifully sent them off to Gill, Karen, Alison and Stuart.

Across the road, there was a museum. We decided to visit. It was small, but informative. The elderly gentleman who, we were told, just happened to be there, gave us an educational tour. I must be old; the items on display were ones I was familiar with. I smiled to myself. Indian relics were also displayed. As he said, with a smile, there were more flint arrowheads than arrows; people make them to sell to the tourists. He pulled himself upright as he said, 'these are my medals, Second World War; that's my Purple Heart – any American wounded in battle is decorated with the Purple Heart.' I felt proud of him. He had lived to tell the tale. One lives to learn.

The weather never lifted. There were sleet and snow showers all day and it was so cold. We had made the right decision. I caught up on my outstanding jobs – cleaned the Goose and washed some clothes. I visited the bank and changed some money into dollars. I also patched my cycling shorts, which were, at last, showing signs of wear. Talking of wear, I only had one pair of shoes which I wore at all times; Shimano cycle shoes. They had also walked a few miles. My cycle gloves stood all the washing and hard wear; one pair only. I could not honestly criticise my cycling gear in any way. My tyres were still rideable. Continental touring tyres: there can't be better on today's market; they are the greatest.

A rest day passes all too soon as there is so much to catch up on. Rightly or wrongly, my Dutch friends decided to spend the night in their tent. They said it was dry. I just shiver at the thought; rather them than me. I bought a supermarket meal. Some supermarkets sold single items of cooked food; collectively they made a good meal, and I didn't forget my breakfast.

The heater in my room was first class; it kept the room and me warm. As I relaxed on the bed I read my good old friend the Gideons Bible. Many people ask if I am religious. My answer is always the same: no – but the Bible has good stories. Good night.

Eureka to Chanute

I woke and looked expectantly out of the motel window at the new day. The sleet and snow were gone. There was no wind, but a heavy frost. I made up my mind that yes, I would cycle. There was no hesitation. I dressed in my thermals. What washing! I packed it in plastic bags, sealing the ends, and bagged up the Goose. The road was traffic-free. I oiled the chain. After a rest day I'm always doubly wanting to be on the road; today was no exception. I ate my apple pie breakfast and drank my tea. My friends were late; I went looking for them at the campsite. All was white with frost, including their tent; it was frozen solid. After a long struggle, we managed to pack it. I was getting cold through lack of cycling. They both looked cold and sorry for themselves. I again vowed never to tent. We didn't stand on ceremony thinking and discussing the day's route; we jumped on our bikes and headed for the nearest roadside café and ate breakfast, my second. So what.

I felt human. It must have made my Dutch friends' day, the warmth of the café, the food and hot drink; they work magic. Within ten miles of cycling I was again cold, especially my feet and hands. I had never been so cold before my 'big C' operation. I wonder if it's my age?

By 11 o'clock it was the opposite; the sun was shining and I had removed some of my thermal gear. The slippery road had changed; the sun had melted the frost. What I saw next I just couldn't believe. After all that cold and frost, the road was now covered in caterpillars of all things; there were thousands and thousands of them. They were all colours: green, red, brown, black. Some were smooth-bodied, others were hairy. The ground was a cascade of moving colours. The next mile the road was now covered in crickets, in their hundreds of thousands. They sounded like one-string fiddles. As we cycled through them, I'm sure the hum of my tyre on the road attracted them. They would leap with such energy at the wheel, only to be chopped up by the spokes.

The dead crickets collected in the brakes; we had to stop and clean them out of the brake blocks.

With the roads now clear of frost we could cycle freely. What a difference. Mile followed mile, the sun was on our backs and life felt good. I couldn't think of anything better to do or anywhere else to be. I was feeling strong; the unscheduled rest day had filled me with energy. We could see the town of Chanute in the far distance. Soon it was upon us; a small clean town with facilities. Martin announced they were stopping there for the night. He wanted to erect the tent to dry it out in the sun. It was understandable, but I did so want to cycle on and cover more miles that day. We had already had a taste of the weather to come and there was a long way still to cycle. I reluctantly agreed. What was the mileage today? I glanced at my cat eye computer; only 66 miles. 'Smile, Mac,' said the Inner man, 'it could have been snow.' I booked into the nearest motel. There was no problem with the Goose, it was allowed in my room. My room was clean; I must give credit where it's due. The small motel rooms in America were usually clean, and credit cards were accepted most of the time.

Again I ate supermarket food of a high standard. I enjoyed my chicken, coleslaw and wedges and completed all my chores. As I rested on my bed I studied the maps. I was unhappy with our progress; I felt we were slowing up. With the end of September approaching, October would soon be here. Time was getting precious. Good night.

Chanute to Pittsburg

As I got up, my first instinct was to pull back the curtain and check the weather. There was no snow; the sky was clear and there was a covering of ground frost. I felt the tension release through my shoulders. I dressed in my thermals, bagged up the Goose and checked the tyre pressures. All systems go. I made my tea and ate my apple breakfast. My Dutch friends met me at an arranged road junction. We checked the maps and agreed to cycle to Pittsburg.

Cycling was cold. There was no wind, but I was hoping the sun would shine later in the morning. As we turned a right-hand bend, we increased our pace and really got into our stride. At this point, we were ambushed by five ferocious dogs; the nearest thing to a pack of wolves. They were full of confidence and fight. What a scatter. Three of them were on Marica; she was shouting louder than the dogs could bark. I ran into one with his teeth in Marica's pannier. I swiped another on the nose with my pump; I think his eyes touched. By now we were all off our bikes. The dogs disappeared as if by magic. No one was hurt or had been bitten by the dogs, though I must admit that we were all in slight shock. We were also lucky that no traffic passed during the fracas. Marica was understandably upset; she was shaking. We stopped and checked out our bags and bikes and caught our breath at the same time. What a start to the day. A dog dazer, a dog dazer, my kingdom for a dog dazer. My dog dazer was at home. Was this the sign of more to come?

Navigational problems. What next? It was turning out to be one of those mornings. There were no road signs. By the way, I can be quite thick at times. The yellow road sign showed an adult holding a child by the hand; it was on a yellow background with the words 'X ING'. It nearly had to bite me for me to realise what it was conveying.

As we cycled on, we soon got into our stride again. The sun came out. We were cycling through farming country with cultivated fields. We came across a field of sunflowers in full bloom; what a beautiful sight. I stopped to take a photo. It was late afternoon when we cycled into Pittsburg. It was a fairly big town with all modern facilities. We were ready for a stop; we had enough highlights to remember this day. As my Dutch friends were tenting, they had to inform the sheriff's office where their tent was. This was a safety measure so that the police could check to see if they were OK.

I checked into a motel of a high standard. I also parked the Goose in my room. I showered, changed into clean clothes, washed my day clothes and put them out to dry. I cleaned the Goose and checked it over mechanically before walking to the supermarket in the direction the receptionist told me. I was feeling strong, fit and well; my health could not be in better shape. I took a vitamin tablet. I must be feeding myself correctly. I ate some tinned mackerel. I eat it most days; if I eat any more I'll grow fish fins. I do like it, that's my problem. I relaxed on the bed. It was a well-decorated room with all facilities. I studied the maps. I was nearly in the state of Missouri. What was that song? 'Got a penny for a poor little robin, walking, walking, walking to Missouri, he can't afford to ride....' and so it goes on. What a doggone day. Good night.

America
Missouri

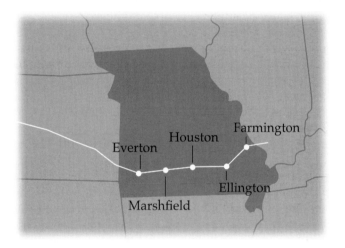

Everton · Houston · Farmington

Marshfield · Ellington

Kansas had come and gone. I was awake at my usual time and glanced out of the window. The weather looked fine; a slight frost. I dressed in my thermals, boiled the water for my tea and ate my apple breakfast. I bagged up the Goose and was soon outside waiting for my friends. I oiled the chain on the Goose as I waited. It was cold. There was no wind and the sky was clear; it had the makings of a good day. It was too early for the rush hour. One or two cars passed, but otherwise the road was quiet. I now wore my thermal socks at all times; when it warmed up, I only changed my thermal vest and gloves.

We were soon enjoying our early morning cycle. The hills came too quickly; hill followed hill. Both Martin and Marica were complaining. I was riding point. We were all, as they say, under the stick. Martin was getting frustrated with himself for not being able to keep up. Marica shed a little tear and I changed down a gear and set a slower pace. It was late morning when we cycled into Gold City. Better than finding gold, we found a roadside café and were inside in a flash. I have never seen the like: homemade fruit pies, individual ones; I counted over twelve different varieties. One pie was the equivalent of four small ones. I could see the pastry was done to a turn. I even toyed with the idea of buying one for my evening meal but had second thoughts; it would soon break up on the bike. The morning break was what we needed. We were all fed with first class food; it gave us our second wind.

We were now on undulating roads. The surrounding country was well-farmed. Even small fields were to be seen near the road. Vintage tractors again stood pride of place outside the farmhouses. Animals were few and far between and birds were a rarity. I could see more birds in Orkney in a morning than I'd seen halfway across America.

We found ourselves cycling through the small town of Everton. It was late afternoon and the sun was shining. Into view came a big period mansion house with a sign saying: 'Everton Continental Bed and Breakfast'. A big red rose was painted in the right-hand corner of the sign.

The house was open-fronted with verandas upstairs and down. The trees surrounding the house and lawns completed the scene. We virtually said it together: 'let's see if we can stay here tonight.' On the front door was a phone number to ring. We found a phone booth and rang the number. 'I'll be there in a minute,' the guy said. 'I only live down the road. And yes, the house is available for accommodation tonight.' We waited at the front door. The guy arrived and let us in. The owner was away on holiday and he was the guy in charge. We asked the cost. 'Thirty dollars.' We paid him there and then. This was a find.

We looked around the house like children exploring a castle for the first time. It had five bedrooms and was full of antiques. Each bedroom had a different colour scheme and everything matched. I felt fully relaxed in the house. Martin flew the American flag from the veranda flagpole. The house was stacked with books; Martin was like a kid with a new toy. He held one book in his hand as he read another. My room was downstairs; Martin and Marica chose to sleep upstairs.

After my shower we walked down to a supermarket and bought our evening meal and I also bought tomorrow's breakfast. My bed was the most comfortable yet; I just sank in the featherdown underlay. Sixty-six miles today. So what. Good night.

Everton to Marshfield

Last night I slept like a log. As I lay in bed I felt relaxed. 'Move your butt, Mac – time to get up.' I checked the weather through the window before dressing. It was a fine day. The branches on the trees were not moving, so there was no wind, only a slight frost. I dressed in my thermals. It was strange to be in a house. I went to the kitchen. A selection of cereals was in the cupboard and there was milk in the fridge. I boiled the kettle and made tea. My, this was just like home. As I finished breakfast, Marica appeared. She looked a bit sombre, I thought. She looked at me, shy-like, and said, 'we are staying another night – are you?' I thought about it. To my mind it was the loss of another day. 'No,' I said, 'I'm cycling on.' Marica said that Martin wanted to stay and read books. So be it, I thought, I'm not my brother's keeper.

I bagged up the Goose and oiled the chain. Martin and Marica were there to see me off. We had been together for quite a number of days. We had grown to know each other's moods; our likes and dislikes; our family backgrounds; what we did and where we lived. We said our farewells. I shook Martin's hand and Marica kissed me on the cheek. I could see a tear in the corner of her eye. I was on the Blue Goose and away. I waved a few times; Marica ran after me shouting and waving. All good things come to an end, as they say. They had been the best friends a man could ever want. Again, I'd like to say many thanks both – I'll never ever forget either of you.

The realisation came at the first crossroads. Map out: which way? I smiled. I was now on my own again. I felt, with all due respect, liberated. I'd wanted my freedom for a while. One can get too involved in someone else's business. I'm sure at times I walked, or rode, a knife edge between the two. I wondered if I would ever see them again.

It rained in the late morning, one or two showers, then stayed overcast and mild. The roads were quite narrow and cars were few and far between. The surrounding land was made up of small fields. I smiled; there were even hedges surrounding some of them. Some woodland now dotted the faraway landscape. Cattle were few. I was soon back into my old ways of cycling alone. I had a good choral morning, singing at the top of my voice. That's a good sign of happiness. I was faced with some steep hills. I pride myself on my ability to cycle hills. Today I got off the Goose twice, and walked; lesson learned. 'Never criticise others,' said the Inner Man. I found it strange cycling along the road with hedges and trees; it felt hemmed in after the open prairie of Kansas. Through persistence I won the day. In the distance I could see Marshfield. I was enjoying my cycle, but at times today the going was tough.

As I cycled into Marshfield I was spoilt for motels. I booked into an above-average motel with a bath. Why not? That's the way I felt. The Goose was allowed in my room. I ran the bath full, slipped in and relaxed; the warm water revitalised me. It removed some of my cycling pains of the day; most enjoyable. It did occur to me to eat tonight in a restaurant, but I changed my mind and walked to the local supermarket. What a choice of ready-cooked meals. What did the sign say? Eight pieces of chicken for two dollars, 99 cents. Eight pieces? That would be too much for me. The chicken, I must admit, did look good. 'How much are two pieces?' I asked the girl behind the counter. 'Two dollars, 66 cents,' came the reply. Crazy, I thought – but then the world is crazy. 'I'll take eight pieces, please,' I said. As I walked away, I wondered who was going to eat all that chicken. 'Guts,' said the Inner Man. I smiled as I walked back to my motel. Good night.

Marshfield to Houston

I was up at my usual time and glanced out of the window; thick fog. I decided it would not be safe to cycle. I'm sure it will lift when the sun gets up. I dressed and ate my breakfast slowly. I thought back to last night, remembering my chicken dinner. I slowly managed to eat five pieces, and ate a sixth piece with determination. If I ate more I'd be flying today. I finished off with ice cream and was as full as a bug. I couldn't wait to get on the road to use up all that stored energy. Within two hours the fog had lifted enough for me to cycle. I oiled the Goose outside and cycled up a somewhat quiet street. The rush hour had come and gone; that's a change.

As the sun's rays increased, the fog lifted. I was late on the road but it was better safe than sorry. I enjoyed cycling through the farms and fields; I could have been anywhere. It reminded me of Pembrokeshire in Wales. I was slowly climbing a steep hill; there was a farm on the roadside near the hilltop. They came out from behind the farm building like two stealth fighters, keeping low but moving fast; two black-and-white sheep dogs. They made no noise. When cycling you can keep your eye on one dog, but with two you don't stand a chance. They positioned themselves at the rear of the Goose as if trained, then each one grabbed a pannier apiece and swung themselves bodily in the air, still holding on to the pannier bags. Have you seen a sheep dog chasing cattle? They grab the cow's tail and hold on with their teeth and swing. This is what they did. I shouted and tried my best to deter them. They went one way, I went the other, and the Goose crashed in a heap. I was lying on my back. As I glanced across at the Goose, I could see the two dogs skulking back to the farm. At least they left me alone, and thank goodness for quiet roads. 'Get up and move your butt,' said the Inner Man. I was lying on my back looking at the sky. 'Thanks,' I said. 'Someone up there loves me.'

I rolled over. I was shaken, but my helmet and cycle gloves had saved me. I checked myself; I was not hurt, thank goodness. I righted the Goose. The rear pannier was hanging off, the brake lever was out of place and the handlebars were twisted out of true. The rear panniers had again saved the derailleur gears. I checked out the wheels and spokes, reset the brake lever and the handlebars and refitted the panniers. I got off lightly; still no vehicle passed. As I walked to the top of the hill, I was aware I was still being observed and stalked by the two farm dogs. They were running back and forth in a threatening manner, as if to say, 'we sorted you out, Boyo.'

I was feeling all right – no shock. I must be honest – I don't like dogs when cycling. I won't be the first or last to say that. Missouri turned out to be dog country. Every farm and house had a dog; there were all sizes and breeds. As you cycled on, one dog's bark alerted the dog next door or down the road, as if to say, 'be on your guard, someone strange is coming.' All dogs have their personal territory to guard. A strong, direct command can turn a dog. I've proved that. If you show fear, you pay the price. Look them straight in the eye. I was back on the road; the Goose was handling fine, no mechanical funny noises.

The road was a roller coaster; as soon as you were up, you were going down. I saw a snake and a tortoise on the side of the road. I kept away from the snake; it had beautiful markings. The tortoise I lifted off the road and headed it the same way I was heading – Houston. I was soon cycling into Houston and was again lucky to find a good class of motel. The Goose was allowed in my room. The sheets were clean and the bed soft. The repetition of one's actions when cycling every day comes naturally: hygiene, bike, food, bed, rest. That's only in the motel; the road rules of survival are different. Good night.

Houston to Ellington

I was awake at my usual time and looked out of the window – I should say I failed to see out of the window; everything was painted in white frost. There were even frost patches on the road. I dressed in my thermals. My – I was thankful I'd purchased the right gear for a cold job. It was 0715 hours. I finished my breakfast, drank my tea, bagged the Goose and oiled the chain outside. I would need to take care for the first few hours, until the sun came up and thawed the frost. Autumn was upon us; the leaves from the trees fell like confetti. I thought I might be stiff after yesterday's fall with the dogs. My ankle was a little stiff, but not really bad. I also thought I might have seen Martin and Marica, but not a sighting. My plan today was to try to cycle to Ellington, roughly 70 or 80 miles away.

What a start. Hills followed hills. It was cold; even through my thermals I could still feel it. There were some patches of fog, but they cleared when the sun warmed up. Farmland and forests were now common; in some places the roads were lined with trees. There were dogs, dogs and more dogs, at every house, every farm. At one farm a rottweiler dog came bounding across the lawn in front of the farmhouse. The dog was about six months old and weighed in at about 10 stone. 'Jesus loves me, yes I know,' I started to sing. I thought I was going to lose an arm or a leg. He bounded up to me; I spoke to him. He did nothing; it was a stand-off.

I was now giving as much as I was taking – and holding my own. It spoilt my cycling; one was surviving until the next dog. Oh! Look at the size of that one. Ride softly, that one is sleeping on the veranda. Some sleeping dogs would wake, look at me, and go back to sleep, just too dog-tired to move. Yes. I know the saying well: let sleeping dogs lie.

I was riding up one of the many steep hills of the day. What was that on top of the hill? Dogs. About five of them. I could see two were sitting and three were standing. That's all I need – a pack of wild dogs. I stopped and caught my breath. What's best to do? I asked myself. Am I going to turn back? Turn back where? Am I going to turn back with every dog I see? As I got closer I could make out two Alsatians, one Great Dane and three 'Heinz 57' breeds. No, I was not going to turn back; I made up my mind. I cycled towards them apprehensively. My awareness was on full red alert, plus. I was ready for anything. As I rode up to them, the three sitting did not even look at me. The two Alsatians just glanced, as if to say, 'we've seen it all before.' The Great Dane sniffed the air. Perhaps he didn't like my aftershave? I cycled on, my butt dry and clean.

I was now cycling in farm country. I came across an accident; two pickups, both women drivers. One was coming out of a farm road on to the main road; the other woman smashed into her. Two mangled vehicles. The women looked OK, if a bit sheepish. I couldn't understand – the road was so open and there was no obstruction. Just a case of not looking, I guess. I turned a corner and there in the field was a herd of white Charolais cows. It was a grand sight. Among the herd was a white mule, or was it a donkey? I couldn't make up my mind. Never a dull moment on the road; one sees life as it's played.

There it was before me in all its glory: Ellington. I glanced at the cat eye computer. It said 72 miles – dog miles. I was pleased. I had arrived in one piece. It had been a tough day in the saddle.

I booked into a motel and the Goose was allowed in my room. I cleaned it there and then. I washed my cycling clothes and showered. To me, that's the way to finish a day – with a shower. I walked to the supermarket and could feel the tiredness in my legs as I walked. I wondered why. Am I paranoid about dogs? No, I love them. Sleeping. Good night.

Ellington to Farmington

I was awake and out of bed and checked the weather. It was frosty, so I dressed in my thermals. I ate my breakfast and drank my tea, then bagged up the Goose. I thought I'd be stiff today, but I wasn't. I must have cycled it out yesterday. I must admit, I did have a few bruises in various places. As I opened the motel door, the cold air engulfed me. I oiled the Goose and we were under way. A few cars and pickups sped by, not in any numbers.

Today will be my last day in Missouri; tomorrow I cross into Illinois. I was looking forward to seeing the great Mississippi River. Looking back on the last two days of cycling, it had been quite demanding in the virtually continuous hill country. Today was no exception. By mid-morning the sun was beaming down. I changed back into my normal cycle clothes; one's actions are not so restricted in them.

I cycled in hill country for most of the day. It requires positive thinking to cycle continuously, hour after hour, in the demanding hill conditions. The scenery helps to hold one's attention. The odd dog wished me the time of day. There was a change of scenery: farms and the occasional house made an appearance. As I cycled, my inventive mind was toying with the idea of devising a dog-scarer for cyclists. The propellant would be party poppers, fitted into either two or four plastic tubes, fitted to the front or rear of the bike. The party popper drawstrings would be drawn together into one pull cord, operated by the cyclist when threatened by dogs. The theory is that dogs do not like fireworks. If you make one, please let me know if it works. I know what you dog lovers are saying; I can hear you now. I also love dogs.

I was thinking again about my Dutch friends; I'd still had no sighting. The sign post said 'Farmington'. It was a very large town, larger than the norm. I cycled through the outskirts making for the centre. It was a clean and well laid-out town. I stopped to check my map. I thought it better to find my road out of town, and if there was a motel there it would save me cycling through town in the morning rush hour. I found towns and cities in America very easy to navigate, as long as one kept to the main street. All other streets branching off were well sign-posted.

I did find a motel. It was a higher class than I usually stay in; it made no difference, the Goose was allowed in my room. It's nice to spoil yourself now and again. I even booked the restaurant for my evening meal. My only pair of shoes were demanding to be cleaned, which I did using shampoo from the bathroom. 'Don't use too much water on the shoes,' said the Inner Man. The power shower was good – it helped me concentrate the hot water on my aches and pains. It was like being hit by a wave. The motel room was warm and cosy. The Goose looked clean so I put that job on a by-pass, washed my cycle clothes and put them on the radiator to dry. I ate my evening meal in the restaurant, to be sociable. You can talk to yourself if you don't mix. I enjoyed the meal and the staff company; service with a happy smile. On returning to my room, I relaxed on the bed, put on the TV, and watched the revealing O.J. Simpson soap opera. Good night.

America
Illinois

What changeable weather. As I glanced out of the window, the sun was shining and there was no frost to be seen. I dressed in my normal cycling gear. I bagged up the Goose, made a cup of tea and ate my apple breakfast. As I met the day through the motel door I could already feel the heat. I oiled the chain. I was in need of a new can of oil; I made a mental note. There was a slight breeze. That was good – later in the day it would keep me cool. As I cycled past a roadside café I could smell the freshly-baked bread. I stopped and bought two blueberry cakes for later in the day.

I cycled for Murphysboro. I soon saw the big Mississippi River. (It's one of the things I remember about school; we were taught how to spell Mississippi.) The morning traffic was building up as I approached the bridge over the river. A pickup towing a trailer was coming in the opposite direction. There was a clattering noise as he drew close to me, and a bang as the trailer hit the road. The wheel flew past me at a great rate of knots. That was too close for comfort; my senses were now on red alert. The road slightly narrowed as I cycled over the bridge; I was being hemmed in. When you've covered as many miles as I have and witnessed so many road accidents, survival becomes a way of life. You become road-wise. It reminds me of a war film I saw. It portrayed a young soldier in a trench in the First World War. This was his second year of fighting in the trenches; he was what you would call a survivor. Yet in an unguarded act of tenderness on seeing a blue spring flower and a butterfly landing on the flower, the young soldier moved to have a better view, and was shot. We all have our strengths and weaknesses. I am morbid today.

I stopped in a lay-by and surveyed the unfamiliar scene. Never in my wildest dreams did I think I'd cycle over the great Mississippi River. I was, to say the least, thrilled. I was now in the state of Illinois. My! The quickness of time; it matches the mileage. The road sign said 'the people of Illinois welcome you.' (Ten yards down the road, on the same side, a big green sign said: 'Route 3, Health Centre, Penitentiary.' Do you think they got it right? I don't.)

I was now out of the hills and cycling on the plains. It was hard, but rewarding. I was closely following the map. I saw a very light green coloured snake crossing the road. It stopped. 'Thanks,' I said. I also saw a stick insect, almost indistinguishable from a normal piece of stick. Nature never ceases to amaze me.

Yes, some dogs made my day; it must be localised to this area. It's definitely not recommended for family cycling. I'm having problems every day: dogs. Yesterday I fought off two packs; today I fought off one pack. The thing is, they go for you in packs of three or four. Not for the faint-hearted.

Murphysboro. I cycled through to find a motel. As I went along, a pickup slowed down, the window opened and a sour puss of a girl with a hissing voice said, 'You shouldn't ride in town.' I was getting used to verbal abuse from young women. It was always a young woman. I'd see them pass, slow down, open their windows and wait for me, then say in a nasty voice, 'Keep your distance, man.' What did I reply? Words I'd hiss back in my best English, with a touch of temper. I'd bark like a dog. 'Don't antagonise the locals,' said the Inner Man. 'Bow wow to you,' I replied, with a smile. I booked in the motel. I'd seen a KFC restaurant down the road. Five dollars, I ate my fill. I returned to the motel and showered, I also cleaned the Goose and washed my clothes. The girl drivers were as bad as the dogs. Ninety miles today. Good night.

Murphysboro to Elizabethtown

I was up with the birds. What birds? I never see any. I dressed in my ordinary cycling clothes; the day looked fine out of the window. I ate breakfast and drank my tea. I always carried double water bottles, filled with fresh water. I bagged up the Goose and opened up the motel door to greet a new day. I oiled the chain with what was left of the oil. I had forgotten to buy another; so much for my mental note.

A man who had just left the motel approached me. We exchanged morning greetings. 'Cycling far?' he asked. 'Virginia,' I replied. 'My, that's some ride,' he said. As we talked he asked where I was from. 'Orkney Islands,' I replied. He shook me by the hand and said, 'My name is McKay, I have relatives in Orkney.' It is a small world.

I had the map out; this was a navigational ritual when leaving town, to find the right road. I was soon heading out of town. It was mixed cycling country; hills were hard to find and the roads were flat as they pushed on through farmland. Three times this morning farm dogs tried to get the better of me, with no success. Trees became plentiful along the road; the autumn colours in the bright sunshine were dazzling. The leaves were red, brown, gold, yellow, green; they danced and shimmered in the sun. Some were dropping through the sky like confetti. One of my sixth senses twitched. What was wrong? I was on the wrong road. Out with the map. I was not that far out, but never have I been so taken with cycling that I took the wrong turn. Five miles out; five miles back: that's ten non-productive miles. Get a grip, Mac. As I said yesterday, one moment's lack of concentration and you pay the price. I studied the map. The sign I'd been looking for had been partially   233 covered. I headed down through a secondary road and a forest. Excuses, excuses. I was back on track, lesson learned. The mistake meant that I arrived in Elizabethtown at dusk. It had been a hard cycle; my cat eye recorded 106 miles. I'd had what they say in America, a good day.

A very well-kept period mansion was a hotel, the River Rose Inn. I tapped on the door. 'Have you a room, please?' 'Yes, we have accommodation,' said a very nice lady, smartly dressed. Her blonde hair was tied back and her blue eyes sparkled. 'I have a secure lock-up garage for the bike,' she said. 'Good night, Blue Goose,' I said to myself as I locked the garage door. I carried my panniers. I was tired. 'Would you like a nice glass of iced beer?' she asked. I thought I was hearing things. She held a clear crystal glass under a barrel tap. 'Now, how does my husband say to do it?' she said. It looked cool. 'There you are,' she said with a smile, handing me the glass of beer. 'Thank you,' I said. As it hit my hollow legs I thought it was indeed the nectar of the gods. Apparently her husband brewed his own beer. I was being spoilt again. Nothing stranger than folk.

'You have a choice of rooms,' she said, as I put down my empty glass. She handed me the hotel brochure. There were five bedrooms, all different and all colour-coded. I settled for the Rose Room. The Scarlet Room, the Captain's Room, the Blue Room and the Magnolia Room were also on offer. My room was described as being a quaint dream bedroom, with private entrance and patio and a Queen's bed. She led me to the Rose Room. 'I'll give you this room at a very reduced rate, as you're cycling our country,' she said. 'Many thanks,' I said, wondering what the reduced rate might be. 'I'll give you a third off the price,' she added. On the door it said 'Rose Room'. She took me in and explained the workings of the room and where I could get an evening meal. She also gave me a time for breakfast in the morning. I thanked her.

I lay on the bed in utter relaxation. If I had shut my eyes I would have fallen asleep. 'Move your butt, Mac,' said the Inner Man. I was soon showering; I was in need of that. There was a heater in the room, so I put my washed clothes there to dry. I changed into my clean clothes. The creases told the story. As Gill says, 'Mac, you can't fold your clothes properly.' I must admit she is right, as usual. I do miss Gill. I wish she was with me tonight. 'Don't overdo it or you'll have me crying in a minute,' said the Inner Man.

I felt a new man. I was hungry. Where did she say the restaurant was? Out through the door, turn right, then right again. I looked back at the house. My, it was beautiful to say the least, and above average; I would say five stars. There was the restaurant. The sign above the door read: 'fish our speciality. Eat all you want.' What's the catch? I said to myself and smiled at my own joke. It was a river boat, a floating restaurant. I'm in – that's for me. On the gangplank I missed the second step, stumbling against the door, which opened. I fell in. I've seen that look before: 'is he pissed?' I smiled that sober smile; the exchange smile was returned. 'Yes Sir, we do have a table.' In my defence, the steps outside were poorly lit.

I was handed the menu. Every conceivable fish was available. I settled for a red snapper. What was that fish anyway? It soon arrived, filling the plate; the veg and brownies were in separate dishes. I was now settled. I looked around the restaurant. It was full; that was a good sign. Half the guys wore their hats; cowboy hats and baseball hats. I really enjoyed my fish supper. The guy next to me had his fill; he was on his fourth plate-full. The waitress asked if I wanted more. I declined. There was a look of amazement on her face. I finished off with a small sweet and a drink of Pepsi. This was a well-run restaurant; something different. It had a charm all of its own. I enjoyed it. Many thanks.

As I left I took care crossing the gangplank. The lights flickered on the river. I made my way back to the hotel. It was Saturday night and the evening was warm. I felt very relaxed. On the veranda was – what was her name? Come on, Mac, you're not the best at remembering names. Elizabeth. I said good evening. She got out of her chair and introduced me to her husband. The golden lab dog sniffed me, giving me a look of approval.

I was invited to sit on the veranda in a relaxing chair. As we talked, I was asked if I would like a glass of beer. Being never one to refuse such an offer, I said yes. It made my day. An hour-and-a-half later, I wished mine hosts goodnight, thanking them for the beer. I patted the dog on the head and retired to the Rose Room. I was tired. I was soon tucked up in bed, in another world. Good night.

America

Kentucky

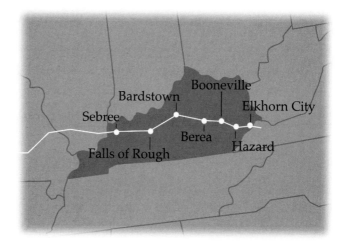

I woke, checked my watch, and was soon out of bed and dressed. I'd overslept by an hour. I can't remember a thing. I slept last night as if I'd been pole-axed. 'Breakfast?' said Elizabeth, as I entered the breakfast room. The table laid out for me was fit for a king. What makes a good meal? It's the way the table is laid, the food presented and the person's attitude. These collective points, and the fact that the background here was above the norm, all add up to an above average meal. I settled for a veg omelette, orange juice, fresh fruit, tea and toast. What a breakfast; the best by far. I thanked Elizabeth. Keep up the standard, folks – it's places like this that make you homesick. The reality of the day returned quickly when I bagged up the Goose. No oil. I was soon cycling down the road. The weather was fine and the traffic light. At least something was in my favour.

Elizabeth showed me a route that ran alongside the great river. I stopped for a photo call. On the river was a long barge being towed by a small tug boat. I suppose the river is different from the sea. As I cycled I had that over-full feeling; I'd soon ride it off. So this was the great Ohio River. On the river bank was a cluster of houses and jutting out into the river was a small jetty. From here, the boat crossed to the other side. It was now on its return journey. Four elderly gentlemen, well dressed (it was Sunday), sat at a provided picnic table. I bade them good morning and we chatted about the ferry and the surrounding countryside. The talkative one of the group told me that the ferry was free, paid for by the two states, Kentucky and Illinois.

I wished them good day as the ferry arrived at the slip. We were all soon aboard and on our way. It was very quick and efficient. A quarter of an hour; that's all the time it took. We were soon disembarking in the state of Kentucky. The weather was overcast but warm. Two cars and two pickups also drove off the ferry. I was soon cycling inland; the Blue Goose was flying. I could have been anywhere in Britain: fields, cattle, houses. I'd been later getting under way. I felt sluggish. 'That's what comes from being spoilt,' said the Inner Man. I looked at my map and decided to cycle to Sebree.

As I cycled in Kentucky I had that euphoric feeling. I was achieving something; I was making headway. I was back in control. It's a great feeling when one only hangs on without too much effort. As I cycled I found it strange to see goods for sale beside the road. The goods, mostly second-hand, were laid out on tables and clothes hung on portable clothes hangers. I have also seen this in the country, out in the wilds; a clearance house stock sale, the very same thing.

Hills were few and far between. I could see a cluster of houses in the far distance that must be Sebree. It was. The cat eye computer read 67 miles. I was happy. I could see a motel and soon checked in. The Goose was allowed in my room. The credit cards mostly used in America are Visa and Master card. I'm glad to say I had both. The room was clean and the bed soft. I soon completed all my evening chores. I showered and felt a new man. I walked up the road to the supermarket and asked the assistant if they sold small tins of cycle oil. She assured me they did, pointing out the hardware counter. I bought my evening meal, which was slightly different from last night: a tin of fish, a tin of pineapple, ice cream and a bottle of Pepsi – not forgetting my breakfast, apple pie. I enjoyed my meal at the motel, and took a vitamin tablet also. The bed looked inviting. As I relaxed, I watched the climax of the O.J. Simpson case. Good night.

Sebree to Falls of Rough

As I awoke, instinct had me looking out of the motel window at the day's weather. It was frosty with some fog. What a mixture, but not enough to keep me from cycling I hoped. I dressed in my thermals without a second thought, ate my apple pie and drank my fill of tea. That's breakfast finished. I could feel the cold as I oiled the Goose. I was on the road in no time and the traffic was light as I cycled out of town. The plan today was wherever my legs would carry me. I knew the direction so I headed down the main road. It ran through farming country. Cattle grazed contentedly in small fields. The corn was still to be harvested. At one road junction I was at a loss; there were no road signs and both road surfaces had the same amount of wear. Across the road in a field I could see two farmers repairing a self-loading trailer. I approached them, wishing them good morning. I asked the direction and they soon told me. One farmer looked at me and asked if I wanted a job for a few months; he could do with a harvest hand. I declined with a smile. Thanking them, I was on my way. A job? I had just retired. The sun came out, chasing the fog and frost away.

As I cycled through a small cluster of houses, a woman called, 'Hey there!' I instinctively stopped. She was a smart, well-dressed lady. 'You cycling far?' she enquired. 'As far as possible today,' I replied. 'Fancy a cup of tea or coffee?' she said, pointing to a very smart house. 'I wouldn't mind,' I replied. 'Would you like some pumpkin pie with your tea?' she asked. 'Yes, please.' Pumpkin pie – I'd never tasted that before. 'We'll take tea on the veranda. If my husband was home, I'd invite you into the house.' The rest, the tea, the pumpkin pie was as if ordered; I thoroughly enjoyed it. We had a good morning chin-wag, as they say.

Thank you Mrs Jean Buttz. Folk can be kind.

As I cycled on navigation became a problem; another crossroads with no sign post. I was scratching my head when a pickup truck stopped. 'You gotta problem, Man?' said the driver in a broad Kentucky accent. I told him where I was wanting to cycle; he gave me directions. He also wanted to talk. I told him I was cycling across America. 'My brother and I in our younger days wanted to ride the states,' he said. 'We never did, though.' He also told me to watch myself today, as it was the first day of the deer shoot. 'Just don't go in the woods. Those townies will shoot anything that moves.' Thanking him, I cycled on. One mile down the road a funny thing happened. A deer came out of the woods, took one look at me and bounded off. Again in the afternoon I was cycling through forest country, pickup trucks were parked alongside the road and not too far away, guns were being fired at a good old rate. I don't like the idea of deer being shot. About five hundred yards down the road three dogs crashed out of the trees on to the road. Not again, I thought. These dogs had been well-worked; they were a smaller version of our fox hounds but darker in colour. They were lost, I could see by their actions. There was no aggression towards me; it was the opposite. They tagged on my tail and followed me cycling at a fast trot, tongues hanging out with the exertion. 'Go home, dogs, go home,' I shouted. The more I shouted the more they hung on my wheel. I reckon they must have followed me for five miles. A tractor pulling a trailer passed me. The dogs did a double-take and were gone. They must have been townie dogs chasing the deer.

It was late afternoon; the sun had given way to black clouds; it was a case of 'it would, but when?' The cat eye computer read 75 miles. A motel appeared as if ordered; the rain had started. I checked in along with the Goose. 'What's the name of this place?' I asked the receptionist. 'Falls of Rough,' she replied with a smile. Lakes surround the Falls of Rough area, she told me, and sailing and boating folk frequent the lakes, along with a high percentage of hikers. 'It's a very picturesque district,' she said. I hadn't seen a lake or a boat. Apparently the sights are to be seen a mile down the road. Thanking her, I retired to my room. The rain had really set in for the day; I was lucky. Before checking into the motel, I had made a mental note of the post office, the shop and the restaurant. As I wheeled the Goose into my room, thunder and lightning added to the rain.

I washed my cycle clothes using travel washing soap I had bought in the supermarket. The clothes did look cleaner. After showering, I decided to eat in the restaurant. I have never been served with such a big helping of dinner before or since. When the waitress saw the dinner on the plate she said, 'that's not enough,' and took it back to the kitchen. She returned with a smile on her face. What a meal; I nearly failed. The waitress was like an old hen, fussing round me. When it came to the sweet, it was piled high on an over-sized plate. 'Here,' she said, 'this will feed you.' I was so full I failed to drink my Pepsi. I paid with my credit card and left a big tip, thanking the waitress. I returned to my room with a slight wobble. I recognised my room; the one with the Coke server outside. I lay on the bed useless; I had eaten far too much. I switched off the light. With that, someone outside played the Coke machine. 'Yes,' said a strange voice, 'I did put the right money in.' Clank, bang first, followed by the boot, then clank, that was the Coke can. I frowned; I hope this Coke machine noise doesn't go on all night.

I had a highly digestible night's sleep; as full as a bug, as they say. Good night.

Falls of Rough (rest day)

I was out of bed at my normal time, early, and looked out of the window; it was raining and blowing a gale. No way was I going to cycle in this weather. I looked at the room instructions. Check out was mid-day. I decided to hold. I ate my breakfast and drank my tea while looking at the rain running down the window.

I cleaned the Goose until it was spotless and cast my eye over the mechanics. All looked to be sound. Mid-day came and the storm was still raging. I checked in for another day. I decided to wash some more clothes; the ones I'd washed the night before had dried. I looked at the weather, complaining about another lost day. With all my chores completed, I relaxed in front of the TV to witness the final day of the O.J. Simpson case. It proved to be dramatic, to say the least. I thought him guilty, but who am I? We were witnessing democracy at work, thank goodness. I must admit it was powerful and highly charged. The day had left me feeling relaxed and rested. My plan was to eat lightly in the restaurant and go to bed early.

The Falls of Rough to Bardstown

I was awake early, fully rested. I had lost that full feeling. I glanced out of the window. The wind was fresh, the sky overcast; the roads were dry, no rain. I dressed in my thermals, boiled the kettle and made my tea. I ate my breakfast – apple pie and yoghurt. I had studied the map yesterday; my route would take me through the lakes. I had already bagged up the Goose and was soon outside. I shot some oil on the chain and the cogs. The traffic was light with only the odd pickup. I was itching to go after a rest day and was soon in among the lakes, with a forest and mountain backdrop. It was picturesque. The lakes were full of boats. I should think, at the height of the season, this would be a very busy place. Photo calls came often; the camera was working overtime. The standard of the roads was good; the surfaces were in an excellent condition for cycling.

The roads stayed quiet. The surrounding country could have been in Wales. For once, the fresh wind was blowing at the rear; the Goose was flying. The autumn leaves were falling and blowing in the wind. The colours on some of the leaves were striking. I stopped and placed two leaves in the pages of my daily log; I have them to this day. At fifty miles, my legs felt strong; I decided to cycle for another fifty miles. The day was still overcast, but no rain. I was enjoying my cycling. As I passed under a line of oak trees the wind freshened; I was showered by a storm of hail like acorns. It was hitting me on the body and bouncing off my hard cycle hat, and the road. I saw a squirrel smile as he chased and collected the acorns.

I cycled past an enclosure full of ostriches. There were also two ferocious-looking guard dogs, free to run with the ostriches. Outside a school, a sign printed in big bold letters read: 'We are what we do. Repeatedly do. Excellence is not an act, but a habit.' I thought it very appropriate. The cycling today went very quickly; a good cycling mixture of flat land and medium high hills. I could see Bardstown in the distance – that's what the road sign said.

Bardstown was a clean fresh town, and friendly-looking. I glanced at my cat eye computer; it read 100 miles. Nearby was McDonald's and a shopping centre, the motel was opposite. I checked in. The receptionist smiled and said, 'just before the rain'. The motel was of a good standard, the reception friendly and helpful. The Goose was allowed in my room. I looked out of the motel window. The wind was freshening and a few spots of rain landed on the window.

I washed my clothes and showered; it was refreshing after 100 miles. I dressed in clean clothes and felt like new. I ate my evening meal at McDonald's and had a salad for a change; most enjoyable. On the way back to the motel it rained. I stopped for a photo call late in the day and the camera did not work; I think it's the battery. I'll have to buy a new one tomorrow. I did try two shops today, but no luck.

Back in my room I switched on the TV for the weather forecast. It was not good; they said that tomorrow the remainder of hurricane Opal would be passing through the area. The rainfall could be as much as ten inches. It said one thing to me: Mac, tomorrow you don't cycle. We'll wait and see. After a hard cycle I needed rest; today was no exception. I

241

was soon in my bed. Good night.

The following day I was unable to cycle because of hurricane Opal. Rest day.

Bardstown to Berea

I was awake early and glanced out of the bedroom window. The weather was overcast; no rain, but a stiff breeze. In my opinion, I was glad to say, I could cycle. Not like yesterday. What a day of wind and rain. I think hurricane Opal has now passed. I dressed in my thermals and bagged up the Goose; I oiled the chain outside on the road. For my breakfast I called into McDonald's. I just couldn't wait to get on the road. I do get fed up on a rest day. In my opinion, it's a complete waste of a day, and that's two days this week. I suppose I did catch up on some work; I bought a battery for my camera, checked my log book and studied maps. I rang Gill. It was grand to talk, and October 4 is my eldest daughter, Alison's, birthday. I ate my evening meal in McDonald's; a ham salad, which I really enjoyed. My plan today was to cycle to Berea. It was too early for traffic as I cycled out of town; only the odd farm pickup passed. The streets were void of humans. I pushed on like a man on a mission. The breeze was from side to face; I wasn't complaining.

The country was vast green plain with trees and forests. Again, animals were few and far between. I had that feeling as I cycled past some farms; they were not prosperous. At one farm near the road I saw two women dressed in long black dresses with big black hats. They were standing over an old-fashioned log fire boiler, as if doing their washing. On some farm buildings, end doors were open and hanging tobacco leaves were drying in the wind and sun.

I was enjoying my cycling; the Goose was flying. I was only here for the ride. In the early afternoon my cat eye computer read 60 miles. I decided to cycle on as I was feeling fresh. I stopped at a roadside café. The notice read: 'no cycles on the veranda.' Your loss, mate.

The weather warmed up in the afternoon; I could feel the heat on my back. The wind had receded. My legs worked like pistons to propel me along. I was enjoying it. I rode two very steep hills. Just when you think you're winning, the hills appear. On the run in to Berea the Goose was gliding along. The Berea town sign said 'population 9,100, all services'. My cat eye said it all: 100 miles. I was satisfied with today's mileage. The town was small and neat and tidy. The motel was near the supermarket. I checked in; the receptionist smiled and allowed the

Goose in my room.

That shower after cycling 100 miles is so relaxing. With the clean dry clothes you quickly feel revitalised. I washed my clothes and hung them up to dry. The Goose was due its clean tomorrow. I checked the tyres; no visual problem that I could see. The supermarket was but a short walk across the road. I bought a salad and tinned fish, most enjoyable. For sweet I had ice cream and Pepsi; it filled the Inner Man. I also bought an apple pie for breakfast. As I relaxed on the bed I wondered what those millions of fans of the O.J. Simpson soap opera were doing tonight now the drama was over. I was fed, watered and relaxed; the highlights of the day stored in my memory bank. Good night.

Berea to Booneville

I was up early and glanced at the weather through the bedroom window. It was overcast, no rain, with a slight breeze. I dressed in my thermals. For breakfast I ate the apple pie and had three cups of tea. I bagged up the Goose and was fit for the road. As I opened the motel door I was aware of the wind. I oiled the chain and was on my way. The traffic was light to non-existent. Soon I was out of town. My, it was cold; the wind was side to face.

For the first ten miles I cycled through farming country; it soon changed to hills. The stiff breeze was in my face as hill followed hill. It was a hard cycle. Dogs were making an appearance. At virtually every farm the dog would bark and the bark would alert the dog at the next farm; just like jungle drums. Each dog had its own individual way of showing he was king of the patch. This was demonstrated by aggression, noise or intimidation.

The local accent intrigued me; it was just like you hear on the American films. I stopped at a supermarket cum petrol station; the shop was also divided into living quarters. Mother and child sat in front of a fire in what I would call a living room. They watched every person entering the shop. The kids waved to me and I waved back.

As I cycled along, poverty was obvious in parts. Caravans parked on the roadside were littered with all the rubbish one sees in unsupervised parks. There were cars and pickups, some with wheels and engines removed, others burnt out. I was surprised the authorities allowed this kind of living. The young kids who played in the debris looked wide-eyed and slum-faced.

It was evening as I cycled into Booneville; it had been a hard cycle. Two town characters sat on a makeshift wooden seat. I gave them the time of day, and asked if there was a motel. They gave me directions.

They were full of questions when I told them of my travels. As the conversation drew to a close, the talkative one took a camera out of his pocket. 'Say, Moss,' he said to his sidekick, 'take my photo with this young man. Do you mind?' 'No,' I said. 'Go ahead.'

I followed their directions and soon found the motel. I checked in and the Goose was allowed in my room. I showered and changed and soon found the supermarket, which was just down the road. I did enjoy the pre-cooked meal. The motel room door couldn't make up its mind whether to stay open or shut. I fixed it with my wedge and put the Goose across the door. As I relaxed on the bed the smell of silage wafted into my room through the open window. I closed it and looked outside. There was a cattle trailer with a cow parked outside my window. Good night.

Booneville to Hazard

I was awake early. As I lay in bed I thought of last night, or should I say, early this morning. Saturday night is the same the world over. The revving of engines first woke me, the revs past the safety limit, then at full throttle the foot was let off the clutch and the squeal of tyres must have woken all the folk in town. The race was on. I bet it woke the cow in the trailer outside my bedroom window. I dressed in my thermals and checked the weather through the motel window; it was dry. I was now getting addicted to my apple pie breakfast; the apple pie was paper covered so it was always fresh. I do enjoy my cuppa in the morning.

I bagged up the Goose and oiled the chain outside the motel. The chain was now showing signs of wear; I'll need to keep a close check on it. I have religiously oiled the chain, that's for certain. I can but hope it will last for the rest of the journey. I was soon out of town, cycling through farming country. There was fog on the high ground and it was cold. The sun made its welcome appearance mid-morning. My mind was thinking ahead; I must be close to the foothills of the Appalachian mountains – the way the hills were appearing I thought I was cycling in the mountains. The water bottles were in demand; the sweat stood off me. It was a demanding cycle. I had been in the saddle seven and a half hours; the cat eye read 40 miles. I could feel the pull on my legs; I was leg weary.

The road sign said 'Hazard'; I was on the outskirts of a small town. There was a motel, or, as they say, a truckers' motel, with an over-sized lorry park. 'Stop,' said the Inner Man. I checked with reception; yes, they had accommodation. I checked into the motel with the Goose. My mind was in gear, thinking. Hazard – it must have been one of the Duke boys beating up the town of Booneville early this morning. It looks so real on *The Dukes of Hazzard*. TV is a powerful medium. It made me smile just thinking about it.

Fifteen miles down the road was a town named Orkney. It was off my cycle route and I'd had enough cycling for today. There were some funny town names: Paint Lick – who in their right minds thought that one up? There was a petrol station shop at the entrance to the motel lorry park; I was lucky enough to purchase my evening meal and breakfast. It was Sunday; a day of rest, so I will also rest. Good night.

Hazard to Elkhorn City

Last night I slept soundly. I was up at my normal time and looked out of the window, or should I say attempted to look out. I couldn't see a thing. I concluded it must be fog. I was soon dressed in my thermals, bagged up the Goose, ate my breakfast and washed it down with tea. As I opened the motel door, I was met with what's best described as a blanket of fog. Talk about a hazard – you couldn't see a hand in front of your face.

I decided that no, I wouldn't cycle in this fog. Cars and lorries passed me with headlights blazing as I stood next to the road; I could just make out the lights. I oiled the chain and decided to play the waiting game. The café next to the motel opened. Why not? I've only eaten a small breakfast. Go on, spoil yourself. I chained the Goose to the rail outside the café window; I could see it while sitting at my table. Better to be safe than sorry. I trust me; whom do you trust? I ordered egg, bacon, beans, toast and tea. 'I'll check if we have tea bags,' said the waitress. I repeated the order; she looked at me real gone like. With her broad Kentucky accent rolling off her tongue. 'Man, ' she said, looking me straight in the eye, 'I could sit and listen to your voice all day.' I smiled and took it as a compliment. Steady, young woman, I thought, I've only come here for breakfast. I enjoyed my breakfast and the good service; I also had time to read the paper. Two hours later the fog began to lift; the sun was making its presence known. I thanked the young waitress for my breakfast, finished off with a big smile. She returned the smile with credit, and a gold tooth sparkled through the wisps of long blonde hair. I wonder what bottle that hair colour came from?

I was soon on the road; I felt as if I'd missed half the day. The fog was still hanging in the trees but the sun was doing a good job of dispersing it. It was fine cycling; the sun shone and the miles passed. The farm country was still dotted with hills; it made hard cycling at times. The road verges were soft in places, with a lot of noticeable lorry tyre debris and litter, making me cycle with care. One or two hills turned to mountains. Halfway up one mountain the sign said, 'God cries for you'; not a truer word spoken, the sign had been placed in a 'give up' area. It gave me a humorous lift. As I cycled down the mountain another sign read, 'I'm sure it helped.' I smiled; it did.

I had now been on the road for ten-and-a-half hours. My cat eye read 90 miles, and not easy miles. I was happy. I checked into a motel with the Goose, found a supermarket, completed my chores, relaxed on the bed and read one page of the Gideons Bible. I was tired. Good night.

America
Virginia

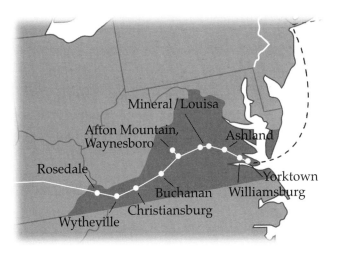

Mineral / Louisa

Afton Mountain,
Waynesboro

Ashland

Rosedale

Yorktown

Buchanan

Williamsburg

Christiansburg

Wytheville

Elkhorn City to Rosedale

As the saying goes, I was up with the birds. The weather was patchy fog, but the sun was making its presence felt. As the weather first thing in the mornings was always cold, I dressed in my thermals. I bagged up the Goose making a mental note that it was due for a clean tonight. I ate my usual breakfast and a few cups of tea. As I acquainted myself with the new day, I oiled the chain. The traffic was light and I was on my way.

I felt excited when I read the road sign: 'welcome to Virginia'. Within 500 yards of crossing into Virginia I saw a road sign I'd not seen in any country before or since. It was yellow with a black lined triangle. In the triangle was a bike motif, and in black letters against a red background it said: 'share the road'. I'm singing its praises because I thought this was the best sign I'd seen since sliced bread. I hope anyone reading this could overcome road hogs by erecting signs like these. Brilliant. I felt wanted. Well done, Virginia roads department.

The cycling today was again demanding. Hills were repetitive, the woods and farmland were giving way to autumn. The dramatic changes in colour painted a picture of beauty, words can't describe the effect: reds, greens, yellows resulted in a golden brown hue of fantastic colours. The sun's rays changed them at will. It was like being on a moving escalator in a picture gallery.

For some reason today the traffic was busy. The roads were not easy to cycle and the soft verges were, in my opinion, dangerous. The roads were also narrow. On one hill, the traffic was nose to tail and the road narrowed. I did my best to hold my line but my front wheel slid into the soft verge; the result of some loose stones and the sudden drop in the road camber. I didn't come off the Goose, but I steadied myself with my right leg and jarred my thigh. My temper showed as I shouted, 'why should I help them? They should help me.' The pain was shooting up my leg. I was not amused. I must admit it was my fault, no one else's. I'd had enough cycling for the day and on the appearance of the first motel, I checked in. As I wheeled the Goose into my room I thought the worst; my leg really hurt. In the shower I bathed the leg and massaged the muscles.

I ate in a restaurant adjoining the motel; it was good food. I begrudged leaving a tip; that was a sure sign of spending too much time in supermarkets. No, I didn't clean the Goose. I was feeling sorry for myself. I rested my leg for the rest of the evening, wondering what tomorrow would bring. Good night.

I opened my eyes to welcome a new day and lay in bed fully relaxed, no pain. I slowly moved to the sit-up position and stood up; still no pain. On taking my first morning step I felt a twinge in my thigh muscle. I made up my mind I would cycle today.

There was no problem or pain during dressing. I bagged up the Goose and glanced out of the window at the weather: patchy fog, but the sun was winning the day. I oiled the chain and was under way. I felt my leg at the first few revolutions of the pedal. I was happy that I could at least cycle.

The hill country I was cycling through was the Appalachian Mountains. I first read of them while planning my route. What a mountain range to cycle. Good job I was a Capricorn goat, otherwise I could not have cycled over them. It was, to say the least, a gruelling hard ride.

My leg was behaving well; there was slight pain but it was bearable. I was again cycling through farming country. During the day I also cycled two mountain passes; those dogs don't sleep, do they? Cycling past his domain he came bounding out across the lawn. Here we go again. My god – he sure sounded the part. What was the model? German or American boxer. I thought it would be either my leg or the pannier bag. He grabbed the latter, swinging first from left to right and vice versa. I had already released the pump before he arrived; he looked like a mean bastard. With my pump I hit him with a lucky swing between the eyes. His eyes crossed; definitely a German boxer. He retired from the field of combat hurt, or should I say, his dignity was hurt. Maybe it will teach him a lesson, I don't know. How I stayed in the perpendicular position on the Goose during combat, I'll never know. I was now on red alert. The adrenaline was flowing and it had an oddly calming effect. I cycled on, thankful that I'd got through that problem unscathed.

I stopped at a roadside grave of a soldier who had died on his way home from the American Civil War. I felt sad and wondered if this was the grave of the first 'unknown soldier'. Trees now hemmed in the roads. It had been a long eventful day. I'd been on the road eleven-and-a-half hours for a grand total of 95 miles.

The sign said 'Wytheville'. In the distance I could see a McDonald's sign, as if to say 'this way, Mac'. The Inner Man said he was thirsty; a Coke and ice cream soon settled that. It's better than a pint of beer. I sat relaxed and watched the world go by. I checked in a motel with the Goose, washed my clothes and cleaned the Goose – not before time. I could feel slight pain in my thigh and right shoulder; that was some jolt.   249

I ate my evening meal at McDonald's – chicken salad. Good night.

Wytheville to Christiansburg

I was awake at my normal time, although I don't have an alarm clock. I glanced at the weather through the window. There was more fog than I'd like, but the sun was making an appearance. I bagged the Goose and checked the tyres; the rear tyre was now smooth. What a way to start a day. 'Change it now,' said the Inner Man. 'OK,' I said, 'don't keep on.' I changed the tyre, fitting in its place a folding Michelin 700+35 tyre I carry as a spare. I also fitted a new tube. I was very reluctant to throw the old tyre away; it had served me well beyond the call of duty. Many thanks, Continental Tyres.

I oiled the Goose and decided to breakfast at McDonald's; cheeseburger, tea and toast. As I swung my leg over the crossbar I felt no pain in either my leg or my shoulder; we were on our way. The day was cold and there was more fog than I'd first realised. I switched on my lights. Navigation was not easy; one needed to be on one's toes. I cycled through two small hamlets. It's a change cycling built-up areas. Traffic was on the increase. I was so glad to see the sunshine clearing the fog. I switched off my lights and vowed not to cycle in fog that dense again.

Cycling through the country, I came across a roadside café and decided to rest and drink a Pepsi. Three elderly gentlemen, or should I say, motorcyclists, sat in the café; I sat with them and talked. They were on a grand tour of the states. They all rode Honda Gold Wings – all singing, all dancing motor bikes. Time flies when one talks. They wanted my photo taken with them; I also took a photo of them. I wished them a safe journey; they did likewise.

Hills to me were now secondary; they came and went. As I cycled down an incline, a group of men were grass cutting. It couldn't be local council workers, I thought; manual work, never in America. As I neared I could see they were all dressed in the same uniform. A single decker bus was parked nearby and a policeman with rifle in hand stood in close proximity. Convicts; I got it in one. I thought, what a good way to pass their time rather than let them vegetate in a prison cell.

As I cycled into Christiansburg I felt I'd had a good productive day. It was a nice clean quiet town. There was a motel; I checked in myself and the Goose. I examined my new tyre, along with the rims and tyre pressure; all was fine. I showered and washed my cycle clothes, and reverted back to supermarket food, including breakfast for the morning. I rested on the clean bed and watched TV. Good night.

Christiansburg to Buchanan

'Move your butt, Mac,' said the Inner Man. Who said I didn't have an alarm clock? I was soon on my feet and dressed in my thermals. The weather was fine and clear; no fog. I looked in my log book – Friday 13th. It conjures up all sorts of funny thoughts in the mind. When Friday and the 13th meet, I am a little superstitious. I think superstitions are inherited from the mother or father. My mother was superstitious; she in turn handed it on to her children. I find that Friday 13th, however, is just like any other day.

The weather turned out to be overcast but mild. Breakfast was the usual apple pie and tea. I bagged up the Goose and oiled the chain. I was soon under way, cycling out of town. There was no traffic to speak of. One thing became obvious as I cycled along, the dilapidated state of so many farm buildings. And the houses were old, most in need of repair. All morning I failed to see a new farm building. I stopped for a photo call when I saw a herd of Aberdeen Angus stock cattle.

I cycled through roads with overhanging trees; leaves and acorns showered me as I went along and the road was covered in a blanket of leaves. I was enjoying the quietness and beauty of the road when my senses were kicked into gear by a now familiar noise; a lorry. I kept my distance from the road edge and the big brute came right up behind me and blasted my butt off with a 95 decibel-plus horn blast. I took immediate action and rode off the road. It was the safest way. What I'd give for a set of super horns to blast the idiot off the road, but then I'd be no better than him. After all, it was Friday 13th. Retreat is sometimes the better part of valour. Hills came often and were high; the surrounding country was something to be seen. Anyone planning a late cycle through Virginia need not worry. The weather can be changeable but the scenery is exquisite. What a wonderful world.

My plan was to cycle to Lexington, but I saw a motel on top of a hill. The background gave it that certain something. To reach the motel I had to cycle across four busy roads. This I did. As I changed to granny gear, I knew the motel was on the side of a hill, or was it a mountain? I reached it eventually and checked in; the Goose was allowed in my room. See how you can get caught? After checking in, the receptionist told me that the restaurant was closed until further notice. At least the petrol station down the road had a shop. I bought some food for my evening meal and for breakfast. My room number was 13. I checked my mileage; the cat eye said 70 miles. The room was of a good standard and the toilet paper was high quality, good for cleaning the Goose. I sat and viewed the roads below. What a spaghetti junction; it was more like a racetrack. I relaxed on my bed and filled in my daily log. Good night.

I was up at my normal time and glanced out of the window. The road was wet, the sky overcast; not a good sign. I dressed with the thought of rain on my mind. I ate my apple pie, heated the water and made tea. The four roads below were quiet, not so much traffic, and the rain was holding off. I bagged the Goose. It was sparkling after last night's clean. I checked the map. Early morning would see me cycle over some fairly flat country, but the afternoon was promising to be a hard cycle over the Afton Mountain. I oiled the chain and checked the not so new rear tyre. I freewheeled down to the road; what an easy way to start the day. Again I cycled through farming country, with fields and forests. There was still corn to be harvested; no change from the other states in that respect.

I was intrigued by the efforts some folk had made to dress their houses for Hallowe'en. Some were works of art; colourful and very inventive. I stopped to take photographs, but they didn't do it justice. The big orange pumpkins played a central role in the staging.

I stopped at a roadside café for my usual morning break and sat on the veranda at a rickety old chair and table. When it was touched, it danced across the floor on one leg, spilling my Pepsi. I saw a notice in the window: gospel singing in the local church at 1900 hours. I would like to listen to that. I asked the shopkeeper if there was night accommodation in the area. She looked at me real dull and said, 'I don't think so.' That settled that. Ride on, Mac. It highlighted the problems I found when stopping in motels; accommodation was not always where you wanted it to be. As I cycled across a railway line I looked left, then right; clear, let's go. The railway lines just stretched to infinity, with no obstruction or deviation. I cycled past a road sign saying 'Afton Mountain'. I should have stopped for a photo, but I didn't. The weather had now changed from this morning; it was overcast and the wind was blowing strongly. Rain was not too far away. I stopped and changed into my wet gear. As I did, it started to rain.

The roadside trees should protect me from the wind and rain, I thought. This was some mountain. I settled for cycling 500 yards and walking 100 yards; the higher I got the more it rained and the wind became stronger. The leaves on the road now became a safety hazard. At times I felt my front wheel slide. The road soon turned to a river, the water rushing down. The wind was now gale force. I was wet, pissed off and far from home. I still battled on. The acorns blown from the trees hit me with a hidden force, bouncing on the road as if running from you. Afton Mountain was turning out to be a mountain and a half. 'Don't moan,' said the Inner Man. 'Get on with it.'

I passed a rubbish dump; one of many, I was surprised to see. I remember in Britain, 40 or 50 years ago, people dumped rubbish in old woodland. This was history repeating itself. By far the most rubbish dumps I'd seen were in Kentucky and Virginia. Old fridges and washing machines littered the woodland. What a mess. What about the environment? I wouldn't be surprised if the Acton charge was still in the fridges. There was a need for the authorities to clamp down on the litterbugs. Talk about bugs. Bugger this for a joke. The storm had now intensified to the point it was impossible to cycle. It was too wet and windy to ride the mountain. I kept walking up and up; my shoes were now under water. Is there a mountain top? I began to wonder.

Only one car had passed me on the mountain road. I was still battling on, when a 4 x 4 stopped in front of me. The driver's window slid down. 'Do you want a lift?' he asked. Don't need to repeat it, I said to myself; I heard it in one. 'If not too much trouble, thanks.' He hopped out and slid his front seats forward. I was too knackered to lift both the Goose and bags as one. I released the bags, lifting them separately. I sat in the back holding on to the Goose. I must have looked like a drowned rat, and felt like one. The driver introduced himself: Mike, and his wife, Martha. I shook hands and gave them my name. 'I'm a keen cyclist myself,' he said. We chatted as we dried ourselves off with towel paper. 'I know what it's like to be caught out in weather like this,' he said. 'There's a motel up the road about three miles.' The wind and rain were now lashing down. The windscreen wipers could hardly cope; they were being blown off the glass. Within what seemed like minutes we were pulling up at the motel. I went in and checked. Yes, they had a room; music to my ears. I removed the Goose and my bags from Mike's truck and thanked both for being so helpful. I also apologised for the puddles of water left by me, the bags and the Goose and offered to clean it up. 'No problem,' said Mike, as we shook hands. I waved as they drove off.

I felt so relieved to be in a motel room. What fine folk, I thought. Who would allow a wet dirty stranger in the back of a new 4 x 4? Not many, I bet. What did the receptionist say? Yes, he would get a TV fitted in the room asap. I removed my bags from the Goose and emptied them out. They were soaking wet, but the plastic bags had saved the contents. The storm was now at its height. The veranda outside saved the room from the buffeting wind. I had taken a photo of Mike and Martha; they must be in their late thirties, early forties, at a guess. Just a down-to-earth couple. I can't thank them enough. I enjoyed the ride and the talk; many thanks both. I looked up; someone was looking after me. I stripped off my wet gear and showered. My clothes were now dry but creased. The wind force had increased again. Outside, the branches on the trees were doing acrobatics; they bent and weaved, as if by some magical force. It was like a scene from a ballet.

The motel was not the best, but it was clean, the sheets were white and the heater worked. I stuffed paper in my shoes and put them with my clothes to dry out. There was a tap on the door, and a guy stood there with a TV. 'I've come to fix it up for you,' he said. 'Carry on,' was my reply. He fixed it and turned it on. I thanked him. After he left, I completed all my chores and finished by drying off the Goose with toilet paper. I sat back on the bed, exhausted. Welcome to Afton Mountain. I smiled and closed my eyes.

I must have dozed off. I woke with a start as it was getting dark. At least I felt rested. The room was now warm and the wind and rain were lashing the window; the wind must have changed direction. There was a restaurant and tourist shops across the road. I decided to eat in the restaurant for a change. I ate fresh fish, not tinned; that was a change. I enjoyed the meal. For my sweet I ate apple tart and custard. It was hot, so I ate slowly. Yes, I did leave a tip. I almost forgot it was Saturday night. I even bought a newspaper and some sweets in the shop. Back in the motel room, I read the paper, noticing it was out of date. I was passing the world by, and it was also passing me by. As I rested on the bed, the wind howled its musical imitations, the notes varying as if conducted. Good night.

Waynesboro to Mineral (Louisa)

I was awake at my usual time and glanced out of the window. The rain had passed but the wind was fresh; the branches on the trees still danced. My clothes were dry. I switched off the heater. I packed the panniers, bagged up the Goose and ate my usual breakfast. I was ready to leave when there was a tap on my door. When I opened it, there stood Mike and Martha. 'Say, Mac – we want to invite you to breakfast,' said Mike. I accepted there and then. 'We have the truck outside,' he said. I locked the motel room door and we were on our way. 'It's only a few miles down the road,' said Mike. I must admit it was strange sitting in a vehicle after cycling. 'Here we are,' he said. The car park was full of cars of all makes and description. The building was like a country restaurant. Martha led the way. We had to wait for a table, the restaurant was so full of folk. I couldn't believe it; it was Sunday. It was self service. What a choice! Spoilt for choice would be more accurate. I reached the pay desk. 'I'm paying,' said Mike. We all had packed plates. When I sat at the table, my hunger let me down. 'Hold, Mac. You say grace, Martha,' said Mike. Martha looked at me. 'Would you say grace, Mac?'

My head nodded like a donkey. 'Yes,' I said. 'For what we are about to receive, may the Lord make us truly thankful. Amen.' Short and sweet. 'We should also ask for Mac's safekeeping,' said Mike. Martha said a few more words. I was starving. I'd eaten less than this for a main meal many times. By the time I'd cleared the plate I felt full. I smiled and said I didn't know if I was fit to cycle after all this food.

Mike was concerned for me cycling down the mountain. 'I expect Mac has cycled worse than this many times,' said Martha. I nodded, smiling. We were soon back at the motel. Again, I thanked them both for their generosity and said if ever they came to Orkney to give me a call. What fine folk. It was sad to say farewell to them both. The time was now ten o'clock; that's two-and-a-half hours for breakfast.

I had not turned a pedal, as they say; what a start to the day. I've come to the conclusion there are more good folk than bad in the world. I oiled the chain. I was now on my way. From the heady heights of Afton Mountain I started the downward spiral. It was a hold-on job; the brake levers were working overtime. It was all downhill and I was knocking up the miles. The strong wind was in my back. I slowed down. What was this beside the road? An old mountain bike in the upright position; the handlebar bag and the rear panniers were red. There was a bed mat roll under the seat. The bike was propped up against six concrete blocks. Alongside was a four-seated table. A green garden hose was lying on the bike with a tap on the end. I took a photo; I'd not seen the like before or since. A simple wooden sign read: 'water for you'. The person who owned the property along the hill road had rigged up a bike water filling rest station. This was for cyclists climbing Afton Mountain. It was five stars. I'm sure there is a call for more of these at petrol stations.

The afternoon saw me off the mountain and making good headway; the miles were piling up. I was feeling strong. The cat eye read 65 miles. No, I decided not to stop. I planned to reach my destination before dark. When I stopped for a Pepsi and ice cream, I lay the Goose against a wooden seat. Damn, I'd broken my rear reflector. I had some tape so I did a running repair. My fault.

Just my luck, the road sign said 'diversion'. I religiously followed the road signs for what seemed like miles before returning to the main route. No, I would not make my planned destination today; the darkness was falling quickly. I switched on my lights, front and rear. The traffic was building up quickly; I was being horn blasted off the road. Some cars came too close for comfort. In other words, they were telling me to get off the road. I cycled up to a petrol station. The sign read 'Johnny's Quick Fix'. I pulled in. It was my idea to get a lift into town; it was only two miles away. I stood at the petrol pumps for an hour; not one pickup pulled in. I asked the pump attendant if there was a taxi available. She phoned, but there was none to be had. I was still reluctant to cycle on the dark road in this traffic. The attendant said, 'I'll ring a friend of a friend.' She tried, with no luck. It wasn't my day. 'I'll tell you what,' she said, 'I'll ring the Sheriff.' 'Hold on,' I said. 'It's OK,' she said, smiling, 'they'll help'. 'Go ahead,' I said. She rang, and with a smile told me they were on their way.

The police car pulled in and out got a smartly-dressed policeman. I don't think I've seen such a smartly-dressed man in all my life, even in my time in the army. His gun just held itself in its holster, as if by a magnet. 'You got a problem, man?' he said, smiling. I told him the situation and he smiled again. 'That's no problem,' he said. I felt good. 'Chain your bike to the counter,' he said. 'Is it in the way?' he asked the girl. She shook her head; 'No problem – we close in half an hour.' I retrieved my panniers. 'Come on, let's go,' said the deputy Sheriff. We pulled into the motel in Mineral; no one was in reception. 'Full,' he said, reaching for his car radio. 'Is there a room in the motel in Louisa?' he asked. 'If so, hold it.' Within minutes the answer came back: 'Yes, room booked.' Ten minutes later we were pulling up outside the motel in Louisa. I checked with reception – yes, they had booked the room. I retrieved my bags from the police car and thanked the deputy Sheriff. 'Ring this phone number in the morning,' he said, 'we will come and collect you.'

The motel room was clean and tidy with all facilities. I'd seen a supermarket across the road when we pulled in. No, I didn't wash my cycle clothes but headed to the supermarket. What a choice of food. I bought my evening meal and my breakfast. The time was now 1900 hours. I returned to my room and thoroughly enjoyed my meal. I showered and filled in my daily log. The mileage today was 90 miles. I was soon relaxing on the bed, or trying to. My mind was active. What a day. Good job they don't come too often. I thought of my Blue Goose. Was it safe? What time did the deputy Sheriff say to ring in the morning? 0630 hours. Where's the card? I found it. 'For God's sake come off the roof and go to sleep,' said the Inner Man. I looked at my watch; it was 2300 hours. Good night.

Louisa to Ashland

I woke extra early although I was still tired. My mind was on Blue Goose. Was it all right? I rang the Sheriff's office. 'A car is on its way,' said the voice at the other end. 'Move your butt, Mac,' said the Inner Man. In double quick time I washed and shaved, dressed and ate my supermarket breakfast, washed down with two cups of tea. I also finished a bottle of Pepsi from last night. I packed my bags and was ready. I sat by the window in my motel room, which had a commanding view of the car park. Within five minutes the police car arrived, with a different driver; he was going off night shift he said. He drove me direct to Johnny's Quick Fix garage. I thanked him for the ride and the unbelievable service. 'No problem, man, glad to be of help.' To both Louisa deputy Sheriffs, Roy F. McGhee and Jeff Sims, thanks a million for everything.

Blue Goose was still hog-tied to the service counter. I was so pleased to see it. I unhitched it and checked it out; all systems go. The girl from last night was still there; I gave her a big smile and a thank you. I asked her if I was in her debt in any way. She returned the smile and said, 'no, man'. I bagged up, oiled the chain and pumped some air in the tyres. I was on my way. The weather was cold with a hard frost. I passed the motel I was making for last night; it must have been one-and-a-half miles from Johnny's garage. I just took everything that happened last night as the norm. It wasn't really. It wouldn't happen in our country – or would it? I looked skywards. Someone is helping me – thanks. The weather changed from frost to brilliant sunshine. My, it was warm. The water bottle levels were dropping at an alarming rate. The heat in the late afternoon made me feel lethargic. I had cycled some big mileage the last two weeks.

The surrounding countryside was, to say the least, picturesque: farms and forests, with trees overhanging the road. I was just toddling along, appreciating life's gift as it unfolded. I stopped to have a Pepsi and an ice cream. With that, six other cyclists pulled in. We chatted as cyclists do; they were cycling across Virginia. Their gear was made up of mountain bikes and backpacks. How do they do it? The straps from the backpacks must cut their shoulders, or at least rub them. Times change. A young guy in the group asked me my age. When I told him I was 60, he was flabbergasted. 'My God, man, you'll live forever,' was his reply. Everyone laughed, me included. I enjoyed the chat; it was just the lift I wanted. There's no better medicine than laughter.

I cycled into a small clean town called Ashland. I think the town was built around the railway station; the rail line followed the streets. There was an old railway hotel which had been renovated to a very high standard. I decided I would check with reception for a room. 'Yes,' said the receptionist, 'we have a single room.' I checked in. 'You'll pay for this, Mac,' said the Inner Man. I was ready to be spoilt. The room was colour-coded; the furniture was period matching. The bed was soft, the sheets sparkling white. I was allowed to park the Goose in my room. I was soon showered and feeling good. I washed my cycle clothes and hung them up to dry. I dressed in my clean, creased clothes. Next door was a home-bake restaurant; it advertised tomato soup, 'the best you'll ever taste.' I did try it and it was good, but not as good as Gill makes.

I was now within one hundred miles of Williamsburg, nearly the end of my journey. Tomorrow's another day. I lay back on the bed and relaxed. I was just lightly dozing when there was an almighty racket; the whole room shook. In my sleepy daze I thought 'earthquake' and sprang bolt upright. It was then the train sounded its horn. I'll sleep well tonight, I thought; but I never heard another train until early morning. Good night.

Ashland to Williamsburg

I was awake early. No, I didn't react to the morning train as I did last night, and I smiled to myself. I had slept well; the rest did me good. I made a cup of tea after I dressed and bagged up the Goose. I had paid to have breakfast in the hotel. Why not? I sat down to breakfast and thoroughly enjoyed it. The weather was frosty and cold; the sort of morning where you have to work hard to retain heat.

On leaving the hotel, some youths were on their way to school. I asked one if he would take my photo with the hotel in the background. He agreed and did it in an expert fashion. I thanked him. That's his good deed for the day. Today traffic was building up on the roads, but it was, after all, rush hour. I had to cycle with care, holding my distance from the kerb. As I cycled it became apparent that in lay-bys, notice boards were strategically placed giving a blow by blow account of the Civil War. I found the boards of great interest and stopped regularly to read them. After all, they were part of the American history.

My mind was slowly focusing on ifs, buts, dos and don'ts. I knew I was within two days of completing my cycle trip. First finish the trip, I thought, before making plans. I should reach Williamsburg today; I had already completed 65 miles and it was mid-afternoon. Navigation in parts was a problem. Cycling through Richmond, I also cycled past the airport. At least that's one option; I made a mental note. As the planes passed low overhead I wondered where they were going and where they'd come from. 'Don't daydream,' said the Inner Man. 'Get on with it.' The Inner Man was also getting hyped up.

It was late afternoon when I cycled into Williamsburg; the cat eye read 90 miles. I was one happy man. I was spoilt for motel choice, this being a top tourist stop. I chose a good class motel, more like a hotel, with all facilities. The Goose was allowed in my room, so I checked in. As I walked round the motel I saw a self-service laundry, so I returned to my room, collected my washing and washed and dried all my clothes. You could buy washing soap from a nearby dispenser. No wonder there were chairs; the drier took an age to complete its task. I ate my evening meal in the restaurant. It was good food but I was now conditioned to supermarket food. This was one of the few times I took a drink while cycling; I went to the bar and bought a can of Bud. As I sat at the bar contemplating, it was obvious I would complete the cycle to Yorktown tomorrow, and, after making contact with the Atlantic, I planned to return to Williamsburg. I sniffed the air. Who's that smelling nice? I looked around and decided it must be me after washing all my clothes. I smiled as I returned to my room. Roll on tomorrow. Good night.

Williamsburg to Yorktown to Williamsburg

I checked my watch three times; dawn was not coming quickly enough. This was my big day; the conclusion of a dream. I was dressed with my bags packed. I checked the tyres and bagged up the Goose. I was ready well before my normal time. I decided to be civilised and have my breakfast in the motel restaurant. I thoroughly enjoyed it. The weather was fine; the sun always shines on the righteous, so it's said.

I oiled the chain and gears and did a visual mechanical check. The Goose was as ready to go as I was. I checked the map and moved out into the morning traffic, which was moderate for that time of morning. I soon cycled out of town; navigational skills were called for to find the right road. The sign said 'Yorktown'; I was on my way.

I had what I'd call a spring in my legs as I followed the course of the river. The main road was quiet. As I cycled I was aware of my feelings. This was a big day for me. As I rode into Yorktown I felt jubilant; dreams do come true. There were no cheering crowds; no welcoming bands. I was alone with my feelings. I'd achieved what I'd set out to do. It was Wednesday, October 18, 1995. As I walked it was as though I was floating on air, and the Blue Goose was floating with me. Anything in this world is possible; I was on a confidence high. I walked across the sandy beach and scooped up a handful of seawater. I washed my face and could taste the salt on my lips. The reality was that I'd cycled across America from the Pacific to the Atlantic. 'Well done, Mac,' said the Inner Man.

What did the sign say? Yorktown pub. No, I would not celebrate yet. I asked a man to take a photo of myself and the Goose for posterity; he duly obliged. 'Come on,' said the Inner Man. 'If we don't return to Williamsburg now, we'll be late for tea.' It was 16 miles, the Goose was flying and as I entered the town I was on a high. I had a rough plan in my mind what I wanted to do next. My overwhelming need now was to get home; it was foremost in my mind. Plan A was to get the train to New York. I cycled to the railway station. 'No sir, we don't transport bicycles.' What a start. 'Can I go by bus?' When sir?' 'Today,' I said. 'No sir, unless you have your bike in a box.' I thanked the guy; at least I now knew my limitations. Damn them all, the Goose was coming home with me.

It was now late afternoon. I checked into a motel near the station; thankfully the Goose was allowed in my room. I checked the phone book. Yes, there was a bike shop nearby. I rode the Goose through the streets; without the bags it felt light in the head. The sign said, 'Bikes Unlimited'. That's the shop. I asked if they would pack the Goose for me. 'Yes, sir,' was the reply. 'Leave it here and we will box the bike; it will be ready for you to collect first thing in the morning.' I walked to the station and booked a bus to New York for early morning. I returned to the motel feeling tired. One more thing I had to do: I rang Gill and gave her the news. She sounded over the moon. 'When are you coming home?' was her next question. I reassured her I was doing my best and would keep her updated. It was grand to hear Gill's voice. I walked to a nearby supermarket and bought my evening meal and tomorrow's breakfast. I had one tea bag left for tomorrow. I would take no rocking tonight, I was ready for my sleep. Good night.

The Journey Home

19th October - 22nd October 1995

I was up early; it was strange not to see the Goose in my room. I dressed in my best clothes: granddad top and cycling trousers, both sun faded, white socks and my cleaned cycle shoes. I was ready to travel. I'd packed my bags; my handlebar bag had a shoulder strap that made it easy to carry. I'd also packed all my immediate needs: toiletries, medical kit and camera, which I found handy.

The bike shop was only one mile down the road. The weather was again fine. By the time I reached the bike shop I found the bags very heavy. 'Yes, sir,' said the bike shop attendant, 'your bike has been boxed and is ready for collection.' 'How much do I owe you?' I asked. 'Twenty dollars.' 'Pay him,' said the Inner Man. 'Don't moan.' I was still in shock. The boxed Goose was heavy and awkward; between the cycle bags and the Goose, I thought I was a weight lifter. The shopkeeper was a chatty sort. 'I lost a bike yesterday,' he said. I nodded, not really knowing what he meant. He went on to explain that a guy came into the shop and asked to try out the new mountain bike. In good faith the guy left his credit card as security. He never saw the guy or the bike again. The credit card was forged. One has to be doubly smart to be in business today. I thanked him. He'll need my twenty dollars to help pay for the stolen bike.

What a job to carry the bags and the boxed Goose out of the shop. It was up a stairway with twenty stairs – I counted them. I did it in two loads. I'm aware of the big bad world out there. I was lucky. The owner's wife was parked outside the shop in a big 4 x 4 jeep. I smiled and in my best persuasive voice asked if she was going near the bus station. 'Why yes,' she said. 'Put the bags and the bike in the truck.' We were there in a very short run. Many thanks, Bikes Unlimited. Twenty dollars was not too dear after all.

I had an hour to wait for the Greyhound bus. I tied my bags to the box handles and sat in the café with a Pepsi and ice cream. I waited and watched the world go by. Greyhound bus, this was it. New York, here we come. Time, 1130 hours; the cost for the bags and the Goose, 50 dollars, plus myself. I handed the bags and the boxed Goose to the driver. On the box I'd written my home address four times, plus I'd taped on the box two envelopes with my address. If the box gets lost, as least my address is on it.

I handed the driver my ticket and I was on the bus. My seat was near the front, so I had a good view. I felt like a child on a first school trip; I was all eyes as we sped past the outskirts of Williamsburg. The route we were taking also went through Washington. I sat back in my seat and relaxed. The bus drove through the Virginia countryside and the sun was shining on my side of the bus; damn, it was hot. The picturesque country passed so quickly it hypnotised me to sleep. After my initial doze I sat and enjoyed the trip. The first stop was Washington bus station. Why is it that bus and railway stations draw weirdos like moths to a flame? One coloured gent with top hat and tails was walking three steps forward and one back; he was going nowhere fast. He came to the road; I hope he made it. I expect he changed his rhythm; he'd need to otherwise he'd be knocked over. The American bus stations have a good working system for catching the correct bus. We also had a change of driver; a coloured lady, slim, of small stature. She looked smart in her Greyhound bus uniform.

At the first stop past Washington a coloured lady got on the bus and sat in the front seat near the driver. Talk! The driver and passenger had not seen each other for a month. They talked above the noise level generated from inside the bus so we were all listening in on the conversation. The subjects discussed ranged from men to money. I soon got bloody fed up with the loud persistent yap. It spoilt my trip. As we left Washington and neared New York the amount of traffic on the road built up. We had some hold-ups. But if the driver was a good talker she was also a good driver. As we entered New York, traffic was nose to tail. We arrived at the bus station and the driver announced in a loud voice: 'New York bus station – all off.'

Now Mac, what's your plan? I retrieved my bags and the Goose and struggled to the information desk. 'What number bus to JFK airport, please?' I asked. 'Yes sir,' was the reply, 'we have an airport bus going every hour on the hour. It used to depart from this bus station, but owing to alterations there is no room. If you go out of this door on to the main road, turn left; five hundred yards down the road turn right – the bus stop is two hundred yards ahead of you on the right.' By the time I'd said thanks and struggled to the outside road, I'd forgotten the direction. Oh yes, I remembered. I followed a dark and dreary road, hobbling along like an over-laden donkey on three legs. It was tough going. I was panting for breath and the hydrocarbon fumes filled my lungs. I sweated and coughed, spit and cursed. Turn right here. Two hundred yards ahead there stood a big beautiful bus. There was no one in the bus and the driver was at the wheel. 'Yes sir,' said the driver. 'JFK airport.' He loaded my bags and the boxed Goose. I had twenty minutes to wait. There was a bus station café down the road, but when I approached and saw the weirdos, I wasn't hungry. I decided to sit and wait on the bus. What a picture of society. Men dressed as women; women wearing their clothes so tight the cheeks of their butts hung over their shoulders giving them bigger boobs. Man, this was more than nature in the raw. It was so sick. It was a minus point of our society. I remembered a conversation I had had in a petrol station shop: 'Where are you going, young man?' said an American. 'Crossing the states,' I said. 'Keep out of them big cities; they will eat you up and spit you out. What gun you toting?' 'I don't carry a gun,' was my reply. He lifted his shirtsleeves to reveal a fair sized arm muscle. 'That's how I defend myself,' he said. I was going to show him the muscles on my legs, but I didn't. He'd think I was queer.

Another two people got on the bus. I was right up the front and had been talking to the driver. He told me this was a part-time job to make ends meet. It was very expensive living in New York, he said. As we drove through the big city he pointed out the places of interest. I was lucky. I was getting a city tour and a commentary from the driver, all for fourteen dollars.

Within an hour we arrived at JFK airport. I had been here once before. What a place. It was now 2200 hours. The burning question was would I get a ticket and flight home tonight? A good question. The answer was no.

The airport ran a continuous courtesy bus around all the main flight players: British Airways, Virgin, American and foreign airlines. I alighted at the British Airways bus stop and collected my bags and the boxed Goose. The day staff had gone home and all was closed down apart from night porters for incoming flights. I caught the courtesy bus again, stopping at Virgin Airlines. There were people everywhere, running, pushing, shoving, crying, lost, happy and unhappy. You name it, all was to be seen on their faces. A lady approached me, 'Can you direct….' I butted in, 'I am like you,' I said, 'I don't know where to go.' She smiled and carried on. Do I look like an airport baggage porter? I suppose I do with the bags and the box. I thought I was a weight lifter. At Virgin Airways the staff were still in their daily cells. 'Upstairs, man,' said one employee in answer to my question. The escalator went up and up. I jumped on. As I reached the top I dropped the boxed Goose near the queue at the booking desk. I queued up. I'd never seen so many Jews in my life. 'Sorry, sir,' said the girl or would-be air hostess. 'we have no more seats for the UK. You can book again tomorrow.' I was mad, I'd let a lot of people go before me owing to the awkwardness of my bags. I turned on my heel feeling pissed off.

I struggled back down the stairs. There was a courtesy phone for hotels and I'd had enough. I lifted the phone. 'Yes sir?' 'Airport accommodation please,' I said. 'Where are you?' said the voice. 'Virgin Airlines,' I said. 'Sorry sir, no accommodation available; it's all booked up.' I was gob-smacked. This can't be the Big Apple, New York. What should I do now? I went out on the pavement for some fresh air. The
courtesy bus stopped. I stepped on with my bags and box. I kept

looking for where we were but there was no need; the tape recorder
tells you everything. I was becoming airport-wise. The bus stopped. The
voice recorder said, 'main reception and waiting area.' I hobbled off the
bus. I had a pain in my right side from weight lifting. I was getting more
and more fed up. I looked at my watch: 2300 hours. 'Balls,' I said. 'I'm
going to sleep here tonight.' I decided to lie on the box with my bags
as a pillow. There were one or two others with the same idea. No one
approached me to say any different and the lounge was warm. Man, I
was hungry. I asked a security guard if there was a café open. He shook
his head; 'no sir, not at this time of night.' I found a sweet in the corner
of my trouser pocket and ate it with relish; what a good dinner and
supper I thought. By midnight I was beyond tired. I stretched out on the
floor and went to sleep; I was knackered. Good night.

JFK airport

The noise stirred me from my sleep; I'd heard it before. I rubbed my
eyes and looked around. I was still in JFK airport main concourse; the
time was 0530 hours. The noise was an electric floor polisher. An elderly
coloured lady waltzed with the cleaner around the floor. I don't think
she was enjoying herself. Her facial expression was deadpan; she was
going through the motions and the machine was walking and working
her. I would estimate a dozen folk spent the night in the main lounge.
They all in turn awoke bleary-eyed. I was now fully awake and the call
of nature was tugging at my butt. The guy who'd slept on the bench in
front of me was also awake. He looked an honest kind of guy. I asked
him if he would keep an eye on my gear as I went to the bog. 'No
problem,' he said, smiling. I shouldered my toiletries bag and made post
haste to the bog, only to find it closed while cleaning was in progress.
I was desperate; I had a high-level alarm up to my back teeth. There
was an escalator. I jumped aboard and on reaching the top the sign
said toilet. What a relief. I washed and shaved and cleaned my teeth. I
glanced in the mirror – I didn't look too bad, considering. I returned to
my baggage. The Goose and bags were still there but the guy had gone.
I was lucky.

The noisy floor cleaner had moved to dirtier pastures; many shoes
undid the work of the polisher. A flight arrived from Israel. There were
Jewish folk, some meeting friends and family off the flight; happiness
was in abundance. One poor chap had a flask filled with something.
He dropped it with a dint as he tried to open it; he did look peeved. As
quick as the lounge filled, so it emptied. Day workers were starting to
arrive, dressed in their smart suits. I was looking at repetitive life; this

was their world unfolding today as every day. I looked at my watch; 0830 hours. It was time to move; British Airways first stop. As I lifted my pannier bags and the boxed Goose I felt a pain in my right side. I must have pulled a muscle.

I caught the airport bus within five minutes and alighted at British Airways flight check-in. First things first; a ticket. I lugged the Goose and my baggage into British Airways main reception area and enquired at the information desk about tickets. 'Up the escalator, man,' said the information clerk. I did my weight lifting act, arrived at the ticket desk and joined the queue. My turn arrived. I requested a ticket to the UK for the Blue Goose and myself, preferably to Glasgow. She copied down the request and fingered the computer. 'All flights to Glasgow today are fully booked,' she said with a smile. How could I negotiate a cheap ticket if there were no seats? 'How about Heathrow as an alternative?' she suggested after fingering the computer again. 'Or Birmingham – change flights to Glasgow?' 'Change of flight?' I said, 'and my bike?' 'Yes sir, and your baggage.' 'I want the cheapest single available,' I said. She announced it was cheaper to buy a return ticket and there were no cheap tickets. I was not in the mood to run around cheap flight merchants looking for the best value. I was on a short fuse as it was. I wanted no hassle. Why can't life be hassle-free, as cycling? In a moment of weakness I said yes, I would take the ticket. 'What time is the flight?' I asked. '1930 hours,' was her reply. 'It arrives in the UK at 0800 hours.' I agreed and paid with my flexi-friend. At least I was booked on a flight. All day at the airport; I'd go spare. I could take up plane spotting. Don't joke.

Progress. With the ticket in my hand I arrived at the baggage check-in. 'Yes, sir, no problem.' I checked in the Goose and my panniers. I was free of the luggage. I was so hungry; I'd only eaten that one sweet last night. The shops and the cafes were in the British Airways concourse area. I chose my breakfast slowly and deliberately; the plate was overflowing. I drank both Pepsi and tea. I sat in a seat with a view and was able to see the aircraft take off and land. I ate, enjoying every morsel; my belly had thought my throat was cut. I felt airport-weary but it was a change to see airport life. I thought of that song, 'Boxes, little boxes'. It said it all; repetition.

As I walked through the shops I remembered to buy a present for Gill. As I lazily gazed over the viewing lounge, a strange aircraft caught my eye. It was the one and only Concorde; it was taxiing the perimeter. I have always wanted to see Concorde. It noisily pulled into its parking bay and stopped; it made my day. As I walked the concourse I saw a man I'd often seen on TV, Terry Waite. By his actions he was obviously lost. I was going to speak to him but changed my mind at the last minute, why I don't know. I ate a light lunch, reminding myself not to eat too much, to keep some room for the meal on the flight. The reclining chairs in the lounge were getting more shaped to my body's contours. I was tired; I dozed off, catching up on my lost sleep.

As departure time neared, I checked in the flight departure lounge. I kept checking which gate; there it was. Boarding now, gate four; flight number 179. I was on my way. Or was I? 1930 hours came and went; I could feel my short fuse burn. These airlines treat us as mugs. An international flight and what did they have the cheek to say was the reason for the delay? The aircraft had to be taken out of service for its regular maintenance schedule. What bloody incompetence. They couldn't organise a piss-up in a brewery. 'Calm down, Mac,' said the Inner Man. The tannoy system crackled into static sound, apologising for the delay, and announced the rescheduled departure time of 2030 hours. I bought a cuppa in the departure lounge café to steady my nerves. What a carry on. I was now feeling more relaxed.

Flight now boarding. We were on the aircraft. 'All doors locked,' said the pilot. This must be it. Get this bucket off the ground. The air hostesses were wearing their working set smiles, with their highly expensive face masks. I looked out of the window. Did we actually move? Yes – backwards. I smiled. I hope he can find the forward gear. There was a crackle as the tannoy system cleared its throat. 'This is your captain speaking. I'm very sorry for the delay, but we have a problem. It's a big one.' He explained that we had now lost our take-off slot; we would now have to slot into a new time and it was up to control as there were approximately twenty flights on hold at that moment. Say no more, Mac. I was fit to be tied. I closed my eyes and willed myself to relax. I was awakened by the acceleration of the engines. We were airborne. The professional air hostesses soon had us all fed, watered and lights out for sleep. I was feeling sleepy; up with the angels, too high for the birds. I adopted the Mac Petrie Cycle Position (see below).

New York to Orkney

Night flight. The person in the seat in front of you invariably adjusts the seat angle, resulting in the back of the seat ending up approximately 12 inches from your face.

The Mac Petrie Cycle Position:
1   Place the in-flight pillow in the small of your back.
2   Place the food tray on the back of the seat in the
    operational position.

3   Place each hand on the brackets attaching the tray to the seat.
4   Place one's forearms lightly on the tray.
5   Place your forehead on top of the seat back in front of you.
6   One leg forward, one leg back.
7   You have now adopted the Mac Petrie Cycle Position.
     (Sleep well.)

I was woken by the announcement on the tannoy system: 'half an hour until landing.' My mind was clear of all the previous day's fuss. I was now thinking straight. I called the stewardess and asked her if I would still connect with the Glasgow flight. She was sure it would be all right; other passengers had asked her the same question. After an all-nighter some of the stewardesses just looked fair; the makeup kept the eyes from sagging. Some were not the bonny-looking girls of seven hours ago. I'm the first to admit they do have a hard life; they do their best against all the odds. It's far from the romantic image that some perceive it to be. Well done girls; many thanks.

We had landed. I felt great. 'For those travellers in transit, please follow this sign.' You know, when some people follow the sign, they have never walked so far in all their lives. It's the nearest walk to a marathon, it's true. Transit lounge. 'Glasgow, sir?' 'Yes, please.' 'Follow me; this way – the flight is waiting.' Six of us followed the leader; a blue goddess with high-heeled shoes and a mobile phone. She collected our boarding cards. We were on our way to Glasgow. That was short and sweet. Within an hour-and-a-half we were landing. I collected my bags in the airport. I waited and waited as the carousel waltzed around case-less. I bet you….I bit my lip and stopped myself mid-sentence. Above the door it said 'enquiries'. I tapped and opened the door. The guy sat behind a desk full of papers and a PC; he looked harassed. I exchanged the niceties of the day and followed up with, 'I've just travelled from Birmingham; where's my bike?' 'What's your name? Where's your ticket?' I produced these in double-quick time. He was on the phone. The expression on his face said it all. 'I'm sorry, sir – your bike is still in Birmingham. 'You bastards!' I had to say it. I'd travelled the world and lost the Goose; I was as mad as hell. 'I apologise on behalf of British Airways for any inconvenience caused,' said the man. Text book reply. I had travelled the world and they had lost my Blue Goose. He carried on to say they would deliver the Goose as soon as possible. What a disgraceful service, and what was annoying was that I'd paid for it. I walked away disgusted. 'Never mind, Mac,' said the Inner Man, 'try and get home today.'

How to get home was the big question. I checked the ticket desk. 'Sorry sir, all seats to Orkney are fully booked. You could book for

Monday.' This was Saturday. The boat went from Aberdeen at 12 o'clock; I was too late. There was the Thurso to Stromness north of Scotland boat, but I'd have to travel all day and stay in accommodation tonight. No. Edinburgh to Orkney afternoon flight? I returned to the ticket desk and booked a flight to Kirkwall. I must now get from Glasgow to Edinburgh. I checked the bus times and yes, a bus was outside the airport almost ready to leave. It was still there, I was in luck. I paid the driver and we were soon under way. I must have looked as I felt: bloody rough. The driver did me a favour on reaching Edinburgh; he dropped me off at the road to Edinburgh airport instead of going into the city. I would have had to catch another bus or a taxi back to the airport.

I walked to the airport trying not to think of the weight of my heavy cycle panniers. I checked in. 'No problem,' said the booking clerk. The flight for Kirkwall, Orkney, was on its way. The last lap. What could go wrong? Nothing, I hope. I sat in the airport café drinking tea and watching the world go by. I had an hour to wait. I looked out the window at the runway as I drank my tea; aircraft were landing and taking off. A small single-seater plane was coming in to land. As it touched down, as if in slow motion, it flipped on its side. The airport fire service was there in good time; the pilot was out of the aircraft safe; well done. I had witnessed an aircraft incident that these days doesn't even make the news or daily papers; it's not sensational enough. The thought did cross my mind that it might hold up my flight home. The Kirkwall flight was called; we were boarding. I had called Gill from the airport phone to ask her to meet me in Kirkwall.

The day was bright and sunny, as if to say, 'Welcome home, Mac.' I always window-gaze when flying. There it was shining like the jewel in the crown: Orkney Islands. We had soon landed in Kirkwall airport. I was out of the aircraft and I could see Gill in the airport lounge. I wanted to run. 'Stay cool,' said the Inner Man.

As Gill and I met and hugged each other, an invisible lock closed on us; only we knew the combination. I had made it home. The adrenaline was flowing; I was on a high. It made up for my scruffy look. The luggage was there. I grabbed my pannier bags and we made for the car. 'Home James,' I said, 'and don't spare the horses.' We arrived. I opened the door to be greeted by my daughters and grandchildren. I was so happy; everyone was talking at the same time. I was swamped by questions. How wonderful. I had been on my own with my own thoughts for six months; I would again have to reinstate myself in the family pecking order. My, how everyone had changed in six months; my grandchildren had grown so much. I must look a different man from when they last saw me. Twenty years older!

Gill had cooked me my favourite meal; chicken in tomato in a hot pot. I cleaned the dish, as they say; I was a contented man. We talked and talked; what a wonderful wife I have. When I woke twelve hours later, I was fully refreshed. When would the Blue Goose be home?

At home in Orkney

It was great to be home. What does one do with six months' mail? The phone was red hot; congratulations received from all conceivable places. Yes, a party was held in the house. We held an open night, everyone welcome; the food and drink flowed. Norma, a family friend, arrived with an iced cake in the shape of the world. On top of the cake was a miniature bike and a flag saying 'well done, Mac'. Stretching across the wall was a colourful banner. It read: 'welcome home, Mac'. Thanks Alison. What a homecoming; what a hoolie of a party. Thank you all for coming; it was the best party I've ever had in my life.

News travels fast. The world press had been on the phone to Gill before I reached home. She had done a good job relating the account of my cycle trip. The mileage was as estimated before the trip. The local press, radio and TV wanted to interview me. The phone rang with requests from community groups and associations wanting me to give talks. I was very busy, to say the least. I enjoyed relating the events of my trip; my brain was on overdrive. My memory was plugged into permanent recall. My daily log was a mine of information, giving more memory recall. In retrospect, I should have written more detail in my daily log; a future lesson to be learned. At the end of my talks I held a question and answer session. I enjoyed the questions; they came thick and fast.

'What did it cost you?' I thought long and hard about this. 'No disrespects,' I said. 'The answer to your question is I don't know, and if I did I wouldn't tell you.' I said this with a smile, not to cause any hurt. The true fact was I didn't know what the trip cost me. As with mileage - 'how many miles did you do?' – to the last mile I could not say. Yes, I did have the cat eye computer, but on local runs and about town I never had it fitted, and in hot climates such as India, the reading liquidised in the heat. My final mileage would be in five figures. I was continually asked questions such as, 'did you ever feel threatened?', 'how did you navigate?', 'did the bike break down?', 'were you ever lost?', 'what was the best country you travelled through?'. Each country has its good and bad points, but the best country I cycled was Thailand. When it comes to ease of travel, I would say France, with its efficient credit card and road sign systems. 'What about your trip across America?' I thought